Praise for *Something from the Oven:*
Reinventing Dinner in the 1950s

"Wittily serious and seriously witty . . . buoyant . . . caustic . . . a truly choice dramatis personae . . . Shapiro describes . . . the myth of the 'trapped housewife' . . . the bullying hard sell of the food industry. 'The food industry is a business, not a parent,' Shapiro reminds us, 'it doesn't care what we eat as long as we're willing to pay for it.' It's a marvelous book."
—*The Times Picayune*

"The story in Shapiro's engaging, droll voice races along, one funny, elegant revelatory sentence after another. If we are what we eat, you had better get *Something from the Oven* to find out why we're eating it."
—*San Francisco Examiner*

"Very funny, and also subtle. [The chapter on Poppy Cannon] reads like a Russian novel."
—*The New Yorker*

"[F]ascinating . . . highly readable . . . illuminating."
—*The Washington Post*

"Shapiro delves into this period of rapid change and comes up with absorbing stories of the era's women . . . [her] graceful, flowing prose makes this history of both cooking and women utterly compelling."
—*Booklist*

"[L]ively and engrossing . . . Shapiro deftly traces the history of both the convenience-loving branch of cooking and the more European-style cooking that emphasized fresh ingredients."
—*Newsday*

Something from the Oven

REINVENTING DINNER
IN 1950s AMERICA

Laura Shapiro

PENGUIN BOOKS

PENGUIN BOOKS

Published by the Penguin Group

Penguin Group (USA) Inc., 375 Hudson Street, New York, New York 10014, U.S.A.

Penguin Group (Canada), 10 Alcorn Avenue, Toronto, Ontario, Canada M4V 3B2
(a division of Pearson Penguin Canada Inc.)

Penguin Books Ltd, 80 Strand, London WC2R 0RL, England

Penguin Ireland, 25 St Stephen's Green, Dublin 2, Ireland (a division of Penguin Books Ltd)

Penguin Group (Australia), 250 Camberwell Road, Camberwell, Victoria 3124, Australia
(a division of Pearson Australia Group Pty Ltd)

Penguin Books India Pvt Ltd, 11 Community Centre, Panchsheel Park,
New Delhi - 110 017, India

Penguin Group (NZ), cnr Airborne and Rosedale Roads, Albany,
Auckland 1310, New Zealand (a division of Pearson New Zealand Ltd)

Penguin Books (South Africa) (Pty) Ltd, 24 Sturdee Avenue, Rosebank,
Johannesburg 2196, South Africa

Penguin Books Ltd, Registered Offices:
80 Strand, London WC2R 0RL, England

First published in the United States of America by Viking Penguin,
a member of Penguin Group (USA) Inc. 2004
Published in Penguin Books 2005

10 9 8 7 6 5 4 3 2 1

THE LIBRARY OF CONGRESS HAS CATALOGED THE HARDCOVER EDITION AS FOLLOWS:
Shapiro, Laura.
Something from the oven : reinventing dinner in 1950s America
p.   cm.
ISBN 0-670-87154-0 (hc.)
ISBN 0 14 30.3491 X (pbk.)
1. Women cooks—United States—History—20th century.   2. Cookery, American—
History—20th century.   3. Convenience foods—United States—History—20th century.
4. Nineteen-fifties.   I. Title.
TX649.A1.S53   2004
641.5'082'097309045—dc21   2003057512

Printed in the United States of America
Set in Bembo, with Park Avenue Display
Designed by Carla Bolte

TO NELL, NEXT IN LINE

Acknowledgments

ONE OF THE pleasures of working on this book has been discovering that everybody has a '50s, even those who experienced the decade only through their parents. And to own the '50s, I found, is to share them. The generosity of friends, colleagues, and strangers has sustained this project from the beginning.

My deepest thanks go to Pat Strachan, who was the first to recognize and encourage the book that lay buried under a welter of inchoate ideas. As I began to shape the topic, conversations with Nach Waxman and Barbara Kafka opened up dozens of possible research paths. Barbara Haber was a wonderfully reliable source for every sort of scholarly help throughout this project, and Barbara Grossman did me the honor of welcoming me to Viking.

The idea for this book was born in the stacks of the Schlesinger Library, and its resources and staff supported my research at every step. My search for Betty Crocker was aided immensely by Pam Becker, Kim Walter, Jean Toll, and Katie Dishman of General Mills, who opened the doors to the company's awe-inspiring archives, and by discussions with filmmaker Susan Marks about her own pursuit of Betty Crocker. Marlene Johnson of Pillsbury made available a trove of material about the Pillsbury Bake-Off, and Daniel Horowitz very generously shared his extensive research and thinking on Ernest Dichter. I'm enormously grateful to Lisa Tuite for allowing me to spend a week with microfilms of the "Confidential Chat" in the library of *The Boston Globe,* and to my own Chat sister, Jan Freeman, for paving the way. Ernestine Gilbreth Carey kindly granted permission for me to delve into the huge and fascinating collection of letters, diaries, and manuscripts that she gave to Smith College. Some of my favorite research hours were spent with Cynthia White and Claudia Philippe, whose abundant memories, reflections, and insights about their mother, Poppy Cannon, greatly informed my thinking. It's impossible to sum up all I have learned about food and life in the course of numerous visits with Cecily Brownstone, except to say that traveling back with her across nearly a century has been a spellbinding adventure and often a hilarious one.

Among the research materials most important to this project have been the books, leaflets, and recipe collections that friends have contributed from the kitchens they know best. For work like mine, these items are splinters from the true cross. I have treasured the chance to handle and study the materials donated by Kim Albright; Charlie Davidson; Bobbie Freeman; Ann Phillips and Wendy Phillips Kahn; Chris Kotowski; Bridget Moore and Meg Moore; Richard Rosen and Carey Rosen; Hal Schiffman; and Suzanne Weil. Other friends introduced me to an amazing variety of culinary artifacts gleaned from their libraries, including Fern Berman, Susan Szeliga, and Mark Zanger. I'm grateful for everything about my long friendship with Susan Riecken, most recently a succession of beautifully wrapped packages full of food books and pamphlets from the '50s, which she located on her Internet travels.

Memory is a resource beyond the reach of any library, and many people have given me access to theirs. My thanks especially to Jean Anderson, Elaine Hanna, Joyce Donen Hirschhorn, Robert Lescher, Elizabeth Moulton, Marion Nestle, Geraldine Rhoads, and Helen Worth. Conversations with Carolyn Goldstein, Joan Gussow, Karal Ann Marling, Anne Mendelson, Quandra Prettyman, Steve Schmidt, and Susan Strasser opened my eyes and mind at many stages of this project. For all sorts of life support during my research, I'm grateful to Dorothy Austin, Cara De Silva, Diana Eck, Ellen Jacobs, Melody Lawrence, Sara Paretsky, Susan Pelzer, Paul Solman, Jean Strouse, Linda Winer, and the members of The Group: Ann Banks, Carol Hill, Diane McWhorter, Ellen Pall, Elizabeth Stone, and Annalyn Swan. I have presented bits and pieces of my research in several venues over the last few years, and the thoughtful responses I have received have been enlightening in a thousand ways. Many thanks to the members of the Feast and Famine colloquium at New York University, the Culinary Historians of Washington, the History Workshop in Technology, Society and Culture at the University of Delaware, and the Women's Association of the Congregational Summer Assembly in Pilgrim, Michigan.

For a writer who doesn't come up with a book all that often, I have been very lucky to work with an agent, Amanda Urban, and an editor, Wendy Wolf, who are the best in the business. They are especially good at spinning gold out of straw, and I have benefited from that miracle frequently. At Viking, Karen Murphy guided the manuscript to publication with apparently limitless resources of kindness and wisdom.

Since the earliest years of our marriage, I have known that my husband, Jack Hawley, could sing highlights from the Muntz TV song. ("There's something about a Muntz TV/There's something about a Muntz TV/There's something about a Muntz TV/There's *something* about a Muntz TV!") Only when I began this project, however, did I discover what a fine native informant he is on every aspect of the '50s, including the food. His vivid recall of Underwood's deviled ham has lighted the way through several of the darker stretches of my work. On this journey as on others, he has been an exhilarating tour guide and a girl's best friend. To our excellent daughter, Nell, this book is dedicated with much love— and many apologies for all the take-out dinners.

Contents

Introduction:
Do Women Like to Cook?

FOR MANY YEARS I have been thinking about the conjunction between women and cooking, an association so deeply rooted that over the centuries it has turned cooking into something tantamount to a sex-linked characteristic, less definitive than pregnancy but often just as cumbersome to deflect. Biology and anthropology tell us pretty much what we need to know about how this relationship came about: Women have the babies, women feed the babies, women feed everyone else while they're at it; hence, women cook. Men cook, too, of course, especially now; but, traditionally, they went to the stove as a job or a profession, to show off for an admiring crowd, or simply for the pleasure of it. Women cook because they're expected to and because the people around them have to eat; happy is she who also enjoys the work. What interests me most about women and cooking isn't so much why they have been entwined all these years, but how that intimacy has affected both parties: the cooks and the food.

In an earlier book, *Perfection Salad,* I looked at what happened when science showed up in the late-nineteenth-century American kitchen with all the charisma of a new religion. Generations of women accustomed to cooking with their senses at the forefront, tasting and touching and remembering, gave way to brides who were learning to maintain a practical distance between themselves and the food. Nutrients and calories bid for attention; standardized equipment and measurements took the place of impressionistic cupfuls; and sanitation became the most demanding deity in the nation's culinary pantheon. Changes like these, which contributed a certain amount of objectivity to the task of cooking, didn't get in the way of talented home cooks. They could absorb the new imperatives or ignore them. And the other home cooks, women who weren't born with the instincts to make food taste good and who struggled to acquire the skills, now had help in getting an acceptable meal on the table. If they followed the written rules, they had a fighting chance. But, inevitably, such changes helped hammer into place a singularly American approach to raw food that was more akin to conquering it than welcoming it home. Nuances of flavor and texture were irrelevant in the scientific kitchen, and pleasure was sent off to wait in the parlor. To cook without exercising the senses, indeed barely exercising the mind, was going to have a considerable effect on how and what we eat.

What gave scientific cookery its staying power, long after the term itself disappeared, was its partnership with the food industry, which was becoming an ambitious new player in the American kitchen. During the last decades of the nineteenth century, factory-made foods began forging their way into homes across the country as rapidly as transportation and income levels permitted. Canned meats, soups, fruits, and vegetables, along with ketchup, pancake mix, granulated gelatin, and baking powder, were among the earliest products to become familiar and then indispensable. As pantry shelves filled up, the food industry began leaving unmistakable fingerprints on the meals and the recipes that characterized home cooking. The ginger ale salad, the canned soup gravy, the pale, puffy bread, and the omnipresent bottle of ketchup became culinary icons that would forever be identified with the American table.

But not until the end of World War II did the food industry take aim at home cooking per se, rapturously envisioning a day when virtually all contact between the cook and the raw makings of dinner would be obsolete. By the 1950s, magazines and newspapers were conjuring scenes in which traditional, kitchen-centered home life was being carried out in perfectly delightful fashion without a trace of traditional, kitchen-centered home cooking. The table was set, the smiling family was gathered, the mother wore a pretty apron, and the food was frozen. Or dehydrated. Or canned. Or prepared from what women were calling a "ready-mix." Do women like to cook? That is, are there any good reasons to cook from scratch, apart from habit, sentiment, and the family budget? The question had never emerged before, but, suddenly, thanks to all the new products, there was a glimmer of space between women and cooking, just enough to invite reflection. Do we like to cook? Is it important to cook? Before the question could even be asked, it was answered with a powerful "Not anymore." The ones speaking up so convincingly were the advertisers.

That moment when the burgeoning food industry confronted millions of American women and tried to refashion them in its own image is the one I explore in this book. It was an encounter that took place chiefly in middle-class homes; for this reason, the book focuses almost exclusively on middle-class women. But if they were the first to engage with the new concept of convenience foods, this was an event that would have overwhelming consequences for the entire nation. The 1950s were a turning point in a process set in motion half a century earlier, back when women discovered canned soup and Jell-O and found out how wonderfully easy they were to prepare. Cooking was genuinely laborious in the 1890s, and such shortcuts had an impact we can hardly imagine today. Once innovations like these settled into place, home cooking would never be the same, not just because the food began to change but because as it changed, Americans began to think differently about eating. Factory conditions imposed strict limits on the sensory qualities possible in packaged foods, making them predominantly very sweet, very salty, or very bland. The more such qualities were reflected in a family's home cooking, the more acceptable they became—so much so that in the worst of the nation's cooking, even dishes made from scratch paid homage to factory flavors. During the first decades of the twentieth century, millions of American palates adjusted to artificial flavors and then welcomed them; and consumers started to let the food industry make a great many decisions on matters of taste that people in the past had always made for themselves. The marketing innovations that would make junk food and fast food a way of life were still far in the future. But by midcentury, when the food industry launched its massive campaign against traditional cooking, manufacturers and processors had every reason to believe that they could lure a critical mass of the population away from conventional meals and into gustatory realms hitherto unexplored.

When I started my research, I assumed I would meet the 1950s—a term I apply fairly loosely to the period stretching from the end of World War II through the mid-'60s—in the version that has long been inscribed in popular history. After all, everyone knows the story of women in postwar America: Conscientiously happy housewives gave over their days to fussing with cake mixes and marshmallow salads, never imagining any other life. Those who dared to feel restless were kept in line by a culture that ferociously enforced the laws of traditional femininity. It took only a little reading to discover the shortcomings of that image. In the course of the 1950s, a rapidly increasing proportion of mothers went out looking for jobs, for instance, and the same women's magazines that ran stories on the matchless excitement of planning birthday parties for five-year-olds were also running stories on the satisfactions of paid work. As for the marshmallow salads, they showed up frequently wherever recipes were published, but so did a wide array of dishes made from scratch, including green salads with vinaigrette dressings and entrées that ranged from meat loaf to shashlik.

The labor statistics spoke for themselves, at least to a certain extent, but the food didn't. Food rarely speaks up at all when the subject is home cooking, for we have very few sources and they're hardly objective. In culinary history, the ordinary food of ordinary people is the great unknown. To track more distinguished cuisine—the sort produced in the best restaurants and in the kitchens of the rich—we can sometimes dig up menus and recipe collections, market lists, bills and receipts, or cookbooks produced by famous chefs. But if we want to know what millions of Americans ate in a certain era night after night and if we're curious about who cooked the dinner and how and why, then the primary source material tends to be elusive. Popular cookbooks tell us a great deal about the culinary climate of a given period, about the expectations and aspirations that hovered over the stove and the dinner table, and about the range of material and technical influences that affected home cooking. What they can't convey is a sense of day-to-day cookery as it was genuinely experienced in the kitchens of real life.

To find out as best I could what was on the table in ordinary, middle-class households, I went frequently to magazines and newspapers. These seemed to me to be closer to the ground than most cookbooks, with the exception of such hardworking classics as *Joy of Cooking* or the Betty Crocker cookbooks. Hundreds more cookbooks besides these flowed through the '50s; many of them sold very well, and they clearly affected the meals of the time. James Beard, Poppy Cannon, Peg Bracken, and others built sizable reputations with the help of their books; I discuss some of

these influential cooks in the chapters ahead. But it's always difficult to know for sure how often women turned to a particular
cookbook, no matter how popular it was. Many home cooks consider a cookbook one of their favorites if they use just two or
three recipes from it. What we do know is that home cooks regularly tore out recipes that sounded good to them from *Woman's
Day, Ladies' Home Journal, Good Housekeeping,* and other widely
circulated magazines. We know because the clippings were saved
for years, sometimes for generations, bundled in envelopes or
stuffed into recipe boxes. We can't ascertain how often those
recipes were used, but plainly they appealed to people. If magazine recipes are imperfect guides to how women cooked, at least
such recipes tell us how women planned to cook or how they envisioned themselves cooking, or maybe just how they wished they
could cook.

My favorite sources were the food pages of daily newspapers,
which by virtue of their place in the community seemed likely to
reflect fairly closely the needs and habits of their readers. And my
favorite bits in the papers that I studied were the recipes sent in by
readers themselves. True, these were recipes from self-selected
home cooks, the most confident and enthusiastic cooks in the
neighborhood and perhaps not the most typical. But they were
sending recipes that brought them success, that friends and family
members loved and applauded. Surely these were recipes in which
I would be able to discern the real appetites of real people. For the
same reason I made use of community cookbooks—those ubiquitous, self-published volumes produced by church groups and
other charitable organizations for fund-raising purposes. The
recipes, gathered by members of the cookbook committee from
everybody in the organization who could be badgered to contribute, were always published over the name of the woman who
offered the dish, not necessarily because she claimed to have in-

vented it, but because it represented her. "This is my kitchen," each contributor said with pride. "This is how I cook."

How such women began to renegotiate the terms of domestic life in the new context of work—a spectre that was everywhere in the '50s, even hovering over women who never so much as filled out a job application—is the question that drove my research. Work changed everything. Yes, women with jobs had to continue fixing dinner, vacuuming, and taking children to the dentist; in that sense, work simply made life more harrowing. But women who worked for pay or contemplated it also started to see themselves, their families, and the world in a different way. The proportions changed and the boundaries shifted; now they were actors on another stage altogether. Whether or not they chose to earn money, they were living for the first time in a world where seemingly immutable sex roles were subject to challenge. Poor and working-class women, who had been in the workforce since the industrial revolution and earlier, were accustomed to inhabiting man's sphere while earning their livings, and woman's sphere when they got home. If anybody understood how porous the border actually was, these women did. But for everyone else it was scripture: The cash economy was for men; the emotional economy was for women. And since scripture has a way of cutting across class and gender lines, many Americans subscribed to this increasingly hazy tradition even if they didn't believe in it, even if their own experience contradicted it.

It was in this discomfiting social atmosphere that cooking—the bride's first chore and the grandmother's last, the very heart of homemaking—came under assault from the food industry. Magazines, newspapers, and radio announcers explained over and over to housewives that a welcome new era of effortless food preparation was at hand. "You don't cook it," promised an ad for Sunkist lemons, brandishing a recipe for making lemon pie in an ice-cube tray. "Just mix and beat as directed, place in refrigerator—*and that's all*." Cookbook author Sylvia Schur assured women that owning a blender "takes the place of years of experience and skill," and Betty Crocker reminded her followers that cake mixes would save them "time, work and the task of following recipes." Yet such ads tell a profoundly lopsided story about the food of the '50s. Most middle-class dinners at home changed far more slowly than the food industry ever acknowledged, despite the mounting importance of paid work in women's lives. Throughout the '50s, good home cooking was far more widespread than frozen fish sticks, as the evidence from women's own hands makes plain. By 1963—when Julia Child launched her first television series—an audience was waiting.

Cooking, it turned out, had roots so deep and stubborn that even the mighty fist of the food industry couldn't yank all of them up. One of the sources I read at some length for its revelations about what ordinary women thought about cooking in the '50s was the "Confidential Chat," a column that has been running in *The Boston Globe* for more than a century. Readers write in with questions about every conceivable aspect of home and family life, and other readers respond with their advice and opinions. All the Chatters, as they call themselves, write under pseudonyms. I studied a swath of Chat letters that appeared from 1948 to 1963, hundreds of them about food, and found women who were constantly testing assumptions as well as recipes. Some were accomplished cooks and satisfied housewives; others longed for work outside the home; and others were like the woman who sent in a cry of distress in January 1948: "Won't someone please come to my rescue? . . . My problem is watery custard and bread pudding. . . . I will sign the way I feel about my cooking. Never Satisfied."

What happened over the next several decades was that Never Satisfied, her sisters, and then their daughters found they had a number of choices. At home, at work, everywhere in their lives they were confronted by more possibilities than women had ever known, and this was equally the case when it came to making dessert. There was homemade custard; there was instant chocolate pudding; there was crème caramel—but they had to know what kind of cook they wanted to be. Many surrendered: They came to believe that cooking really was difficult and time-consuming unless ready-made ingredients defined the goal and led the way. Others learned to treat their kitchens the way Julia Child did: as a place where they were in charge, where even failures tasted better to them than packaged perfection. But whether dinner on a given night was boeuf bourguignonne or a canned soup casserole, by the early '60s a great many women were figuring out how to come to their own rescue. Was one of them La Mesa? She wrote the last of the 1963 letters in my survey of Chat sections, heading her contribution simply "Chatters—". She didn't have a question, and she didn't need help with any problems; she just wanted to share her favorite recipe for a batch of peanut butter cookies. I have to admit I've taken the liberty of reading confidence and pride between the lines of her utterly honest ingredients.

Chatters—

½ cup peanut butter   1 ¼ cups flour
1 stick butter or margarine   ¾ teaspoon soda
½ cup white sugar   ½ teaspoon baking powder
½ cup brown sugar   ¼ teaspoon salt
1 egg

Chill, form into tiny balls. Flatten with a fork. Bake in 375-degree oven 10 to 12 minutes.

—*La Mesa*

Something from the Oven

Chapter 1

The Housewife's Dream

Theadora Smafield clasps her hands with joy: She has just won the Grand Prize in the very first Grand National Recipe and Baking Contest, better known as the Pillsbury Bake-Off. The contest was staged in a ballroom at the Waldorf-Astoria Hotel in New York on December 13, 1949. Among the one hundred finalists were such attention-getting entries as Patio Picnic Casserole, Company's Coming Cashew Pie, and Ruth's Dotted Swiss Cake; but Mrs. Smafield's No-Knead Water-Rising Nut Twists triumphed over all. She took home $50,000 and later opened Life magazine to find a glossy picture of herself in glory. (Photo: Martha Holmes/Time Life Pictures/Getty Images.)

Toward the end of February 1954, James Beard was at work in his Greenwich Village kitchen doing what he most loved to do: cooking delicious meals. One night he made lobster à l'américaine for a dinner party; a few days later he entertained guests with a quiche of sautéed bay scallops, then served them fillet of beef with a Marchand de Vin sauce. The next day he set about braising octopus in olive oil and garlic, and while it simmered slowly in red wine, basil, and parsley, he wrote a quick note about the recipe to his friend and gastronomic soul mate, the California cookbook author Helen Evans Brown. "Smells divine," he told her contentedly. With five cookbooks out, most recently *Paris Cuisine,* and several more being readied for publication in 1954, Beard was well settled at the forefront of his profession. Later that year *The New York Times* would bestow upon him the title that would accompany his name for decades to come: "Dean of American Cookery." And yet, as he often complained to Brown, American cookery seemed to be barreling off in quite a different direction from their own culinary styles. For every dinner like the one Cecily Brownstone, food editor at the Associated Press, offered him that summer—they dined in her garden on shrimp with dill and tarragon, steak in a garlic and ginger butter sauce, and baked pears with praline—time and again he encountered recipes for its evil twin, a cuisine he bemoaned as "the Home Ec side" of cookery. "I have been going over a brunch cookbook for *House and Garden* because someone forgot to put in the wines," Beard wrote to Brown in 1960. "Such a mess of stuff. There is actually a recipe for rolling white bread with butter and a sprinkling of Lawry's salt and toasting it in the oven. I nearly popped. What wine you might choose for that is problematic. I would say an old pre-phylloxera Mogen David Concord, with added sugar, myself."

Beard, Brown, and their like-minded colleagues would spend years gloomily monitoring the disappearance of old-fashioned good cooking. Successful though they were in their own careers, they felt powerless as processed foods rolled across the nation like an invasion welcomed by the multitudes. "Where, oh where, do you find a real apple pie, oozing with juices and covered with a flaky brown crust?" he wondered. "Or a fine, well-grained chocolate cake? Or a buttery piece of genuine pound cake?" Not in Portland, Oregon, his home-town. When he arrived for a visit in 1953, the food page of the local paper was rejoicing over Pineapple Betty (marshmallows, pineapple, graham cracker crumbs, and nuts). The nation seemed to have lost its ability to cook with skill or to taste with pleasure. As far as Beard was concerned, what he and Brown undertook in the kitchen and at their typewriters was "missionary work"—bringing the gospel of fine homemade meals to Americans pathetically satisfied with short-cuts and fake pizzazz. Small wonder that when he heard about the daily cooking segments on NBC's lavish new *Home* show, he was aghast. "Try to get to a television set," he urged Brown. "Poppy Cannon is the food person, and she did a vichyssoise with frozen mashed potatoes, one leek sautéed in butter, and a cream of chicken soup from Campbell's."

Beard himself had been making vichyssoise—real vichyssoise, with cream and a little nutmeg and a rich, homemade broth—at least since 1939 when he and his partners in a chic Manhattan catering company used to put up vats at a time and sell it for an impressive two dollars a pint. Now here was Poppy Cannon, au-thor of the immensely popular *Can-Opener Cookbook,* blithely de-ranging a great soup on national television. Her creed—for she, too, was a missionary—was exactly the opposite of Beard's. "It's

easy to cook like a gourmet, though you are a be
nounced in *The Can-Opener Cookbook*. "We wa.
just as we do that in this miraculous age it is quite po
it's fun—to be a 'chef' even before you can really cook.
Beard, she made lobster à l'américaine, but hers started with a c.
of tomato soup. Her "French" and "*so* romantic" variation on
floating island called for lemon Jell-O in the shape of little hearts,
dropped on a "small golden sea of soft Royal Custard sauce." The
food industry was no enemy to her; it was Aladdin's lamp.

To Beard, everything that was wrong with American cooking
in the postwar era was symbolized by the remorseless Poppy Cannon. Yet the two of them had more in common than a look at (or
a taste of) their respective vichyssoises might have indicated.
Beard's antagonism to the food industry would relax considerably
when he started working as a consultant to food companies. And
while Cannon had deep and sometimes inexplicable loyalties to
the industry, she was hardly its slave—as we shall see in another
chapter. What really separated culinary purists like Beard from industry enthusiasts like Cannon wasn't their assessments of American cooking, it was their views of the American cook. Beard
believed the housewife was losing her way, forfeiting her skills,
mindlessly surrendering to packaged foods whenever they beck-
oned. Cannon saw that same housewife heading smartly into the
future, reinventing great culinary traditions with the help of epicurean new products.

Neither of them had it quite right. During that winter of 1954,
just a few weeks before Cannon made her appearance on the *Home*
show, the women's page editor of *The Boston Globe* was hit by an
unexpected torrent of angry mail. The paper had published an
enthusiastic story on New Year's Day about a speech by a food industry consultant trumpeting all the advances made possible by

odern science: frozen food, milk in cartons, fresh vegetables available year-round, electric mixers and toasters. "How long is it since you spent a day without the benefit of science?" the industry expert demanded. "Our kitchen culture may be founded on tradition, but each year science has made its gifts to the homemaker." These sentiments inspired a rush of responses from readers who were not only ungrateful for the latest "gift" they encountered on supermarket shelves, they were downright suspicious. "We've had repercussions—but plenty!" the editor wrote in a follow-up story, and quoted from a few of the letters that had poured in. "Just how much more do packaged foods cost?" "How much time do we homemakers save when using packaged food?" "How does packaged food assure a healthier family? Both my Grandparents lived to be over 90 and they bought their flour in a barrel."

Undoubtedly, these readers were glad to bring home their carrots washed and their flour free of bugs, but they weren't abandoning culinary tradition with the zeal the food industry had been counting on. By the time they sat down and wrote to the *Globe,* in fact, some of these women had been wooed by the food industry for nearly a decade, and they still weren't ready to make a commitment. There was a future for frozen spinach—nobody in the food industry doubted that, and most housewives knew it, too. But it wasn't going to be the future everyone expected, the future that Beard so dreaded and Cannon so joyfully anticipated. It wasn't going to be the glittering future that food companies had been charting since the end of World War II when they turned their attention from military to civilian appetites and began to glimpse the tantalizing profits that lay ahead. Winning the loyalty of American home cooks would turn out to be a lot more difficult than the inventors of instant mashed potatoes and frozen chopped liver ever imagined.

It was a sweltering August day, the air-conditioning in his office was broken, and Joe Graham was worried sick about the price wars that posed an increasing threat to his frozen-food distribution business. Suddenly an old-fashioned electric fan, mounted overhead, fell off the wall and bonked him senseless. When he woke up, it was half a century later—August, 2000. Helicars flew back and forth overhead and parked on the roofs of buildings; and instead of unbearable heat the weather was lovely, for as his friend Marty told him, "Now the entire city is air-conditioned. Huge atomic blowers keep a mass of cooled air in circulation." Joe was so dazed by everything he saw that Marty invited him home for the evening, and that's where Joe encountered sights even more amazing, at least to a frozen-food devotee. Marty's wife, Janet, was delighted to see Joe, for this was one wife who had no problem entertaining unexpected guests for dinner. The meal would be ready in five minutes, she told the men, and strolled away into the next room. At her approach, a segment of one wall slid away to reveal shelves of frozen foods. She selected several packages, placed them in a small compartment in the sliding wall, pressed a button for a few seconds, and announced, "All defrosted and ready to cook." In another room, she inserted the food into a metal square and waited exactly one minute. Then she called the men to the table. "This is some kitchen," Joe remarked, and Janet laughed. "That's a word I haven't heard in a long time," she told him. "There's no such thing as a 'kitchen' nowadays. . . . Just freezer space, electronic cooking, automatic dishwashing. Life's really simple nowadays—science has emancipated women right out of the kitchen."

"Frozen Foods 2000 A.D.: A Fantasy of the Future" was published in *Quick Frozen Foods,* the industry's leading trade journal.

To cook by choosing food packages, to watch the home kitchen fade away into unsentimental memory—Joe's professional Utopia went straight to the heart of the food industry's grandest vision for postwar America. "My predictions are based on current trends and their possible final form," explained E. W. Williams, publisher of the journal and writer of the story. "May we dare to hope that some as yet unborn reader of *Quick Frozen Foods* on some long-distant day will take up this article from a dusty shelf and exclaim, 'Well, whatdyeknow, they had it figured out 50 years ago!' "

They did have it figured out, or at least they devoutly hoped so. Back in the mid-'40s, as World War II was ending, the food industry found itself confronted with the most daunting challenge in its history: to create a peacetime market for wartime foods. Manufacturers and packagers had put considerable expertise into the war effort, not only keeping grocery stores adequately stocked but turning out an array of specially designed foods that could accompany the armed forces anywhere—from camp to jungle to high in the air. Now a great deal of new technology was in place or under development, and factories were ready to keep right on canning, freezing, and dehydrating food as if the nation's life still depended on it. But peacetime shoppers, unlike soldiers in foxholes, had a choice. If a product didn't seem appetizing, it was going to be wonderfully easy for people to ignore it. What the industry had to do was persuade millions of Americans to develop a lasting taste for meals that were a lot like field rations.

Some of the new foods eagerly sent to market right after the war were, in fact, field rations. "Foods formerly manufactured solely for army use will now be put on the civilian market," announced *American Cookery* magazine in 1946, hailing a bonanza of canned meats. "Only 12 different varieties were available before the war, but postwar shelves will boast 40 varieties." Along with the indestructible luncheon meats known as Spam, Treat, Mor, Prem, and Snack, there were canned-ham-and-sweet-potato dinner, canned pork with applesauce, and canned bacon. Dehydrated potatoes and powdered orange juice were ready for market as well. The magazine also welcomed Tatonuts, "a new potato tidbit" notable for its "strong resistance to weather conditions." According to the manufacturer this product would remain "crisp and crunchy" for months. Other foods crossing over from military to civilian life included canned deep-fried hamburgers and canned fruit gelatin, although the latter had to be reformulated for consumers not likely to be serving it under battle conditions. The original version had been created to army specifications, resulting in a jellied dessert so stiff with pectin that it could be gripped by a soldier without losing its shape. For peacetime, the manufacturer was trying to work up a somewhat lighter consistency.

It was a heady time for visionaries in the food business: If you could dehydrate orange juice, why not wine? An ingenious New York engineer set about drying sherry, port, muscatel, sauterne, and chianti, hoping sophisticated diners would come around to the idea of selecting an appropriate powder at dinnertime and adding water and alcohol. Another company spent the war years perfecting frozen coffee ("Froz-n Coff-e"), which came in a package of six paper cups, each holding an ounce of coffee extract. Housewives would simply squeeze the frozen extract out of its paper cup into a coffeepot and add boiling water. And just a year after the war was over, Maxson—a frozen-food company that had been supplying complete meals to wartime fliers, to be heated up on the plane—began offering similar dinners to be served aboard civilian airlines. Steak, meat loaf, beef stew, and corned beef hash patties were the first specialties, accompanied by vegetables, each item in the meal arranged in its own compartment on a plastic plate. "From its reception by travelers it seems a success," remarked *Better Food* magazine, adding that Maxson contemplated entering the retail market as well. Would families give up "the vital element of choice . . . as to which vegetable goes with what?" *Better Food* thought they would, "in return for ease of preparation and excellence of product."

Perhaps wisely, marketing efforts for some of the new foods skipped "excellence of product" and went straight to "ease of preparation." At General Mills the first shortcut product to be unveiled after the war was Pyequick, "an entire pie in a package." A box of Pyequick contained a bag of dehydrated apples and a bag of crust mix. "With a few simple movements, Mrs. Homemaker can have America's favorite dessert ready for the oven," the company asserted in a bulletin, and went on to illustrate the point with motion-study photographs taken in General Mills's test kitchen. A researcher rigged out with tiny electric lights on her fingers made a pie the old-fashioned way and then made one with Pyequick, while a cameraman tracked her motions both times. The old-fashioned method resulted in a picture showing a messy tangle of white lines, suggesting how frantically her two hands had worked to assemble the pie. Making a Pyequick pie, by contrast, produced fewer and simpler white lines, suggesting a process so relaxed that Mrs. Homemaker might have been plucking daisies in a hammock. (Both photographs displayed the same agitated welter of lines over the pastry board, inadvertently revealing that rolling out the crust, at least, was much the same task whether Mrs. Homemaker used Pyequick or made her pastry from scratch.)

Of all the new products the food industry was inventing and dispensing right after the war, the ones that appeared most clearly destined for greatness were frozen foods. Freezing seemed to offer everything: It eliminated nearly every trace of work for the cook, and it captured an illusion of freshness that no other manufactured product could equal. With proper marketing there was no logical reason why the new frozen foods should not simply replace their competitors—the canned and powdered foods that had been around for years and all those messy, bothersome fresh foods that had been around even longer. Gazing into the future, frozen-food manufacturers loved what they were sure they glimpsed. "Fresh produce for retail consumption is a thing of the past," Marty says proudly to the time-traveler, and Joe's envy is heartfelt. In 1959 the authors of a textbook called *Food: America's Biggest Business* announced that a frozen-food Utopia was already at hand. They offered the example of a typical if hypothetical homemaker who decided one morning to serve an entire day's meals out of her freezer. Breakfast was juice, coffee cake, and fish cakes, with a cup of coffee made from a cube of frozen coffee concentrate; lunch was chicken croquettes, french fries, brownies, and lemonade; and at night the TV dinners came out. Cheese and salad greens were the only fresh foods she had to handle. "No pots or pans, no serving dishes, a plate which you throw away when you are finished," the authors sighed happily. "This is a housewife's dream."

A few frozen products had been on the market since the 1930s, but most Americans were not introduced to the startling concept of making dinner from hard-frozen blocks until the war years. Manufacturers of canned and dehydrated foods directed their resources to feeding the military, especially overseas, for the duration, while the frozen-food industry helped supply the home front. The industry was still so young that relatively few grocers even owned a frozen-food display cabinet. Nevertheless, once rationing was under way, every grocer in the country had to display an official poster showing the value in ration points of different foods, including frozen products, whether or not the store actually carried them. These posters, along with newspaper ads that ran regularly and featured the same information, gave many shoppers their first inkling that such foods existed. And for shoppers trying to use their ration points efficiently, the posters made frozen foods look like a very good buy. Supplies of canned foods were limited, because tin was being shunted to war industries, but frozen products were abundant; so frozen fruits and vegetables cost less in ration points than their canned equivalents. Moreover, some frozen products weren't rationed at all, including experimental lines of codfish cakes, chicken à la king, baked beans, and welsh rarebit. At the same time, of course, many traditional foods were hard to obtain. Homemakers who couldn't shop as usual decided to give the new items a try. Sales of these novelties took a jump, but only until the end of rationing, when families went right back to the foods they preferred. As early as 1944, admitted the publisher of *Quick Frozen Foods,* frozen baked beans had become "a drug on the market." Apparently 25 million pounds were available, and pretty much remained so.

Nonetheless, the brief wartime boom in frozen foods made the new industry seem so promising that fledgling companies rushed into the business in the late '40s, processing and distributing an enormous array of hastily conceived items. In 1948, plain frozen fruits and vegetables were joined by bouillabaisse, pâté de foie gras, oyster gumbo, deviled crab, and chocolate chip cookies, as well as what were called "dinner plates" with an entrée, potato, and vegetables. Most of these products and companies quickly disappeared, but if skeptics had any doubts about the sky-high potential for frozen food, orange juice made them believers. During the war, the National Research Corporation of Boston found it could produce powdered orange juice using a vacuum process originally developed to make penicillin and blood plasma. Unfortunately, the only customer for powdered orange juice was the army, and once the war was over, demand was nonexistent. With the help of scientists at the Florida Citrus Commission, however, the company that had been producing the powder—Vacuum Foods, which later became Minute Maid—took another look at the process and found that with certain variations it could be used to make a frozen orange juice concentrate. All the customer had to do was add water, and the juice was remarkably close to the real thing.

Easier than fresh and tastier than canned, frozen orange juice had genuine appeal. By 1950 a quarter of Florida's orange crop was going into concentrates, and oranges that had once been so cheap that growers were letting them rot on the ground now sold for $3.50 a box. A jubilant Minute Maid flooded the floor of its Plymouth, Florida, plant with orange juice and sent out three showgirls on ice skates to do a cancan. But it was 1952 that brought the statistic that frozen-food enthusiasts were waiting for; at last, frozen appeared to be pulling ahead of fresh. According to a study, about 28 percent of the juice served at home that year was frozen, and about 25 percent was squeezed fresh. Canned juice still dominated overall, but the more affluent the family, the less canned juice it was drinking. A year later, frozen juice slightly outstripped canned among the highest income families, and it remained more popular than fresh at all income levels except the lowest. These were triumphant statistics in what *Quick Frozen Foods* called the "battle of fresh vs. frozen." In yet another skirmish, experiments proved that housewives saved eight and a quarter minutes when they used frozen concentrated orange juice instead of squeezing oranges. Here, surely, was the first product destined to leave its fresh equivalent behind in the dust, and there didn't seem to be any reason why dozens more shouldn't follow.

Milk, for instance. The dairy industry, as well as the frozen-food industry, watched what was happening with orange juice, and they were starry-eyed with hopes for milk. Production always exceeded what could be sold fresh; dried milk had no appeal apart from its price, and the advantages of a frozen concentrate over fresh liquid supplies were obvious, at least to accountants. Frozen concentrated milk could be stored for up to six months, then reconstituted; and according to its partisans, no change in flavor could be detected. After a couple of years of hard effort, however, discouragement reigned. In terms of sales, frozen concentrated milk was "as dead as the dodo," admitted the president of Borden. "We have marketed the product experimentally in many Illinois communities and elsewhere," he told *Quick Frozen Foods* in 1951. "Consumers have not been enthusiastic about it here or in any other area where it has been introduced." Apparently, homemakers could see no reason to store, thaw, and reconstitute milk when fresh was always available and the price was the same.

If not milk, what about . . . water? E. W. Williams of *Quick Frozen Foods* thought frozen concentrated mineral water might appeal to consumers; they could buy a six-ounce block of distilled mineral water and just add water. But his colleagues had their attention fixed on juice. Processors started concentrating and freezing every fruit they could squeeze or crush: apples, grapefruits, lemons, pineapples, grapes, tomatoes, limes, tangerines, and cranberries. The apple industry in particular had big dreams, because it needed a way to process a constant oversupply of Delicious apples, which were too bland to be used by themselves in canned applesauce. Scientists at the U.S. Department of Agriculture helpfully designed a new method of concentrating apple juice that permitted Delicious apples to be used exclusively, but consumers didn't like it. Nor did they like most of the other frozen juice concentrates, with the prominent exception of lemonade. This was so much easier to prepare in quantity for children than fresh lemonade that the product became the next huge seller among concentrates. Frozen concentrated tomato juice, on the other hand, flopped hard, despite bearing a much closer resemblance to its fresh counterpart than canned tomato juice, which was a thicker product with a slightly cooked flavor. The problem was that people liked canned tomato juice and, more important, recognized it as tomato juice. Nothing else was going to earn that title, not even the juice of tomatoes.

The next orange juice turned out to be fish sticks, which Birdseye introduced cautiously in a few test markets in 1952. Two years later fish sticks had become a frozen-food legend. More than 7 million pounds were produced in 1953, and 30 million in 1954. Most people ate little fish in the course of a year, but fish sticks were breaded and fried—a treatment that effectively eliminated the taste of fish, especially after the liberal application of ketchup. "This is the way folks love fish!" exclaimed an ad for Hunt's tomato sauce, showing a picture of fish sticks doused with sauce. "Besides, it's a perfect recipe for busy homemakers and career women—ready in a jiffy." Numerous companies raced to get into the fish stick business, while still others headed to the laboratory and emerged with chicken sticks, ham sticks, veal sticks, onion-flavored poultry sticks, eggplant sticks, and dried lima bean sticks. These alternatives failed to extend the category as planned. By the same token, frozen tuna potpie was never able to inherit the mantle of the popular chicken potpie, and while frozen dinners in partitioned trays eventually won favor, the frozen breakfast in a partitioned tray ("Honeymoon Breakfast for Two") attracted no following whatsoever.

Time after time, in fact, frozen-food manufacturers rushed into the marketplace with products nobody wanted, fell back defeated, and jumped up to charge forward once more. The pages of *Quick Frozen Foods* practically bristled with irritation. Why wouldn't people buy frozen Camembert cheese? What prejudice kept women from trying frozen whale steaks, especially since they were "Papal approved" for Fridays and Lent? When would the market be ready at last for frozen eggplant, advertised as "Eggplant—the new wonder vegetable"? Even such practical items as bread and rolls didn't stir much interest. "If the truth were known, the average housewife does not do a good job of home baking," fumed a vice president at Frigid-Dough in 1949. His company made frozen bakery items for women who largely ignored them.

One reason frozen food was making little impact at that time was that few people had any sort of freezer space. In 1952, there were 155 million people in the United States, according to the most recent census, and they owned about 33 million refrigerators—that is, nearly every family had one. But only about 4 million families owned home freezers, and most lived on farms. In a small study of homemakers in two upstate New York communities, conducted in 1952, a Cornell Ph.D. student found that 80 percent of the farm households had access to a freezer, either at home or in a nearby food locker, compared with about 10 percent of city dwellers. No wonder the industry's most cherished new products weren't selling: Farm families tended to fill their freezers with vegetables from their own gardens, not packages of frozen bouillabaisse. The very people whom the industry had identified as the likeliest consumers of frozen food, namely working couples and small families in cities and towns, had no place to keep frozen food. Most of the new refrigerators coming on the market had separate freezing compartments, but families who still used their old refrigerators barely had room for a few ice cubes in the tiny interior compartments. Worse, from the industry's point of view, they seemed convinced that they just didn't have space for a freestanding freezer if they lived in a small house or apartment. With a tiny kitchen and no cellar, where could they possibly put a bulky new appliance? This was a problem the industry believed it could solve. Surely there were places all over the home where a freezer might be slipped in unobtrusively among the other furnishings.

International Harvester was one of the first to experiment with the decorative possibilities of the home freezer: In 1953 the company put out both a refrigerator and freezer trimmed with plaid fabric slipcovers. Plaid kitchen curtains completed the ensemble, and a selling point was the ease with which housewives could redecorate simply by changing to new fabric. Then *Quick Frozen Foods* commissioned a designer to come up with ways to get the freezer out of the kitchen entirely, integrating it into the living room, the hallway, and even the bedroom of a typical small dwelling. A top-opening freezer, for instance, might be camouflaged by coating it with a laminated wood veneer that would make the appliance look exactly like a credenza, especially with decorative grillwork hiding the motor opening. A small upright freezer, also covered in wood veneer, would be practically invisible if a drop-leaf tabletop rested on it. One design showed a freezer built in the size and shape of a radio cabinet, with "radio dials" that were actually freezer controls, and fake straw grilles. According to *Quick Frozen Foods*, ideas along this order "might increase the sales of home freezers by as much as a million units a year."

Freezer sales did increase, mostly because people moving to new homes in the suburbs had more room—in the kitchen or basement. Meanwhile, the hopes of the industry gathered around a new product, one that had been emerging slowly and haltingly since the end of the war and by 1952 was finally beyond the experimental phase. That year the first frozen dinners—turkey, potato, and vegetables—in oven-ready aluminum trays began to arrive in grocery stores. If frozen food was ever going to take its rightful place at the center of American home life—an ambition that was an article of faith in the frozen-food industry—the vehicle would be the complete dinner.

Inexplicably, at least to the industry, such work-free dinners caused very little stir at first. Most shoppers barely noticed that the housewife's dream had come true.

These particular frozen meals, harbingers of a product that would eventually symbolize the cuisine of an entire era, were devised by a company called Quaker States Foods, which sent out its brainchild under the One-Eye Eskimo label. Along with turkey, One-Eye Eskimo offered Swiss steak and pot roast dinners. Around the same time, Frigi-Dinner unveiled its own frozen dinners for the retail trade: beef stew with peas and corn; veal goulash with peas and potatoes; and a Chinese platter with egg rolls, fried rice, and chicken chow mein. More companies quickly began planning inroads into the full-meal market, but it took Swanson, a well-known Omaha producer of canned and frozen poultry, to give the concept landmark status and a generic identity. Swanson came late to the full-meal idea—its segmented dinner tray didn't show up in stores until 1954—but the company added three ingredients to the formula that made the product stand out instantly from the crowd. The first was the Swanson brand name, already widely recognized around the country. Second was voluminous national advertising, including a full-force promotional effort nicknamed "Operation Smash" to accompany the dinner's debut. Third, and perhaps most important, Swanson came up with the inspired term *TV dinner*. Television was still a young medium, but it was spreading so fast that by 1955 nearly two out of three families owned a set. Previous frozen dinners had never gotten beyond the novelty stage, but the first year Swanson TV dinners were on the market, Americans sat down to an estimated 13 million of them. "The day of the complete meal has dawned for good," rejoiced E. W. Williams in a *Quick Frozen Foods* editorial. "The public is 'conditioned' to prepared foods. . . . It is no longer thought odd to make a meal of a precooked item such as fish sticks, chicken or meat pies, chow mein, ravioli, and similar items. The gap has been bridged. First, we had single items such as french fried potatoes, then the partially complete meal such as pot pies and now—the 100% meal such as turkey or chicken dinners, fish dinners and meat dinners. The field is open!"

And it was—but chiefly to Swanson. While the company hurried to bring out more varieties—fried chicken came next, then pot roast—other manufacturers scrambled to compete as fast as they could think up attention-getting menus. Swiss steak, roast beef, and "beef patty" dinners appeared; a Mexican dinner showed up, and a second Chinese dinner was introduced, this one featuring chop suey, chow mein, rice, and—mysteriously—a helping of tomato sauce. None posed any serious challenge to Swanson, even the ones that offered very similar meals. It was the phrase *TV dinner* that found a permanent place in the culture and made the product an icon.

The flavor of Swanson's dinners—entrancingly metallic, as if tray and turkey were one—clings even now to the palate memory of anyone who encountered those magic meals in childhood. But contrary to the industry's expectations, they didn't replace cooking. Children ate them when their parents were going out, and husbands made do with them when their wives weren't home. A TV dinner occupied the time and space of a meal and fulfilled its function, but nobody confused a TV dinner with the real thing. In 1958, *McCall's* magazine invited 105 subscribers to assemble for a discussion of their domestic likes and dislikes at an event called the Congress on Better Living, staged for the benefit of advertisers. While many of the women participating commented favorably on TV dinners, they made it clear that these occupied a different and humbler category than actual cooking. "When I'm having a dinner party for guests, the TV dinner does come in handy for the children eating early," said one. "We never have them as a meal," said another, "but if I am ever by myself . . . I buy one because I don't like to cook for myself alone." Two years later, marketing researchers at *Life* magazine asked more than a thousand women what they thought about frozen foods and heard similar responses. Would they serve a frozen meal if the boss was coming to dinner? Almost unanimously, the women said no. As *Quick Frozen Foods* put it in a rueful analysis of the survey, "They felt that frozen foods are lacking in prestige."

It was supposed to be the housewife's dream, but in reality the housewife was wide-awake and leafing through her recipe file. Despite statistics that the frozen-food industry loved to quote— for instance, by 1954 consumption of frozen foods had jumped from 17 to 36 pounds annually per capita—most families were buying relatively few such products. Only 3 percent of consumers accounted for 80 percent of the purchases of frozen chicken and beef pies in 1954. A year later about half of all families were buying frozen foods at least occasionally every month, but for the most part they were buying frozen vegetables and juice; everything else lagged far behind. In comparison to other kinds of food, frozen was still obscure. Even frozen vegetables, the leading product in the industry and its first staple, were barely registering their presence at the dinner table. Americans were eating about 190 pounds of vegetables per capita in 1954; of that amount, about 145 pounds were consumed fresh, 40 pounds canned, and a little under 6 pounds frozen.

The food industry's crusade, launched with such confidence right after the war, was winning far fewer converts than its visionaries had predicted. Processed and packaged foods were making themselves known and in some cases necessary throughout the 1950s, but they didn't come near to dominating the American table. A study conducted in 1955 by the U.S. Department of Agriculture showed that homemakers were spending only 7 cents of every food dollar on canned and frozen fruits and vegetables, which were among the most frequently purchased processed foods. "New convenience foods still have had relatively little impact on the total food market," concluded *Advertising Age* in its report on the study. Even frozen orange juice was making a less spectacular showing than indicated in the food industry's own studies, most of which were carried out and packaged to emphasize the most favorable view possible. According to the USDA figures, only a fifth of the families it surveyed were drinking frozen juice, though these included nearly half of the families in the highest income brackets. Fully half of all the families were still squeezing oranges.

Five years later the numbers were up, but convenience products continued to play only a minor role at mealtime. From the spring of 1959 to the spring of 1960, the USDA studied purchases of 158 popular convenience foods—everything from canned spaghetti to frozen orange juice to devil's food cake mix—and found they accounted for no more than about 14 cents of every dollar spent on food. In 1960, too, *Parents Magazine* published the results of a survey carried out among a random sample of subscribers who were asked detailed questions about the food they served their families. One of the more widely used frozen products was fish sticks. A little over half the subscribers bought them, but most families had them only once a month. They also ate frozen potpies occasionally, and about a third of the families bought frozen dinners; few of the other heat-and-eat specialties had much of a presence at all. The picture emerging from all this research showed a homemaker who typically made use of a package of frozen peas, a can of peaches, or maybe a box of Jell-O or instant pudding in the course of planning a meal. Sometimes she heated up a can of spaghetti for the children's lunch, and in the summer perhaps she kept frozen lemonade on hand. "To date the average homemaker

has used convenience foods only to a limited extent," acknowledged the advertising expert Janet Wolff in 1958.

There were many reasons why homemakers proved far more
difficult to woo than the best minds in the food business had predicted. Wolff thought it was in part the taste and cost of packaged
foods that kept women at a suspicious distance, and she was right,
but those were only the most obvious of the problems clinging to
the new boxes, cans, and jars as they lined up on grocers' shelves.
Packaged foods per se were hardly novelties to Americans: Canned
goods and pancake mixes had been pantry staples for decades; and
by the late 1930s grocers were carrying Bisquick and other dry
"ready-mixes," along with the first efforts coming from the
frozen-food industry. But prices for many such prewar products
were high, and except for canned goods they had scant effect on
most people's eating habits. During the war, some housewives
turned to packaged foods out of necessity—if they couldn't buy
sugar, they could a least buy a box of cake mix—but shortcut baking didn't become widespread until years later. Similarly, as we
have seen, homemakers tried frozen foods when rationing made
them attractive, but dropped them as soon as familiar products returned after the war. The fact that shops were carrying new and
different packaged foods in the late '40s just didn't matter very
much to most housewives. Like the legendary women of Boston
who already had their hats, home cooks already had their family
meals, and they didn't need new ones.

What's more, many of the products that were hurried onto the
market right after the war simply could not be translated into appealing or even recognizable food. Powders and mixes, for instance, tended to produce wholly inadequate imitations of
whatever was pictured on the box. Dried milk had its niche solely
because it was cheap and lasted forever, cake mixes were uneven in
quality until well into the '50s, and instant coffee made only weak

and helpless gestures toward the flavor of real coffee, in part because the powder was full of peculiar-tasting carbohydrate additives. (As *Consumer Reports* wrote, after a tasting in 1947, "Most of the 16 brands tested had no aroma at all, or if they did, it was not that of coffee.") Within ten years most companies were marketing pure instant coffee and sales were rising. Yet even then coffee lovers found it so reprehensible that Janet Wolff called it the one convenience food that was popular in spite of its terrible taste. Canned foods were accepted more easily than anything else, because they had been around for so long that Americans had become accustomed to the way the canning process sorely depressed the flavor and texture of fruits and vegetables. Canned peaches, canned pineapple, and canned tomato juice had little resemblance to their fresh counterparts, but they needed none; the canned versions had won popular identities of their own. When homemakers encountered some of the new canned foods, however—foods they had never before taken from a can—they balked. Canned hamburgers had no place in the category of hamburgers and no place in the category of canned food. They fell flat.

Frozen foods at least had the virtue of looking relatively the same as the originals, but the industry was haunted by poor products right after the war, as novice companies rushed into the business with little experience in processing, packaging, or distributing. A team of food technologists from the University of California tested samples of frozen fruits and vegetables, purchased from grocery stores in 1947 and 1948, and found peas with "stale" odors, mixed vegetables with "hay-like odor and flavor," asparagus that was "inedible because of stringiness and off flavor," and spinach "about as tasty as a wet piece of cloth." A decade later, quality across the industry was much improved, but shoppers interviewed in a San Francisco supermarket still described frozen peas as "tasteless," frozen spinach as "lots of green ice," and frozen broccoli as "frozen green mush." They complained that chicken pies should be called "gravy and potato stew" and that frozen poultry was all bone and skin.

Quality would never prove to be a particularly reliable standard for packaged foods, since any realistic assessment of flavor would have dealt a harsh blow to innovation. In 1962, for example, a "taste panel" at the USDA evaluated twenty-eight of the new freeze-dried foods then on the market. The panelists, all from the food quality laboratory of the Human Nutrition Research Division, tasted beef, chicken, and seafoods, and rated them on the basis of appearance, flavor, juiciness, texture, and tenderness. Five panelists took on each food. They found the diced beef "tough," "fibrous," and "stringy"; the beefsteaks "mushy" and "dry, yet oozing juice"; the chicken stew "off-flavored"; and the chicken and rice dinner "cardboardy, chalky and powdery." "A definitive aroma described as 'wet cardboard' was noted while the dinner was being prepared in the laboratory," commented the author of the report. Seafoods received similarly doleful ratings; as the author noted, "Flavor seems the key palatability characteristic lowering the general acceptance scores." What these responses amounted to in the end were ratings of "acceptable" for nearly all the products. None of them was judged a failure.

Price, by contrast, was often less forbidding than the food itself. Packaged specialty foods—frozen egg rolls, canned macaroni and cheese, pudding mix—were indeed more expensive than the cost of making the equivalent products from scratch. But by the start of the '50s even frozen foods, which were the most expensive of all the packaged products, could be competitive with fresh in the category of plain fruits and vegetables. In January 1952, fresh peas in the pod cost from 29 to 45 cents a pound in New York, but once they were trimmed, the price effectively jumped to a range of 72 cents to $1.12 a pound. In season during 1951, the post-trimming price had been 31 to 62 cents a pound. Meanwhile, frozen peas cost between 29 and 35 cents a pound, with relatively little seasonal fluctuation. Women seeking good-quality produce at a decent price had reason to investigate all the choices—fresh, frozen, and canned—especially since each choice provided a completely different food.

In the course of the '50s, homemakers did start thinking about produce that way. Canned fruits and vegetables remained popular for their low price and easy availability, while frozen produce gradually changed its identity from novelty to staple. But packaged specialty foods—the entrées and dinners and desserts that were supposed to set women free—budged very little from their original place out at the distant margins of home cooking. It's not that women didn't want help in the kitchen. They had long been accustomed to sharing the work with family members or visitors, and a friendly voice from a cookbook was always welcome when it came time to prepare a meal. But never before had the food itself tried to elbow a woman away from the stove, and few homemakers welcomed the intrusion. What's more—and this was a possibility the food industry had never in its wildest imaginings entertained—the postwar years turned out to be exactly the wrong moment for the industry to try to persuade home cooks to quit cooking. Prohibition, the Depression, war, and a culinary history replete with ketchup and canned soup had all done their parts to pose serious threats to the tradition of decent cooking in American kitchens, but it had never disappeared; and in the '50s its prospects were looking brighter than they had in a long time.

It's true that much had been lost in the past hundred years, thanks to an increasingly industrialized food supply and the changes in culinary technique and style that accompanied the rise of food processing in the nineteenth century. By the '50s, cottony white bread in cellophane was the standard in homes up and down the economic scale; the notion of a green salad was frequently iceberg lettuce drenched in sweet, bottled dressing; and more and more cookie jars were filled by Nabisco. Increasingly, too, there were changes under way in the nation's farmlands that would pose a threat far greater than Oreos to the American table. Agriculture was fast becoming a matter of technology and chemistry as farmers began to select seeds with long-distance shipping in mind, not flavor, and to rely on new pesticides to increase yields. Still other chemicals were coming into use in the raising of livestock and poultry. In the '50s and early '60s, a few food writers were already starting to complain about the quality of fresh produce. "With the fresh tomatoes on the market so dreadful (there is no other word for it), you must turn for real tomato flavor to the can," wrote Poppy Cannon in *House Beautiful* in 1956. James Beard said he was "getting scared" about what seemed to be happening to beef and poultry. "Our Thanksgiving turkey was about as interesting in flavor as soap," he wrote to Helen Evans Brown in 1962. "The chickens they sent from Maryland for the school last week looked beautiful and tasted like absolutely nothing. . . . I bought a steak the other night from the butcher down here—$5.50—tender but no beef taste or quality of aging, a complete dud." But it would take another couple of decades before criticism of supermarket fruits and vegetables became widespread, and the extent of the environmental devastation across America would not become a national scandal until after the publication of Rachel Carson's *Silent Spring* in 1962. Hence, the '50s were largely sheltered from the trepidations that would beset consumers later on. A crisis and a crusade were waiting around the corner, but most home cooks were simply pleased to find nice, fat chickens neatly cut up in the supermarket and fresh fruit all year round.

In many ways the fifteen or twenty years following the end of World War II constituted a genuine good-food era in American life. Regional culinary traditions were still manifest in those pockets of the nation where food lovers had long been accustomed to enjoying their meals and had no intention of quitting: California and the Northwest, Louisiana and the South, along the New England coast, and in the ethnic neighborhoods of cities everywhere. While a succession of pies, pork chops, and other plainspoken favorites continued to reign over countless dinner tables, a scattering of homemakers had begun to explore different culinary territories—and some were serving livelier dishes than their families had eaten in generations. These ambitious cooks belonged to a fast-growing class that was learning how to spend its discretionary income on food, and they were fascinated by the potential represented by herbs, spices, wine, butter, and cream. On their trips to Europe they remembered or discovered the pleasure of wonderful food, and at home they entertained zealously.

Many of these newly awakened gastronomes were working their way toward a desirable mode of existence known as *gracious living*. Women's colleges sometimes evoked this lofty goal when they encouraged students to learn how to sit on a sofa, cross their ankles, and sip demitasse, but gracious living had an important commercial component as well. Incomes had been rising steadily since the war, boosting millions of Americans into the middle class and encouraging millions more to dream about it. From 1950 to 1960 the number of home owners nearly quadrupled, and postwar magazines were stuffed with ads and editorial copy aimed at helping readers furnish and equip their new lives. Leafing through hefty magazines bulging with pictures and advice, readers could revamp their taste as they examined furniture and kitchen equipment, stately silver, charming tableware, and even carefully selected paintings and record albums. *Living,* "The Magazine for Young Homemakers," started publishing in 1947 specifically to reach women with up-and-coming husbands and a future bright with disposable income. Stories in every issue described home life in America the Sophisticated, starring one blithe couple after another who cooked with wine, tossed big green salads in wooden bowls they never washed, and served their guests casual yet dramatic dishes such as authentic French onion soup, "the runniest Camembert," "a wicked curry," or maybe just ham—"but make it ham de luxe, cooked in champagne!"

Party stories like the ones in *Living* were a staple of gracious-living journalism, and *Life* easily perfected the genre. In 1954 the magazine visited four splendid homes for a feature called "Ten Minutes Before the Party," dropping in on notable hostesses as they put the last touches on their table settings. Designer Bonnie Cashin was poised to serve paella to eight; novelist Kathleen Winsor, hovering over her table arrangements in a strapless gown, planned a "simple supper" of lamb; Mrs. Owen Cheathan of Augusta, Georgia, was readying a massive buffet of ham, creole shrimp, biscuits, and wild rice; and Gloria Braggiotti and "her artist husband Emlen Etting" were expecting company for an after-concert spaghetti supper in Philadelphia. Even *Forecast,* the monthly home economics magazine, tried to get into the spirit of gracious living with a first-person party story, this one contributed (as were many *Forecast* articles) by a representative of the food industry. "Here is my favorite menu for entertaining at Sunday night supper," wrote a home economist at Ralston. Her menu featured Ralston cereals in every course, from hors d'oeuvres to dessert, and the photo showed four guests gamely holding up Ralston appetizers: morsels of Vienna sausage between bite-sized shredded wheat biscuits, each tiny sandwich speared on a toothpick.

Cookbooks of every sort began piling up in shops during the '50s, so many that Jane Nickerson, food editor of *The New York Times,* predicted the market could never absorb such a number—

forty new cookbooks in the spring of 1952 alone, she wrote in amazement. Among them were *French Country Cooking* by Elizabeth David and *West Coast Cook Book* by Helen Evans Brown, both widely acclaimed on their arrival and now regarded as classics. Charlotte Turgeon had already translated the popular French family cookbook *Tante Marie's French Kitchen* and was about to coedit an American edition of *Larousse Gastronomique*; and Buwei Yang Chao's *How to Cook and Eat in Chinese,* first published in 1945, had gone back to press five times by 1950. When the renowned radio personality Mary Margaret McBride published her own cookbook in 1957, she acknowledged in the introduction that "news of dehydrated steaks, faster mixes, even food squeezed from tubes" was constantly bombarding Americans. "So you may ask: Why a cookbook at all in such times? Well, I recently came on a consumer survey which reported that in the midst of this mad whirl of no-hands cooking, the sale of baking powder has increased substantially!" She went on to predict that homemade biscuits and cakes would never lose their appeal, "just as no satisfaction will ever equal the joy a woman finds in setting those biscuits and other delicious products of her own skill before her family."

Newspapers and magazines were teeming with recipes, from the plainest to the most elaborate, that made no mention at all of packaged ingredients but comfortably shared space with the numerous industry-inspired stories about frozen salads and speedy desserts. At the *Ladies' Home Journal*, editors Bruce and Beatrice Gould went so far as to instruct food editors to limit the use of packaged foods in recipes, lest they lower the tone of the magazine. In this spirit, the *Journal*'s resident philosopher-cook, Ann Batchelder, charmed readers for many years with tips on fried oysters, crème brûlée, ham hash, and chicken curry served in a pineapple shell. *Life* ran a series of spectacular food stories throughout the decade, elaborately photographed and accompanied by recipes for a fearless range of dishes: Szechuan noodles, pressed duck, bouillabaisse, kidney-liver kebabs. Nearly all the major magazines featured wine stories at least occasionally, spurred in part by a wine trade trying to resuscitate itself after years lost to Prohibition and the war. As guests of the wine industry, writers went off to tour vineyards in Europe and California, then returned home to write enthusiastic articles about grapes, regions, harvests, and wine-making methods, accompanied by appropriate recipes. Prompted by the wine industry, writers often tried to persuade Americans to stop feeling intimidated by wine and just go ahead and put a bottle on the table, European-style. Don't worry about vintages, they begged; don't worry about the size and shape of the glass. "The best of the experts agree on one simple, cardinal rule," instructed *Life*. "If a wine tastes good, it is good."

At *Ebony*, which began publishing in 1945 as a *Life* magazine for middle-class blacks, food editor Freda De Knight published recipes of her own along with many more that she gathered from famous black entertainers, public officials, society women, and chefs. Her popular column was called "Date with a Dish," and although she often featured such standards as curried chicken, lemon pie, and macaroni salad, she had a wide-ranging taste for foreign dishes as well. Written up with notes, photographs, and step-by-step instructions, her recipes revealed a sharp appreciation for the taste, smell, and texture of good cooking. In 1948 she brought out a cookbook based on her columns, and *Ebony* gave it a warm welcome, calling her a "food impresario" whose recipes were influenced by "the finest in Spanish, English, Italian and East Indian eating, as well as the conventional barbecues and other dishes so relished by colored gourmets." The magazine, which typically placed pictures of brand-name products right in the food photography in an effort to court national advertisers, at the same time had a commitment to serious food coverage. In 1949 a test kitchen was installed in *Ebony*'s Chicago headquarters, and a year later De Knight took a trip to Paris to study for three months at the Cordon Bleu. Her teacher was chef Max Bugnard, the Escoffier-trained master who happened to be teaching another American woman that year, a foreign service wife named Julia Child.

Ruth Ellen Church, the "Mary Meade" who edited the food pages at the *Chicago Tribune,* was full of praise for De Knight's "intriguing" recipes, including the East and West Indian dishes that De Knight prepared at a Chicago cooking demonstration in 1950. De Knight, noted Mary Meade in a column, was "the only home economics trained Negro food editor" and hence much in demand as a lecturer around the country for audiences interested in what Meade called "the Negro angle." But De Knight stood out from her colleagues for reasons that had nothing to do with race. Although she cooperated just as they did with the food industry, frequently acknowledging the convenience of shortcut products—and becoming a spokeswoman for Hunt's as well—she never missed a chance to urge her readers to cook from scratch for the sheer pleasure of the work as well as for the results. Her culinary convictions went very well with *Ebony*'s view of African American women, summed up in the headline over a two-page editorial that ran in 1947: "Goodbye Mammy, Hello Mom." According to the editors, it was time for "Negro" women to quit work and stay home with their families. In an era of high employment, an increasing number of men would be able to support their families, freeing women at last from the years they spent in the white woman's kitchen. "Today in thousands of Negro homes, the Negro mother has come home," the editors proclaimed. "The cooking over which the 'white folks' used to go into ecstasies is now reserved for her own family." With this editorial support, De Knight could give full rein to an enthusiastic understanding of food. "What is the secret of wonderful French food?" she reflected on her return from Paris. "I am convinced there is no single basic reason, but a combination of the fertility of the French soil and the genius of French housewives." Most food journalists wouldn't think that way for another twenty-five years. "The French love to eat as well as cook," she added feelingly. "Their foods are cooked to keep the flavor *in*."

Although other African American publications ran women's sections with food stories and recipes, few could afford coverage that was as knowledgeable and distinctive as De Knight's. At the *Amsterdam News* in New York, most of the food stories came from syndicated columns and food company press releases. But like *Ebony*—and quite unlike the paper's news columns—the women's section and its food articles bore no consistent racial stamp and were aimed at a middle-class readership that might have been living in any socially ambitious community in the country. "If one has been compelled to decline a dinner invitation, should one make a call later?" was one of the questions posed in a Q&A column called "Modern Etiquette." ("Yes; this is the proper and courteous thing to do.") The paper offered its readers a steady stream of packaged-food recipes, using the same Ritz crackers, Jell-O, and Pream that were being featured in recipes throughout the mainstream press; but from time to time, the editors featured such company dishes as lemon chiffon pie, cocktail-sized deviled meatballs, and raspberry soup—"chilled, of course, for summer dining pleasure." On these occasions the tone became as properly lofty as the food. For this readership, food represented a way to climb up and perhaps out, but at the same time it seems to have enjoyed a secure status in its own right. The emphasis on these pages was on widening a reader's world and opening up new ones. "Integration took place over the dinner tables—menuwise—long before laws were passed," noted food editor Betty Granger in 1957, describing a recent fund-raising dinner at an African American church in Brooklyn. The committee in charge of the dinner had decided to make it a smorgasbord, and rounded up recipes from a Swedish restaurant as well as from friends and various cookbooks. Travel posters from Sweden were hung around the church auditorium, and among the standout dishes were Swedish meatballs and a cottage-cheese aspic mold.

Canned-soup casseroles were thriving everywhere, and it was hard to beat the thrill of watching Reddi-wip unfurl in a swoosh from beneath a fingertip, but homemakers who wanted to learn more exotic ways in the kitchen were eagerly signing up for cooking classes. The British-born cook Dione Lucas had opened her Cordon Bleu cooking school in New York in 1942. By the mid-'50s she was known across the country as well, appearing on her own television program five nights a week and traveling widely to give demonstration classes. In Kansas City one morning in 1955, more than nine hundred women packed an auditorium to watch her cook. Helen Worth had been attracting socialites and affluent homemakers to her handsomely equipped cooking school on Manhattan's East Side since 1948; her devotees called it "the Radcliffe of cooking schools." And James Beard, whose expertise and celebrity made him a sought-after figure for all sorts of cooking demonstrations around the country, finally opened his own highly regarded school in 1956. In Minneapolis, women went to Verna Meyer, a Cordon Bleu graduate, to learn to make soufflés, lobster thermidor, and brioche. In Princeton, New Jersey, housewives studied with Evelyn Patterson, author of *The Gourmet Kitchen,* or drove to Montclair for an introduction to Italian wines with Mrs. Robert Caruba, founder of the Wine and Food Tasters of New Jersey. In San Francisco they could learn Japanese,

Cantonese, and northern Chinese cooking at the YWCA; in Baltimore the Y offered a course in Eastern European pastries; and in Detroit and Denver housewives signed up for classes in foreign cookery through local adult education programs.

In this dizzying atmosphere, some of the old charmers in the American kitchen repertoire were starting to look frumpy. "You are *dated* if you top your desserts with a maraschino cherry and whipped cream," counseled *House Beautiful* in 1951. "You are *up-to-date* if you serve your peaches in orange juice, your figs in sour cream, and your ice cream with a blazing sauce." Reviewing a flock of new cookbooks in 1954, a critic at the *Saturday Review* said she pitied the poor souls who might be served one of the recipes she came across in a children's cookbook, a dish she described as "that bridge-club pest of yesteryear." It was the venerable candle salad: half a banana standing in a ring of canned pineapple, with a cherry on top. In its day decades earlier, this had been the very emblem of creativity, but although many Americans were still eating it, the experts had moved on. And with them went an increasing number of lay eaters. "I particularly enjoy your articles on food, which I find above the usual 'tuna, potato chip and mushroom soup casserole' category," wrote a pleased subscriber to *Living*.

No wonder, then, that the most spectacularly successful advertising campaign for a food product in the postwar era—arguably one of the most successful promotions in the history of the modern food business—was the Pillsbury Bake-Off. Shortly after the war, while the companies producing frozen cookie dough and dehydrated pie filling were helplessly brandishing their no-work desserts in front of an inattentive public, Pillsbury launched a celebration of home cooking that went straight to the heart of millions of women and made the term *Pillsbury Bake-Off* a domestic totem in American culture. It shouldn't have worked: The prevailing wisdom on women and cooking was running in exactly the opposite direction when the Leo Burnett advertising agency dreamed up the idea in 1949. Many sages in the food business thought that such a massive campaign in honor of plain, all-purpose flour had to be one of the riskiest ventures conceivable. The costs were huge, the logistics were overwhelming, and the potential for legal problems was immense. What if a finalist's assigned stove didn't work on the big day, and she sued? And while Pillsbury's Best Family Flour had a respectable history as the company's core product, flour was the humblest of all grocery items, with little to distinguish one bag from the next. It was going to take unheard-of quantities of publicity to get people to look twice at such a pedestrian product. Indeed, why buy a bag of flour at all when instant piecrust was available? But Pillsbury decided to take a chance, and by the time *Life* magazine captured Theadora Smafield of Detroit clasping her hands and shrieking with delight over her victory, it was clear that the gamble had been a smart one. Pillsbury's Best attracted 700,000 new customers in 1949, and as a satisfied executive told stockholders, "The goodwill we earned alone paid for the cost."

The event was officially titled "The Grand National Recipe and Baking Contest," but well before contest day in December, everyone including the press was calling it the Pillsbury Bake-Off. Entry blanks were available at grocery stores, and grocers also distributed "mystery tokens." If one of these plastic tokens accompanied a winning recipe, the cook would receive double the prize money. Pillsbury sent out 5 million tokens to grocers and then had to resupply them almost immediately; in the end, 32 million were handed out. Meanwhile, a professional contest-running company was taking charge of the thousands of recipes that poured in. A team of home economists examined each recipe and chose two hundred of the most intriguing for a first round of test baking.

More testing followed by a second team of home economists, until half the two hundred were eliminated. Then Pillsbury contacted one hundred thrilled home cooks and invited them to travel to the Waldorf-Astoria Hotel in New York, all expenses paid, to compete in the Bake-Off. They would prepare their dishes in the morning, and a fresh assortment of judges—4-H officials, newspaper and magazine food writers, perhaps a movie star or two—would taste and discuss the entries. The next day the winners would be announced at a celebratory banquet. That first year three men and ninety-seven women from thirty-eight states and the District of Columbia made it to the finals.

Contest day opened with a flourish: In a formal procession led by company president Philip Pillsbury, all the contestants marched into a ballroom outfitted with one hundred electric stoves provided by General Electric and got busy measuring and mixing, while crowds of hometown and national press hovered nearby. Pillsbury officials had assured the finalists that next to their stoves they would find every ingredient they needed for their recipes; even so, a Wisconsin woman brought her own fresh eggs, and Mrs. Smafield was forced to use a brand of yeast she had never seen before. Nor had she ever cooked with an electric stove until she arrived in the ballroom. "I was real discouraged," she told *Life*. But the judges were charmed by the fancy sweet rolls she called No-Knead Water-Rising Nut Twists. They weren't hard to make, and Mrs. Smafield used a quaint, all-but-forgotten method with her yeast dough: She wrapped it in a tea towel and submerged it in warm water, where it gently expanded until it rose to the surface. The next day, Eleanor Roosevelt herself arrived to bestow the prizes. She handed Mrs. Smafield a check for $50,000, and the two women gazed at each other with a mixture of pride and amazement as flashbulbs popped.

Second prize went to Laura Rott of Naperville, Illinois, who was inspired to invent Starlight Mint Surprise Cookies when she received a box of chocolate mints as a gift. She made a rich cookie dough, wrapped a small portion around each mint, and placed half a walnut on top. Miss Rott's ingenuity won her $10,000. A classic layer cake won third prize: Aunt Carrie's Bon-bon Cake, which had a creamy white filling and chocolate frosting. Mrs. Richard W. Sprague of San Marino, California, called it a cake "that all men like" and took home $4,000. Every finalist received $100 or more in payment for his or her recipe, since Pillsbury would be publishing it, and all one hundred of them went home with their electric stoves, courtesy of G.E.

Pillsbury had planned to start making the recipes available in March, first running ads featuring the three top prizewinners, and later publishing a booklet with all one hundred recipes. But the publicity generated so much demand for the recipes that grocers urged the company to step up the schedule. In mid-January, just four weeks after the contestants left New York, the ads began to appear, and by the end of February grocers had distributed 18 million copies of the recipe booklet. Clearly the Bake-Off was on its way to becoming an indelible feature of Pillsbury's public image. Plans for number two were already in the works, and although it was going to be difficult to top Eleanor Roosevelt as the guest of honor, the company expected plenty of publicity for its choice: Next year's overjoyed winners would receive their checks from the gracious hand of the Duchess of Windsor.

Hundreds of thousands of women and a handful of men submitted recipes to the Bake-Off during the 1950s. The chief rule was a simple one: Each recipe had to include at least half a cup of Pillsbury's Best Family Flour. Using mixes, even Pillsbury mixes, was not permitted. Cake recipes were most abundant and regularly won the big prizes, but contestants offered up a flamboyant array of breads, desserts, and main dishes as well. "Submit a recipe that is *different* from any you have ever seen," suggested Della Ruth Emerson of Cochocton, Ohio, whose Swiss Chocolate Cheese Cake made it to the finals in 1959. Cheesecake was certainly different to her—she had never tasted one in her life—so she studied a cookbook and then assembled an original version featuring chocolate and shredded coconut. Other contestants tried, failed, and tried again. Beatrice Harlib of Chicago submitted a recipe for butter cookies three times, but it never got to the finals. Deciding to try a fourth time, she had just mixed the dough when she had to leave the kitchen to answer a phone call. While she was away, her two sons fooled around with the dough, rolling pieces of it into balls and pressing them on top of pecan halves. "Look, Mom, they look like turtles!" they exclaimed when she returned. Coated with chocolate frosting, Snappy Turtle Cookies won $25,000. Bertha Jorgensen of Portland, Oregon, was another contestant with determination: She sent in her mother's yeast-roll recipe six times unsuccessfully. Then she tried filling the rolls with a mixture of confectioners' sugar and ground hazelnuts, and made them sweeter still with an orange juice glaze. Pillsbury happily christened them Ring-a-Lings and awarded Mrs. Jorgensen a grand prize in 1955. Leona Schnuelle of Crab Orchard, Nebraska, tried cake, pie, and dessert recipes, but none of them impressed the judges. Finally, she started wondering about a bread she traditionally made with buttermilk. Maybe if she used cottage cheese instead. . . . And since a recent winner had featured sesame seeds in her recipe, Mrs. Schnuelle went to the cupboard and pulled out a jar of dill seed. At last the judges perked up: her Dilly Casserole Bread won $25,000 in 1960. "When your recipes do not win, then *dare* to go beyond the conventional," she advised would-be contestants. "Dream—experiment—measure. Of course your finished product must taste and look good."

Amaizo was marketing its first instant pudding in 1949, the year the Bake-Off was launched, and Betty Crocker was urging house-wives to try her new "cake in a box." These were quick and easy desserts, and they had a future. But so did Ring-a-Lings, Snappy Turtle Cookies, and thousands of other ingenious confections that flowed from American kitchens for years in a quest for glory. The Bake-Off triumphed because it celebrated far more than dessert, far more than even the romance of home cooking. The Bake-Off celebrated the applause. When Marjorie Child Husted, an execu-tive at General Mills, surveyed housewives right after World War II, one of the questions she asked them was "What do you think women need most to make homemaking a full and satisfy-ing career?" The answer that came back again and again was ap-preciation. "Encouragement and appreciation from those we serve," wrote one woman. "Appreciation and recognition of the work we do," wrote another. The Bake-Off was all about recog-nition, all about taking justifiable pride in one's work, all about the rewards that might blossom for a woman who stood at the kitchen counter and prepared food with her own two hands. And the recognition that came with the Bake-Off wasn't just senti-mental: Pillsbury backed up its rhetoric with money and national fame. For the first time ordinary home cooks were invited into a glamorous public forum to display their work, surrounded by re-porters and photographers, cheered on by Eleanor Roosevelt, the Duchess of Windsor, Margaret Truman, Art Linkletter, and Arthur Godfrey. The miniature kitchens lined up in the ballroom became one hundred little stage sets, and the stars were women like Mrs. Patrick Sullivan of Lawrence, Kansas (Orange Glory Rolls, 1951), and Ella Pauline Schulz of Racine, Wisconsin (Cashew Caramel Yummies, 1955). No wonder some homemakers put the Bake-Off squarely in their sights and kept it there, fighting their way from rejection to rejection until they came up with a winning recipe. When Mrs. Herbert Thurston of Needham, Massachusetts, arrived back home after the 1961 Bake-Off, she was disappointed not to be carrying a fat check for her Regal Chocolate Cake, but she gratefully counted up her prizes. "My first plane ride, my first electric range, my first mixer, and my first experience winning," she reflected. And there was something else, the prize she treasured most from all those months of cooking, testing, tasting, and perfecting: "The precious feeling of suddenly having fortune smile on me—really and truly so." Women like Mrs. Thurston knew very well what a labor of love was, for they worked under those auspices every day; but the Bake-Off was delightfully different. Here for once was a labor of love that went public and earned its reward in the tangible coin of the realm.

Chapter 2

Something from the Oven

How to make dinner...and the double feature too

Serve Swanson TV Brand Dinners
You (and all happy eaters!) will appreciate their extra-good taste! Swanson TV Meat Loaf Dinners, for instance. Juicy beef, with tomato sauce of rare distinction . . . plus whipped potatoes and garden peas. Brighten your next busy day with Swanson TV Dinners (six delicious kinds).

FROZEN
SWANSON
"TV" DINNERS

Made only by *Campbell* Soup Company

Only Swanson comes so close to your own home cooking

"TV" and "TV Dinner" are registered trademarks

In 1954, Swanson introduced what would become the most famous and enduring culinary icon of the postwar era. This ad was published around 1960, when TV dinners were no longer a novelty but hadn't attained the status of a genuine, adult meal. They never would, despite efforts like this one to justify frozen dinners as crucial time-savers for busy, modern women. (Swanson® is a registered trademark of CSC Brands, Inc. Used with the permission of Pinnacle Foods Corporation.)

Not all home cooks in the postwar years were talented and imaginative; on the contrary, many were ordinary, resentful, or inept. But straight through the 1950s women kept cooking. Willingly, haphazardly, in a lousy mood or a panic, sometimes with enjoyment and sometimes hardly noticing the food—they cooked. And straight through the '50s, the food industry and numerous other observers insisted that women weren't cooking; they didn't want to cook, they had no time to cook, they had quit cooking long ago. Stories rejoicing over the way packaged foods had transformed cooking began showing up in the press long before most women had so much as opened a box of Bisquick or tasted instant coffee. "Women who gave up laborious home preparation for processed foods a generation ago are learning to use packaged and prepared foods with new skills," *Look* magazine announced confidently in 1950. By this account, women's wholehearted conversion to the new foods "a generation ago" predated many of the convenience foods themselves. "When the food manufacturers moved into the kitchen, the housewife was waiting with outstretched arms," asserted a 1952 *Business Week* story headed "It's a Revolution in Eating Habits." "Today, prepared foods make up about three quarters of all we eat." A year later *Fortune* published a special report titled "The Fabulous Market for Food" analyzing the popularity of convenience foods, which the story described as occupying the very center of the American diet. "The loathing with which American women seem to regard prolonged labor in the kitchen has been often noted and much interpreted," the story pointed out, underscoring women's "insistence on convenience in the kitchen" and their "relentless pursuit of convenience items." Like other magazines, *Fortune* claimed that most of the food that families were eating in 1953 was packaged. "When the American housewife shops her supermarket, she has a choice of 4,693 short-cut foods—the most dazzling array of prepared, precooked and ready-to-eat foods the world has ever seen," wrote Helen McCully in a 1955 *McCall's* story. "These amazing short-cut foods—in cans, glass and packages—have revolutionized cooking habits in every home in the United States."

Only by defining the term *packaged foods* in the broadest possible sense could these publications legitimately make such claims about American homemaking. It was true that by the '50s the staple products Americans ate all the time had undergone some degree of processing and packaging before women bought them, including sliced and wrapped bread, ground beef, bagged potatoes, and trimmed lettuce. But when it came to partially prepared foods, the ones that needed only to be heated or mixed with water, the real picture was very different. Far from standing in the door with outstretched arms welcoming the new foods, housewives tended to be deeply suspicious of them, as the frozen-food industry kept discovering. The widely evoked image of women carrying home bags and bags of such products and serving them in place of traditionally prepared meals was simply unfounded. As late as 1960, according to a survey, more than half of the subscribers to *Parents Magazine* still baked pies, cakes, and cookies from scratch every week—thirty years after what *Look* had described as the death of home baking.

Virtually no independent research backed up this vision of the homemaker who "loathed" making dinner. In fact, the overwhelming consensus of scholars examining the question was that women liked cooking better than any other household task, or at the very least disliked cooking less than they disliked their other chores. Between 1938 and 1961, ten studies involving more than two thousand women were carried out by Ph.D. students in home economics; only one of these found homemakers who put cooking in second place, and the women who put it there were young mothers whose favorite and still-novel task was caring for children. In his thousands of psychological interviews, the pioneering consumer research expert Ernest Dichter found few homemakers who were averse to cooking. Pierre Martineau, another influential researcher specializing in consumer psychology, said 95 percent of the women he interviewed expressed positive feelings about cooking, far more than the number who had anything good to say about the rest of their housework. Although Dichter once claimed in a study of women's attitudes toward new appliances that women preferred cleaning to any other household chore, he admitted he had no statistical evidence to back up the notion. Other studies, including a 1949 poll conducted by the *Woman's Home Companion* and a 1951 Gallup poll, found that women favored cooking over all other household tasks by a wide margin.

What's more, despite the uniform depiction of the homemaker as "Mrs. Busywoman," as *Quick Frozen Foods* referred to her—so rushed every day with housework, children, the PTA, and maybe a job that she couldn't possibly cook a traditional dinner—the evidence showed otherwise. Most women on most days had no trouble finding enough time to produce a typically unadorned American meal for their families. (Taking a stab at paella or *nasi goreng* was another matter, but those were company dishes.) By the 1950s, making dinner from scratch was an easier, faster job than it had ever been. Except in rural areas, nearly all households had running water, refrigerators, and gas or electric stoves. Women could buy their chickens plucked and ready to cook, their vegetables sorted and trimmed; they had butter and milk on hand in the refrigerator.

True, housework on the whole was taking about the same amount of time in the 1950s as it had in the 1920s—about fifty-two hours a week, according to surveys, even though women at mid-century had such time-saving advantages as indoor plumbing and modern electrical equipment. But while women no longer had to boil vats of water for laundry or arduously black the stove each evening, they did put in hours every day on such new chores as shopping, laundering clothes that had been worn just once, or chauffeuring children around town. The one job that took significantly less time in the '50s than it had in the '20s was cooking. Women spent about twenty-three hours a week preparing food and cleaning up in 1926, and about seventeen or eighteen hours a week on those tasks in the late '50s. Certainly, the use of convenience foods contributed to the difference, especially such popular staples from the supermarket as bread and ice cream, but efficient new stoves and a taste for smaller, less elaborate everyday meals were also instrumental in making food preparation a speedier enterprise. Canned hamburgers and frozen crêpes suzette, by comparison, generated enormous excitement in the food industry and were credited in the press with freeing women from hours of tedious labor, yet they showed up on only a scant number of dinner tables before disappearing altogether. When a Los Angeles company asked customers who bought its frozen prepared Swiss steak dinners why they were purchasing the product, the answer time and again was that people liked the flavor. Convenience was hardly mentioned.

Women themselves rarely complained that cooking took too much time, at least when they were asked by researchers conducting studies. As one Ph.D. student in home economics pointed out, women in the surveys tended to begrudge the time spent on domestic tasks they hated but apparently didn't mind spending time on work they liked. When a doctoral student surveyed 210 families in Pennsylvania in 1958, women were asked if they had enough time for cooking, and nearly three-quarters of them said yes. Then they were asked what they did when they were pressed for cooking time. Did they buy convenience foods, did they cook ahead of time, did they eat in restaurants? Most reported that they prepared meals ahead of time; only 11 percent resorted to convenience products. In a study conducted by two psychologists at Michigan State University, 242 homemakers in Lansing described how they decided what foods to buy. Despite the widespread assumption that women couldn't wait to get out of the kitchen, "food preparation time" was a relatively unimportant factor in their decision making. What mattered most was how much they had to pay and what their friends and families liked to eat.

Mirra Komarovsky, the sociologist who studied fifty-eight working-class families in 1958 for her book *Blue-Collar Marriage*, found that few of the women felt "harried" or "overburdened" by housework. They worked all day at their chores and child care but had no trouble getting everything done. Among these women, she reported, time was not a particularly scarce commodity. Komarovsky compared this response to an earlier study she had conducted among college-educated homemakers who did complain about not having enough time for all their responsibilities. It wasn't the demands of housework that differed between the two groups, Komarovsky concluded; it was the extras in the lives of the wealthier women: taking children to dancing lessons, finishing the latest issue of a magazine, feeding the children before the babysitter arrived so the couple could go out in the evening. Sure enough, consumer surveys showed that it was better-off families such as these that purchased more convenience foods.

Even employed women, long targeted by the food industry as a ready and waiting market for convenience foods, didn't show much interest in them. Informal polls and small-scale studies consistently indicated that working women bought convenience foods at pretty much the same rate that full-time homemakers did.

In 1955, for example, two professors in the Department of Agricultural Economics at Michigan State University surveyed some four thousand families in Grand Rapids and Flint concerning their purchases of frozen meat. Families in which the wife held a job bought frozen raw meat and poultry more frequently than the other families did, the professors found; but when it came to genuinely time-saving products, such as fish sticks and frozen entrées, there were no differences. Another study, this one conducted by graduate students in home economics at Syracuse University, found that working mothers purchased no more labor-saving kitchen equipment than full-time homemakers. Yet throughout the postwar era a powerful association between women's employment and the rise of shortcut cooking was taken for granted by nearly everyone who commented in public on either subject.

So obvious did this cause and effect seem to the experts that the first major study of working women and convenience foods wasn't published until 1968. The study was based on a survey of 7,500 households and examined the buying habits of families with employed wives against the buying habits of families with at-home wives. Purchases of ten products were compared. The favorite in both camps was packaged instant potatoes, purchased by 31 percent of the full-time homemakers and 31.8 percent of the employed homemakers. A few products, namely gravy mixes and "powdered instant breakfast drink," were slightly more popular with the at-home wives; the rest were slightly more popular with the working wives. But differences were minuscule. Working women appear to have handled their time problems, at least through the early '60s, by doing less cooking per meal—buying dessert, skipping the homemade biscuits—rather than by playing the role so often attributed to them and leading a national stampede toward instant foods.

Day after day in the pages of newspapers and magazines, homemakers and the food industry played out a visible struggle between traditional home cooking and the new packaged foods. The food industry—which supplied the ads and greatly influenced the editorial matter, especially in the food sections of daily newspapers—pummeled the media with tales of magical entrées and desserts that needed only a few finishing touches to become flawless representations of real food. Simultaneously, the readers took advantage of every opportunity to speak up and indicate that they preferred home cooking as usual. At *McCall's,* for instance, where the food section sometimes reprinted recipes from past issues when readers requested them, the editors were startled at the popularity of a long, traditional recipe for spaghetti and meatballs that called for beef, pork, veal, salt pork, garlic, onion, pepper, parsley, cloves, nutmeg, wine, tomatoes, and more. "Frankly, we were surprised at the number of letters received from readers asking us to republish this recipe," the editors wrote in the November 1954 issue. "We *knew* it made the best spaghetti we ever tasted, but we also knew it took a lot of time and an assortment of ingredients." Two pages later came a story created by the editors themselves, featuring the sort of recipes women were supposed to be seeking: Mock Jambalaya, made with instant rice, canned shrimp, and Vienna sausage, and Chipped Beef De Luxe, made from chipped beef, olives, white sauce, mayonnaise, and angostura bitters.

Newspaper food sections had long invited readers to send in recipes for possible publication, sometimes awarding a small cash prize if one was selected to be the Recipe of the Day. These reader-supplied recipes tended to be very different from the recipes that ran in staff-written food stories or were gleaned from industry press releases. The proud home cooks who saw their best recipes in print generally favored plain, conservative preparations, cooked mostly from scratch, perhaps with a modest touch of glitter. Tuna croquettes, bread-and-butter pickles, and rhubarb crisp were typical of the winning recipes in the *Denver Post* during the mid-'50s; meat loaf baked on a bed of canned pineapple was one of the more daring contributions. It was the paper's food editor, not a home cook, who suggested making a rarebit from canned tomato soup and a jar of cheese spread.

At *The Boston Globe,* similarly, traditional American dishes predominated when women sent recipes to the "Confidential Chat," a long-running readers' exchange on domestic topics that was published daily. Casseroles, pork chops, meat loaf, stews, and innumerable baked goods filled the columns of the Chat in the postwar era. These women didn't shun packaged foods, but when they made use of Jell-O, Bisquick, and other shortcut products, it was often for very specific reasons that had to do with the needs of the day and the dish. "Could a double-crust lemon pie be made using package filling?" queried a reader in 1948. "We live quite a distance from the shopping center, so rely on package fillings as it is more convenient." Some Chatters took for granted the use of cake mixes in their own and other homes ("Tried your tip on adding oil to cake mixes and, like you, I'm sold on them"), but this generally accepting attitude toward mixes coexisted very smoothly with a nonstop zeal for desserts baked from scratch. Day after day Chatters urged one another to try Luscious Date Cake, Mystery Mocha Cake, Ambrosia Cake, Black Midnight Devil's Food Cake, and hundreds more of their beloved specialties. The inspirations never let up, and very few called for a ready-made ingredient of any sort.

At the same time, one of their highest terms of praise for any recipe was "easy." They greatly valued simple procedures and assured results, and often shared ideas for shortcuts. Yet outbursts of the peculiar creativity endemic to professional test kitchens were unusual in their recipes. If Chatters prepared tuna Stroganoff (described by the *Globe* as "a quick and easy entrée, with a continental touch") or followed another *Globe* tip and baked a loaf of luncheon meat with blue cheese topping, they certainly didn't crow about it in their letters. They were reading spectacular full-page ads for new products, they saw the enticing packages in supermarkets, but few of them seemed tempted to make fundamental changes in the way they put three meals a day on the table.

This clear reluctance on the part of readers to give up their eggbeaters and paring knives only spurred the editors to emphasize again and again that a dramatic revolution had swept over the American kitchen. "Is Home Cooking on Way Out?" inquired a *Globe* headline in 1954 over a story reporting on a food convention in New York. At the convention, one of several such events in the '50s, newspaper food editors from around the country gathered to hear representatives of major food companies describe the latest developments in frozen, dehydrated, and instant products. News stories that emerged from this generous procession of luncheons, dinners, demonstrations, and parties generally pronounced home cooking to be an irrational vestige of grandmother's day and predicted its quick demise.

Despite such commercial rhetoric, it was clear to the food industry that few homemakers were surrendering themselves heart and soul to convenience products. The question that plagued the industry was why. Opening a couple of cans, mixing the contents together, sprinkling the contents of a box on top, and putting the whole thing in the oven was such an easy way to prepare dinner that it just didn't make sense for women to resist. What mysterious and ineffable forces could be restraining homemakers from sweeping ready-made piecrust, dehydrated puddings, and frozen dinners right off grocery shelves? In an effort to explore the depths of the female psyche, the industry turned to the new science of consumer psychology. Women were avoiding ready-made foods for fear of "shirking their duties as housewives," reported Ben Duffy, president of the advertising agency Batten, Barton, Durstine & Osborne. They resisted products that took over too much of the work they considered their special responsibility, advertising expert Janet Wolff believed. "How often have we heard a wife respond to 'This cake is delicious!' with a pretty blush and 'Thank you—I made it with such and such a prepared cake mix,'" wrote Mason Haire, a marketing research expert. "This response is so invariable as to seem almost compulsive. . . . In ready-mixed foods there seems to be a compulsive drive to refuse credit for the product, because the accomplishment is not the housewife's but the company's."

What they were talking about was a slew of anxieties that many women simply felt as guilt—a vast and murky guilt that seeped across issues of work, love, identity, and responsibility. Aside from raising children, cooking was the job that led all others on the list of chores that defined homemaking and ruled women's daily lives. And cooking wasn't just a chore; in many ways it was a responsibility similar to taking care of children. The emotional component was huge, the day-to-day necessity was relentless, the social pressure to perform well could be imposing, and there was no mistaking failure. No matter how appealing the prospect of doing something as utterly labor-free as opening a can of macaroni and cheese, spooning the contents into a pan, heating it up, and serving it, very few women were able to convince themselves that they had produced a meal. The moral obligation to cook simply was not satisfied. Where was the personal dimension, the hospitality, the sense of a gift from heart and hands that had characterized the notion of home cooking for millennia? Clumsy cooks, harried cooks, bored cooks, and adequate cooks weren't so different from good cooks in at least one regard: They felt duty-bound to cook. That meant producing the meal, doing the work, putting their hands in the food, moving about the kitchen, and making it happen. It didn't mean opening boxes and jars, then summoning the family.

Even homemakers who went ahead and used the new products sometimes found themselves grappling with their own uncertainties, seeking the right rationale for avoiding work that was supposed to be intrinsic to a woman's identity. Ruth Ellen Church, whose widely read "Mary Meade" food columns in the *Chicago Tribune* featured a great deal of scratch cooking, often discussed convenience foods as they came on the market, in part because the *Tribune*'s food section was beholden to its advertisers and in part because she knew her readers were uncertain about how to react to such products. "I was a little slow to register enthusiasm about the packaged roll mixes, for I felt as many women do about making their own breads and rolls—it's really a creative job and one that's particularly rewarding," she wrote in a 1948 column. "But I must admit the excellence of a mix which will turn out fluffy rolls, a coffee ring, or a loaf of cinnamon bread in record time and with no kneading. There are times when shortcuts are necessary in the life of every busy homemaker! I am not too proud to keep pie and roll mixes on my pantry shelf." That undertone of apology clinging to Mary Meade's strong defense of the new foods was inextricably attached to the very idea of "pie and roll mixes." The products might be useful and the results might be tasty, but opening a box of gingerbread mix was a different level of activity from truly baking gingerbread, and everybody knew it. Packaged foods held out the temptation of perfect results every time, yet there was something distinctly shady about using commercial shortcuts to fulfill what amounted to an eleventh commandment.

Just how shady became clear in the spring of 1950 when the *Journal of Marketing* published the results of a study designed to expose housewives' real feelings about convenience foods. This was not a food industry study but an experiment in psychology aimed at helping market researchers develop better techniques for eliciting information from consumers. The idea was to prompt more instinctive reactions from study participants by probing their feelings indirectly instead of asking simple questions about people's preferences and receiving the usual self-edited statements in response. To this end a team of researchers drew up two grocery shopping lists, exactly the same in every respect except that the first list specified Nescafé instant coffee and the second list specified Maxwell House drip ground coffee. They gave the lists to one hundred women—fifty received the first list, and fifty the second—asking each person to write down her impressions of the housewife who created the list.

The results were devastating. By huge margins more women described the Nescafé buyer as lazy, disorganized, a spendthrift, and a bad wife than described the Maxwell House buyer in such terms. "Apparently, she likes to sleep late in the morning," commented one respondent about the Nescafé woman. "She must appear rather sloppy, taking little time to make up in the morning. She is also used to eating supper out, too. Perhaps alone rather than with an escort. An old maid probably." Meanwhile, both of the mythical shoppers were buying canned peaches, but this was a convenience product of such long-standing familiarity that it broadcast no particular character failing. It did, however, back up whatever assumptions the respondents were making about the housewives based on their choice of coffee. On the Maxwell House woman's list, for instance, canned peaches became evidence that this warmhearted housewife wanted to give her family a treat. On the Nescafé woman's list, they were simply one more sign of how lazy she was. Finally, the researchers added a new component to the study. They asked another group of women to respond to the same two lists, but an extra convenience product was written into them: "Blueberry Fill Pie Mix." This time the respondents not only demolished the Nescafé woman, they gave the same treatment to the Maxwell House woman, finding her almost as inadequate as her wretched sibling.

Clearly, the food industry had its work cut out for it. Unpleasant images were swarming like an invasion of red ants over the boxes, jars, and cans that represented the industry's best efforts and highest hopes. For their own stubborn reasons, many women still shared, perhaps even treasured, a powerful understanding of what it meant to cook for loved ones at home, and they had relegated convenience foods to a minor role in meal planning. Such products didn't seem to count as food; using them wasn't considered cooking; serving them was a cause for shame. This had to change. Somehow the industry had to rid shortcut products of their slatternly image and instill in the women who used them a sense of pride and competence. Merely persuading shoppers to try this or that new grocery item—in other words, business as usual—wasn't going to be enough to dislodge an emotional certainty built up over lifetimes and generations. The challenge to the food industry was stark: Homemakers needed a different way to think about the task of feeding people. They needed a different approach to cooking—to every aspect of cooking, starting with the very definition of the verb *to cook*. Working in concert with the media, the food industry spent the postwar era radically overhauling the popular view of making dinner. The result was a new cuisine.

Unlike its traditional counterparts, this cuisine was detached from the usual sources of culinary invention—the weather, the crops, the special occasions for feasting, the daily needs of home cooks. Instead, packaged-food cuisine was created deliberately to showcase new foods and new methods. Emerging from professional test kitchens, packaged-food cuisine flowered in magazines, newspapers, home economics classes, and cookbooks, crisscrossed the nation, and settled at last in the messy drawers or bulging envelopes where women stashed their favorite recipes. Like French cooking, it was rigorously true to its principles; like Italian, it made the most of the ingredients that inspired it; and as with Chinese cooking, it was the banquet version that became best known. Although packaged-food cuisine never fully conquered the nation's kitchens, it had a lasting effect on the American appetite, in part because many of its dishes became classics and in part because it was able to exert a powerful influence on the role Americans assigned to cooking itself.

The industry faced two major challenges as it set about persuading housewives to adopt packaged-food cuisine: one was the strange new food, which families would have to learn to like, and the other was the strange new way of cooking, which women would have to learn to respect. As it happened, the food turned out to be far easier for Americans to accept than the cooking. Few middle-class homemakers, after all, were such purists by mid-century that they spurned all packaged foods. Nearly everybody made use of canned soups, fruits, and vegetables. Jell-O was all but universal, and pancake mixes were as familiar as pancakes. Women could employ such standard shortcuts without damage to their sense of culinary propriety. Even more important, from the point of view of manufacturers hoping to recast the American meal, a long tradition of using such packaged foods had encouraged Americans to develop a strikingly resilient sense of taste, one that tended to perceive imitation as plenty good enough.

Ever since the turn of the century, when a newly scientific and mechanized food supply began reshaping the nation's eating habits, American cooking had been characterized by a blatant irrationality that stunned European visitors. Culinary values bred in the factory—blandness and uniformity, interrupted by sudden jolts of novelty—became pleasing to many appetites, while subtleties of flavor and texture lost their importance. Some of the nation's best-known culinary ideas had been spawned in the course of industrializing the food supply, ideas dreamed up by home economists and food writers bent on combining ingenuity, nutrition, and the earliest commercially processed foods. Their brainchildren—canned soup casseroles, flamboyant gelatin salads, a steady drumbeat of marshmallows throughout the meal—were widespread emblems of home life by World War II. When packaged-food cuisine began to appear after the war, millions of Americans were well accustomed to meals that careened between the predictable and the outlandish, with sweetness the dominating flavor. If home cooks shied away at first from postwar convenience products, it wasn't for gustatory reasons. There wasn't much the food industry could do to repel a nation that was already stirring chopped tomatoes and pickles into strawberry Jell-O for a Red Crest Salad.

This 1930s recipe, and hundreds more for such staunch Americanisms as mock apple pie and frozen fruit salad, became the building blocks for packaged-food cuisine. But if there was a longtime flavor template that made Americans susceptible to the new foods, there was no such cultural template. Some of the dishes created by the food industry in the name of packaged-food cuisine were too peculiar for even an American to absorb, lurking as they did at the far reaches of culinary tradition without visible ties to any known combination of foods. One of the most distinctive features of packaged-food cuisine, in fact, was the mysterious nature of many dishes that seemed to follow no apparent culinary logic. In large part this was a tribute to the commercial underpinnings of the cuisine: Each recipe was wholly in thrall to the product being promoted. Hence, canned fruit cocktail was reborn as a cole slaw ingredient, peanut butter forged its way into stuffed sweet potatoes, and frozen lemonade made a surprise appearance in salad dressing. A cook who actually decided to follow the suggestion in a Heinz booklet and fold a quarter cup of ketchup into beaten egg whites, thus arriving at a ketchup meringue, might well have wondered what on earth to do with it until the concept of spreading a topping over a meat pie swam into focus.

Some recipes created for promotional purposes were so ingenious that they were impossible to classify as breakfast, lunch, or dinner. In a story on cooking with bananas, *Household* magazine suggested sprinkling cheese on tomatoes, topping them with banana slices and mayonnaise, and then browning them in the oven, but offered no hint as to when the "unusual treat" should be served. English muffins covered with canned apple slices, spread with heated red jelly, and then broiled; frankfurter rolls cut in half-inch slices, toasted, and then rolled in butter, cinnamon, and sugar; half a doughnut covered with a slice of canned cranberry jelly, topped with cottage cheese—none of these had a readily discernible place in the day's eating. Nabisco promised that anyone could "sophisticate" a strawberry by placing it on top of a saltine spread with cottage cheese, but to label this combination "an easy dessert" was surely wishful thinking.

Ultimately, the creators of packaged-food cookery were forced to try inventing new meals or at least seek out hitherto unsuspected eating opportunities to absorb some of the products pouring into grocery stores. Betty Crocker decided there was time toward the end of the day for a fourth meal—"the fun meal, anywhere from nine to midnight"—when the most appropriate food would be cake made from a Betty Crocker cake mix. The fourth meal never did attain permanent status with the other three, but a great deal of attention went to breakfast, where food companies saw real potential for expansion. The days of meat, potatoes, and pie first thing in the morning were disappearing with family farms, and cold cereal was fast becoming the standard. That left plenty of room for fresh ideas. Campbell's thought a bowl of soup would fill out any breakfast menu nicely: chicken with rice, for instance, to go with sausages, toast, fruit, and milk; and vegetable beef to accompany cold cereal. "Gone are the days of skipping or skimping on breakfast!" announced a Quaker Oats ad, which featured a testimonial from Elizabeth Murphy, a New York City widow and mother of five. How did she make sure her children ate a good breakfast every day? " 'Easy!' says alert, capable Mrs. Murphy. 'I just put bits of chocolate or of a candy bar on creamy-delicious hot Quaker Oats.'" Another novel perspective on breakfast came from the makers of Cream of Wheat, who suggested serving it with a scoop of ice cream on top. "Honestly, it's good!" exclaimed the ad. "Kids love it. . . . It takes ideas to keep kids interested in breakfast." Hovering restlessly between breakfast and lunch was the pancake sandwich, or "pan-san," as the *Chicago Tribune* food section called it: two pancakes made from a mix, each topped with a slice of processed cheese and two strips of bacon, the whole served with butter and maple syrup.

Whether or not many home cooks ever tried such recipes, they helped to alter the nation's culinary consciousness simply by virtue of showing up so often in magazines and newspapers. To the extent that homemakers ignored the pan-san or resisted topping cereal with ice cream, their objections most likely had less to do with flavor than the sheer oddity of the idea. But that left plenty of scope for the food industry—and homemakers themselves, in time—to come up with more acceptable recipes. Perhaps it seemed extreme at first to stir 7-UP into a boiled dressing or add it to a child's glass of milk ("Mothers know that this is a wholesome combination"), but plenty of homemakers proved willing to bake cakes using a bottle of soda as the liquid. Flavor was an infinitely flexible standard as far as many Americans were concerned, and the food industry had every reason to believe it could corral millions of appetites as its campaign went on.

The more daunting obstacle that confronted the creators of packaged-food cuisine was that women seemed unaccountably attached to cooking. They would buy convenience products, it was clear, but only for certain narrowly defined purposes that kept the hierarchy of the kitchen unchanged. If a homemaker opened a can of tomato sauce to use in a casserole or tossed a bouillon cube into a stew, she was employing shortcut ingredients as mere helpers—behind-the-scenes assistants to the real star. What the industry had to do was create leading roles for their products while quietly turning home cooks into stagehands.

One of the most important steps in this process was to refurbish the problematic term *cooking* by changing some of the popular assumptions that had long accompanied it. To cook, first of all, was to work. It meant sifting, mixing, beating, pounding, frying in spattering fat, hovering over pots, peering into ovens—using physical strength, in other words, and feeling tired at the end of it all. Everyone liked easy recipes, and women who cooked a lot generally came up with their own ways to make the work lighter, but some degree of hands-on labor was an essential part of the enterprise and justified much of the sense of achievement that constituted one of the chief rewards of cooking. Packaged-food cuisine, by contrast, was painless. That was its main selling point, but it was a drawback as well. One approach to this challenge was to try to make packaged-food cooking look like work, albeit very simple work. When Kraft introduced miniature marshmallows ("You don't have to cut them up!"), they were featured in newspaper ads that pictured a recipe card neatly headed "Marshmallow Surprise Lemon Pudding." The ingredients appeared in standard recipe format:

1 pkg. lemon-flavored pudding
1 cup Kraft Miniature Marshmallows

Then came the directions:

Prepare the pudding according to directions on the package. Cool. Fold in the marshmallows. 6 servings.

Other advertisers and food writers handled the problem by lifting work right out of the cooking process and dismissing as outmoded any chore more laborious than applying a finishing touch. "Cooking is *not* work," announced Virginia Stanton, a food columnist for *House Beautiful*, in 1949. She went on to explain that cooking no longer had to mean slaving over a hot stove all day. Instead, women could do what she did and use their heads. Nobody had to know how the food got on the table. "When they rave about my applesauce or whatever, I never let on, and let them assume I spent hours paring apples. In reality, I opened a can of applesauce, added two tablespoons of mint jelly, two leaves of fresh mint and diced currant jelly. Whatever I did, I spent only about five minutes doing it. But the result passes for either Escoffier or Grandmother's—even with the nosiest gourmets."

Stanton and many other authorities were fond of contrasting easy, modern cooking with its old-fashioned counterpart, which was always depicted as a task of staggering dimensions. Since their favorite point of comparison tended to be the traditional cooking of fifty or a hundred years earlier, they had a good deal of evidence on which to draw. When Street and Street, the publisher of *Living,* celebrated its centennial in 1956, the editors produced a special issue in honor of the event and took the occasion to look back pityingly on cake baking as it was practiced in the nineteenth century. Pounding the sugar, stoning the raisins, boiling the milk, weighing the ingredients—it was a two-day process that took all the domestic help available, the story pointed out. But in 1956? "One opens a box of cake mix, adds the liquid, plugs in the mixer, adjusts the oven to the proper temperature and then reads a book." What the editors omitted, of course, were all the advances that made baking from scratch relatively simple in 1956, including modern refrigerators, reliable electric stoves, and ready-to-use staple ingredients.

Using mixes took less time, however, and at the heart of the industry's new definition of cooking was a ticking clock. Homemakers had always valued recipes for dishes that could be prepared with dispatch, and the concept of saving time by using this product or that recipe had been a familiar theme in food writing and advertising for decades. In its classic formulation, speed was associated with emergencies, and emergencies generally amounted to unexpected guests. Novice cooks were always advised to keep a well-stocked pantry in case visitors dropped by. But during the postwar era, time became an obsession of the food industry and eventually of American homemakers as a manufactured sense of panic began to pervade even day-to-day cooking. Advertisements and stories plowed across the media reminding readers again and again how busy they were, how frantic their days, how desperately they needed products and recipes for quick meals. "If you're a typical modern housewife, you want to do your cooking as fast as possible," wrote a columnist at *Household* magazine who was promoting instant coffee and canned onion soup. Not even cold cereal got to the table fast enough. According to Kellogg, what mothers really liked about the new Corn Pops was that the cereal was presweetened, a boon they found to be a great time-saver. "In this fast-moving era, everyone is concerned with saving time," emphasized a teacher who was submitting her favorite recipe to *Forecast,* the home economics magazine. "I, in company with innumerable other women, feel the pressing need of entertaining my friends well but with a minimum of time and energy spent in preparation." Her solution was to use a can of baby food as a lasagna ingredient. In the pages of *Forecast* and other magazines, it wasn't the arrival of sudden company that threw a household into emergency status—ordinary life was sufficient. "Baby fussing? Dinner to get?" inquired an ad in 1953. "When baby wants attention and daddy wants dinner, your best friend is *quick-quick* Minute Rice!" Soon no excuse at all was needed, and stories simply promised "Hot breads—in a jiffy!" "Quick fix desserts!" "Suppers that beat the clock!" Here was one claim that manufacturers could stand behind; and when it came to some foods, this was probably the sole claim that could be made with any credibility. "It's just 1-2-3, and dinner's on the table," exclaimed a story in *Better Homes & Gardens*. "That's how speedy the fixing can be when the hub of your meal is delicious canned meat." The five menus included several recipes of a type that would become legendary in the annals of packaged-food cuisine, including "Twenty Minute Roast"—wedges of Spam glazed with orange marmalade—and a pan of Vienna sausages broiled with canned peaches, which this story identified as a "Harvest Luncheon."

But the insistent rhetoric of high-speed cookery had to be handled with care. The faster the cooking, the less it was going to feel like real cooking, and the greater the potential for guilt on the part of the homemaker. A woman who felt she herself had contributed almost nothing to the dinner she served her family wouldn't buy those particular items again, advised Ernest Dichter, whose theories about the psychology of advertising guided promotional campaigns for a range of consumer products. He and his staff at the Institute for Motivational Research interviewed thousands of women over the years, and his analysis of "today's lady consumers" reverberated widely throughout the food industry. In the old days, he explained, women felt they were obligated to live up to the most exacting standards of housekeeping. Modern women were shaking off these demands, but not entirely. They were glad to be rid of the hard work but unwilling to give up the rest of what they saw as the important role of housewife. Their solution—and this became Dichter's major contribution to packaged-food cuisine—was an approach to cooking he called "creativeness." He spelled it out in the form of a dialectic:

Thesis: "I'm a housewife."
Antithesis: "I hate drudgery."
Synthesis: "I'm creative."

Dichter's chief example of the dialectic in action was the housewife who used canned foods to save time and effort but never, ever served them right out of the can. Instead, she developed a skill for "doctoring up" the contents, thus convincing herself she was personally involved in preparing the meal. "She may spend less time in the kitchen and she may buy canned food," he wrote, "but *she makes up for it by greater creativeness*." This analysis proved to be an immensely useful concept for the food industry. Creativity was the personal touch that would turn an ordinary dish into an epicurean one, and creativity was how women trained in political science or ancient Greek would find complete satisfaction in housework. Above all, creativity was the fairy dust that would transform opening boxes into real cooking. Even Thanksgiving dinner, tradition and all, could be summoned from cans if enough creativity was applied to the task, according to Edalene Stohr of *Forecast*. "The question is often asked 'Does the modern homemaker take the same pride and receive the same satisfaction from preparing a meal that her mother and grandmother took?' " she acknowledged. Her answer was a resounding affirmative. Modern women were very proud of their ability to create "unusual combinations of canned foods," she reported, not to mention their skill at "adding original touches that may be their very own."

Yet modern women, as we have seen, at first displayed notably less confidence in the creative possibilities of packaged-food cookery than advertisers and food editors did. It was creative to put cranberry jelly and cottage cheese on half a doughnut, all right, but there was no clear reason to eat it. What finally did lure many homemakers to packaged-food cuisine was a culinary technique that came roaring out of home kitchens and test kitchens alike during the '50s, a technique that turned cans and boxes into party food. The women responding to the Nescafé housewife had made it abundantly clear that instant cookery was tainted cookery, no matter how creative it might be. A homemaker could doctor up a can of beef stew, but that didn't make it worthy of the best china. To shop for such products with the intention of serving them proudly in their own right was unthinkable. But to manipulate these products in such a way that they approached gracious living—to use them, that is, as symbols of affluence, ease, and good taste—boosted both the cook and her cooking a few notches up in the social scale. Back in 1941 a magazine dedicated to the high art of fine dining had appeared; it was called *Gourmet*, and its appeal was mostly confined to a circle of the rich and leisured. Now, however, the exclusivity of the word *gourmet* was dropping away. Prewar gourmets made coq au vin from scratch; some postwar gourmets did the same, and it was also possible to fashion coq au vin from canned chicken and cooking wine and call yourself a gourmet, too. All it took to become a gourmet the easy way was a simple technique known as "glamorizing." The food industry flogged it mightily, but for once home cooks needed little prodding. "The show in Cleveland was rather fun, because people were eager to know more about the use of cognac and what glamorizing meant," James Beard wrote to Helen Evans Brown on his return from an out-of-town cooking demonstration. Glamorizing, in fact, meant cognac—or wine or a can of shrimp or a swirl of fanciful frosting. An economical cake made with just one egg would normally be served only to family, but as a 1952 recipe feature in *The Boston Globe* made clear, Betty Crocker's new one-egg cake "lends itself to glamorizing" and with a few touch-ups could be offered without contrition to guests. As the concept of easy haute cuisine spread from kitchen to kitchen, often via pantry shelf items, it banished the dowdy image of packaged foods and gave them a powerful boost toward the ranks of company cooking.

Anybody who could splash sherry over the peas or set fire to the dessert could glamorize, and soon, it seemed, everybody did. Glamorizing food was a lot like doctoring it up, but the aim wasn't merely to be creative, it was to achieve an unmistakable impression of luxury and sophistication. Sometimes glamorizing just meant adding a single attention-getting ingredient—anything from frozen strawberries to canned truffles—and sometimes it meant assembling an entire cast of plain and fancy ingredients to be combined in the name of sheer luxe. According to *House Beautiful,* women who cooked this way were doing precisely the opposite of doctoring up: They were using as their takeoff point the principles of haute cuisine—"the most elegant and most glamorous version of how to cook"—and achieving them by simpler means. "For instance, a really good main dish, made entirely of easy-to-get canned ingredients, is made with a can of cream of mushroom soup, a can of cream of tomato soup, a pound of crab-meat, a teaspoon of curry powder, and two to four tablespoons of sherry," advised a *House Beautiful* food expert. "It's as gourmet as anything, yet it can be put together in about ten minutes." It was the crabmeat, the curry powder, and the wine that imposed a clear distinction between yesterday's doctoring-up (which probably would have quit after the tomato soup had been stirred into the mushroom soup) and today's glamorizing.

Glamorizing sounded expensive, but it was utterly democratic. Canned mushrooms were all it took to glamorize cheap cuts of meat, according to *Forecast*; A1 Sauce performed the same service for a crustless meat pie baked in a cake pan and titled Beef Pizza; and a story in *Household* asserted that canned fruit turned just about any mixture into "salad glamour for summer," including a molded fruit salad made with cooking wine. Even instant coffee shed its miserable image when *Living* glamorized it with a little curaçao and pineapple juice. Canned pineapple was such a widely recognized glamorizing device that a Wellesley College professor confidently added it to a bowl of raw, shredded rutabaga. Sure enough, her recipe for Rutabaga–Pineapple Salad won a coveted spot in the college's fund-raising cookbook. For numerous other homemakers, canned crabmeat performed the alchemy. A housewife in Topsfield, Massachusetts, combined it with frozen spinach, cream of mushroom soup, and Cheez Whiz, arriving at a recipe she called Gourmet Crab. In Milwaukee a member of the Junior League mixed canned crab and canned shrimp with mayonnaise, sprinkled crushed saltines and Parmesan over the top, and then passed it around the living room as Sea Food Spread.

The day that housewives in Topsfield applied the term *gourmet* to a dish made with Cheez Whiz was a proud one for the food industry, but still to come was an achievement that ranks as perhaps the greatest of all in packaged-food cuisine. This was its success— however incomplete—at winning respectability for the cake mix. Here was a truly hard-fought battle, one that took place over decades and across the most sensitive territory in the entire realm of home cooking. Frozen dinners were never perceived as real food no matter how often a family ate them, but cake-mix cakes ultimately did cross over, reconfiguring as they did the emotional landscape of domesticity itself.

Few products emerging from the American kitchen have the sentimental heft of the classic frosted layer cake, universally recognized as a triumph of love as much as skill. "Can you think of anything more symbolic of the loving comfort and security of home than the fragrance of good things baking in the kitchen?" Marjorie Husted asked a conference of gas company salesmen in 1948. They couldn't, and neither could the editors of *McCall's* when they made publishing history in 1950 by becoming the first major women's magazine to put food on the cover—a picture of a cake. Since colonial days women had been marking holidays and festivities with the best cakes their households could afford. Many of these celebratory cakes were rich, fruit-studded yeast breads, but by the early 1800s pound cakes and sponge cakes had moved to center stage, with special reverence attending those that rose majestically into the air thanks to quantities of eggs and hours of hard beating. With the invention of baking powder in the mid-nineteenth century, it finally became possible to achieve light, handsome layer cakes with fewer eggs and far less kitchen labor, and the American cake sailed into its heyday. "Cakes from every land have been introduced to America—but none is so glamorous as the typically American cake developed in this country—the gorgeous concoction of richly tender layers, crowned with luscious creamy icing!" wrote Betty Crocker in a 1942 recipe booklet, and she went on to brandish one sentiment-laden symbol after another: "The beautiful cake for the announcement party . . . the triumphantly towering wedding cake . . . children's birthday cakes, blazing with candles . . . the proud cake celebrating the silver or golden wedding. . . ." It was rare for Betty Crocker to indulge in such rhapsodic prose. Even when she evoked the homemade bread of yesteryear in the same booklet ("the full wheaty flavor of the buttered slice!"), she wasn't able to summon the angel voices that soared when the subject was cake. But cake had a grip on the heart that bread simply couldn't match.

Betty Crocker had another motive for polishing her adjectives when she talked about cake: At General Mills and all the other flour companies, sales of flour for home use had been declining since the late 1920s. Despite what everyone felt about homemade bread, baking sufficient quantities for the family's needs all week was a major chore; and as white, airy loaves became more widely available in stores, fewer and fewer women baked their own every week. Eating patterns were changing, too, with rising incomes and a greater popular awareness of the role of vitamins. Americans were consuming less bread and fewer potatoes, and more fruits, vegetables, and meats, than they had at the turn of the century. The crowning indignity, as far as the flour companies were concerned, was that bread was getting a bad reputation: Women thought it was fattening. For all these reasons, by the 1940s families were keeping much less flour on hand. As a Pillsbury executive put it, "The era of the hundred-pound sack was drawing to a close." The flour companies didn't try to revive home bread-baking, its day seemed so definitively over, but instead put their hopes in the other baked goods that traditionally came from home kitchens—biscuits, muffins, cookies, pies, and cakes.

The first great instrument designed to spur homemade biscuits and muffins was Bisquick, which General Mills introduced in 1931. Like pancake mixes, which had been on the market since Aunt Jemima launched hers in 1889, Bisquick was based on self-rising flour; the innovation was that it was already mixed with shortening. All the homemaker had to do to make biscuits was add water or milk; and she could make a host of more elaborate baked goods by adding eggs, sugar, or other ingredients. But the eventual success of Bisquick did not automatically blaze a trail for cake mix. Cake was different. It was never just dessert. "*Betty Crocker says:* A gift you bake is a gift from the heart," ran a typical flour ad from General Mills. At General Foods it was "*Remember, men love Swans Down cakes (and the girls who bake them!).*" To sell Calumet baking powder: "Love and Kisses to the gal who bakes this luscious cake!" Or Swift-ning shortening: "He'll think he married an angel! Can you blame him? One taste of this homemade beauty is enough to convince any man he's in heaven!" Or as Pillsbury summed it up, "Nothing says lovin' like something from the oven." Cake was love, femininity, happiness, and a man around the house. Not that the women who glanced at the ads in newspapers and magazines needed much reminding. "When my beloved husband reached home this evening, he as usual gave me a big hug and kiss and asked: 'Did you make a cake or pie today?'" confided a reader of *The Boston Globe* in a letter to the "Confidential Chat." Luckily, she had just taken a two-egg cake from the oven.

Cake recipes sent in by readers who wanted to share them with their Chat sisters ran constantly in the *Globe.* In 1959, when the paper's food editor invited readers to submit their very favorite recipes out of all those they had ever clipped from the *Globe,* nearly half were for cakes. "What recipes do women ask for most frequently? Cakes!" announced Mary Meade in the *Chicago Tribune,* introducing a "Cake of the Week" recipe feature in 1948. The response was so enthusiastic that even she was taken aback. "My staff and I have known for a long time that women love cakes, but we were somewhat surprised at the popularity of this weekly cake presentation," she wrote when the feature had run for nearly a year. The plan was to move on to a "Dessert of the

Week," but some readers still begged for cakes. Two hundred women—Meade called them "cake addicts"—telephoned the paper in a fury the day a recipe for Orange Lemon Sunshine Cake appeared too blurry to read.

But cakes could be as treacherous as they were powerful. Baking was a precarious enterprise; much could go wrong even in an oft-used recipe, depending on such factors as the weather, the size of the eggs, or the freshness of the baking powder. When a 1953 Gallup poll asked respondents to name the dish providing "the real test of a woman's ability to cook," both men and women put apple pie in first place, showing a healthy respect for the demanding nature of pastry. In second place men put "roasts," while women—who did most of the baking and knew very well what could befall them—put "cake." Whenever homemakers were offered the chance to ask a cooking expert for help with their kitchen problems, questions about cake were paramount. *Household* magazine, published in Topeka, Kansas, for a largely midwestern readership—that is, for America's prototypical home bakers—ran an advice column called "Kitchen Questions" that featured cake problems more regularly than any other aspect of cooking. "Before my sponge cake is cold, it falls out of the pan." "Why does the brown coating around my angel food cakes always stick to the pan?" "Here is my recipe for Milk Chocolate Cake which is much darker than it should be." Irma S. Rombauer, the personable author whose beloved *Joy of Cooking* went into its fifth edition in 1951, attracted a great deal of mail from women who used the book, and many of them wrote to her about cake. A Connecticut woman couldn't manage to make the Velvet Spice Cake properly; it came out "thick and horrid." A San Francisco woman loved Rombauer's pound cake, but the fruit kept settling on the bottom. A Cincinnati woman wondered about baking fruit cakes in small pans. And a woman from the Bronx mailed Rombauer a family member's recipe for walnut torte, wanting to know why it always fell. (Rombauer scribbled her analysis in a quick note to herself: "recipe no good.")

The stakes were high and the journey was perilous; no wonder the food industry sensed a market for cake mixes. Such a product might make up for the languishing sales of home flour and of course could be sold for a higher price. Duff cake mixes were the first to appear, starting with gingerbread in 1931 and later including white, spice, and devil's food cake. Other manufacturers followed—more than two hundred of them by 1947—but most of these rudimentary products were distributed only regionally. The concept itself didn't begin to take root until the two biggest players, General Mills and Pillsbury, launched cake mixes after the war. General Mills was first out of the gate with Betty Crocker Ginger*cake*—so named, complete with italics, because it was made with Softasilk cake flour and was a lighter product than the term *gingerbread* would have implied. Pillsbury was right on Betty Crocker's heels with white cake and chocolate cake mixes, both introduced in 1948. That same year General Mills came out with devil's food and a product called Party Cake, a mix that became white, yellow, or spice cake depending on what the homemaker added in the way of eggs and spices. The possibilities didn't end there: By following the frosting recipes that came with each package, the homemaker could actually make sixty-four different combinations of cake and frosting.

With the power of national distribution and advertising, especially TV advertising, three giant companies—Pillsbury, General Mills, and General Foods—quickly swamped or bought their smaller competitors. Pillsbury launched the first angel food cake mix in 1951; Swans Down followed, and General Mills jumped in two years later. Meanwhile, Nebraska Consolidated Mills, an Omaha flour company, had been experimenting with cake mixes, and in 1951 it launched its own, packaged under the Duncan Hines label. Thanks to the power of Duncan Hines's name—Hines was a homey food writer who published a popular series of restaurant guides—the company gained 10 percent of the cake-mix market within a year despite limited distribution. Throughout the '50s these four industry leaders battled furiously for the affection and loyalty of homemakers.

As far as most home cooks were concerned, cake mixes were still quite new in the late 1940s and early 1950s, but to the food industry this brief span of time was the product's golden age. The prototypes on the market in the 1930s had mysteriously failed to take hold among consumers. Now at last women were waking up, and so were sales. In 1947, just before the big companies introduced their first mixes, shoppers spent about $79 million on cake mixes. By 1953 they were spending more than twice that amount. "These were the days when cake mixes were miracles; when using them was like having the essence of the modern world in your own kitchen," a Pillsbury executive remembered fondly in 1960. His nostalgia was understandable, for after the initial excitement, the rate of increase dropped significantly, with only a 5 percent gain between 1956 and 1960. Worse, the industry wasn't attracting new buyers. Through the latter years of the 1950s, the number of home cooks using cake mixes hardly budged, not even reflecting population increases.

Cake mixes had definitely arrived, but the industry had no clear picture of the extent to which they were supplementing or replacing traditional baking. Published estimates ranged wildly: In 1953, General Mills decided that 20 percent of homemade cakes came from mixes; two years later, the company raised the estimate to 50 percent, and that same year Pillsbury claimed that 70 to 80 percent of families were using mixes. More plausible numbers, albeit gathered from a very small survey, appeared in the 1958 study referred to earlier in which a doctoral student interviewed 210 Pennsylvania homemakers and asked about their meal-planning habits. She found that 68 percent of them baked cakes from scratch. She also found that nearly all the women, including the scratch bakers, kept a variety of mixes on hand—cake mix, Bisquick, muffin mix, piecrust mix, and more—and used them from time to time.

Plainly, baking mixes of all sorts had a permanent place in the American pantry by the late 1950s, but when it came to cake mixes a lot of women seemed to be balking. They made use of cake mixes but were still distinguishing between cake-mix cakes and real cakes. The flour companies preferred to talk about great leaps in the sales figures, but they knew their customer base was stagnant. In fact, they had been puzzling over women's reluctance to discard traditional baking ever since Duff's first gingerbread mix made its debut. Back then, despite the tremendous sentiment that surrounded a homemade cake and the attendant nervous frenzy about baking one, the prospect of serving a cake that took no skill just wasn't very alluring. Good cooks were proud of their handiwork. And struggling cooks had enough problems coming to terms with their inadequacy in a world where food is love without being forced to deal with what looked like guilt in a box. There were women, of course, who latched on to cake mixes with enthusiasm, but they weren't always the consumers that the industry had expected to reach right away—namely, novice cooks, brides, and working wives in the city. The homemakers who were buying cake mixes disproportionately were farmwives—women who had to put big meals on the table for hungry men, including family members and farmhands, two or three times a day.

Homemakers who weren't producing meals under such pressure all day long might not have been particularly impressed by the amount of time they saved using a cake mix. When home economics students at Hood College conducted a study in 1950 comparing cake-mix cakes with traditionally made cakes, they found that mixes saved only three to fifteen minutes per cake. In 1954 a study at Michigan State College pinpointed the time saved at exactly thirteen minutes and made a point of noting that apart from measuring out the ingredients, similar work was required for both kinds of cake. Other studies (these projects were very popular in college home ec classes) tended to find that cakes baked the old-fashioned way were more "palatable" than the ones that came from a box. Too much sugar and too much artificial vanilla doomed the cake-mix cakes in the Michigan State study. In the long run, quality would prove to be an imprecise measure of cake-mix acceptability, but at least in the early years women seemed to feel that the extra minutes they put into their own scratch baking paid off.

Looking for reasons why so many women who could benefit from cake mixes seemed to be ignoring them, advertisers and consumer experts chose to embrace the egg theory. Ernest Dichter had come up with this analysis in the course of a study he was carrying out for General Mills. After interviewing women and exploring the emotions that surrounded cakes and baking, Dichter reported that the very simplicity of mixes—just add water and stir—made women feel self-indulgent for using them. There wasn't enough work involved. In order to enjoy the emotional rewards of presenting a homemade cake, they had to be persuaded that they had really baked it, and such an illusion was impossible to maintain if they did virtually nothing. "This is typical of what the average housewife said: 'Yes, I'm using a cake mix; it saves me a lot of trouble but I really shouldn't,'" Dichter wrote later. His advice was to leave the homemaker something to do—for instance, add the eggs—whenever she made a cake from a mix. She would feel she had contributed something of herself, and the mindless nature of the task would no longer plague her.

According to Dichter, his client—and, by implication, the other manufacturers—seized on this wisdom and promptly reformulated their mixes, leaving out the dried eggs. Women started adding their own fresh eggs, stopped feeling guilty, and cake mixes became a success. Over the years this story came to be a favorite among other consumer experts, who often rounded up more psychological studies to reinforce Dichter's analysis. The egg theory, with its emphasis on the homemaker's personal investment in the cake, set the tone for much subsequent advertising ("You and Ann Pillsbury can make a great team") and has been widely acknowledged as the insight that saved cake mixes.

But while Dichter's work was influential, its precise role in the success of the cake mix is unclear. It's true that the earliest mixes were what the industry called "complete"; the box included dried eggs and everything else except water or milk. And these were the mixes that failed to catch on, prompting Dichter's study. But manufacturers did not quickly or unanimously fall in line behind him. When Pillsbury and the other big companies were working to develop their cake mixes in the 1940s, the question of whether or not to include dried eggs was a major in-house debate. Paul Gerot, the CEO at Pillsbury in this period, called it "the hottest controversy we had over the product," and he noted that even after the mixes made their debut, the arguing went on for years.

For the industry, the problem wasn't so much that dried eggs deprived the housewife of her contribution, it was that dried eggs produced inferior cakes. They stuck to the pan, the texture was poor, the shelf life was shorter, and they sometimes tasted too prominently of eggs. General Mills, which conducted a great deal of technical research on dried and fresh eggs as well as commissioning Dichter's study, staked its fortunes squarely on fresh-egg mixes and made a point of saying so. "Unlike most cake mixes, there are *No dried egg whites, no dried egg yolks, no dried eggs of any kind in* Betty Crocker Cake Mixes," announced a 1952 ad in *Life*. Three years later, on a Betty Crocker radio show, Betty Crocker told her listeners about a recent trip to Alaska, where she chatted with the wife of the Barrow Airport manager. This Arctic home cook preferred Betty Crocker cake mixes to all others, and why? "Because she can add fresh eggs to the mix," Betty Crocker said firmly.

Pillsbury conducted extensive research as well, including surveys of consumers to gauge their preferences for either complete mixes or fresh-egg mixes. The company found that people tasting both kinds said they preferred the fresh-egg mixes but indicated they would be more likely to buy the complete mixes. Rather than try to decode this particular message, Pillsbury simply made the decision to go with complete mixes. By 1955, General Mills and Pillsbury shared most of the cake-mix market between them despite wholly contradictory egg philosophies.

Chances are, if adding eggs persuaded some women to overcome their aversion to cake mixes, it was at least partly because fresh eggs made for better cakes. But Dichter rightly perceived the overwhelming weight of the moral and emotional imperative to bake cakes from scratch. His research spurred countless ads and magazine articles aimed at persuading women to differentiate between the plain cake layers—"merely step number one," according to *Living*—and the finished masterpiece. "Now, success in cakemaking is packaged right along with the precision ingredients," Myrna Johnston assured readers of *Better Homes & Gardens* in 1953. "You can put your effort into glorifying your cake with frosting, dreaming up an exciting trim that puts your own label on it." For modern women, these authorities proclaimed, the real art of baking began after the cake emerged from the oven.

This perspective changed the nature of the traditional challenges facing home bakers. Flavor and texture were no longer at issue, and they had little importance anyway in a cake that was destined for a great deal of imaginative frosting. Cover a quick angel food cake with apricot glaze and icing, and surround it with ladyfingers cut to size, the experts suggested. Or split the cake, fill it with buttercream, border it with chocolate, and top it with chocolate-dipped cherries. Fill and frost layers of yellow cake with butterscotch pudding, dot the top with salted pecans, and call it a torte. Cover an oblong cake with chocolate frosting and sprinkle it with green decorating sugar—that's the football field. Use white frosting for the lines, and stick candy for the goalposts. A piece of banana covered with melted chocolate is the football. Cut a hole in the center of an angel food cake, fill it with partially jelled orange gelatin and canned peaches, frost the whole thing with whipped cream, and cover that with toasted coconut. *McCall's* gave directions for making a Humpty-Dumpty cake—there were thirteen steps to it, including making three different frostings, painting the cake with food coloring, and assembling the various parts with wooden skewers and drinking straws. It took about twelve hours, though much of the time was spent waiting for various layers to dry. The thirteen steps didn't include making the cake itself from two boxes of mix.

A huge, lavishly frosted layer cake, opened up wide so the viewer could gaze at the tenderness inside, became the presiding image in cake iconography. Ads for flour and cake mix, as well as for baking powder, shortening, chocolate, and coconut, invariably displayed a cake in this posture. Like models whose mesmerizing, inescapable faces define beauty in their time, these cakes set the standard for perfect festivity and made most others look humble by comparison. The standard itself was purely visual. Flavor would never count for much in an industrially produced cake, because simple sweetness was so easily achieved in the factory and so widely acceptable. But the distinguishing attributes of the iconic cake—its height and lightness—were just the qualities that technology could achieve with ease. Cake mixes never completely lost their aura of being second best or their near-indelible association with cheating. To this day, guilt follows many of those boxes home from the supermarket the way Jiminy Cricket followed Pinocchio—his conscience always with him. But the promise of a foolproof cake became more and more tempting, especially for a housewife who didn't trust her own hands. At *McCall's* Congress on Better Living, the forum staged for advertisers in 1958 at which homemakers offered their views of household products, one of the few delegates who voiced no compunctions about opening a box instead of baking from scratch was a woman who said forthrightly, "I really don't know how to bake, and I wish I did." She told the group that she had finally worked up the nerve to try baking a cake and had deliberately started with a mix. The whole procedure delighted her. "I never enjoyed anything so much as knowing I couldn't make a mistake," she reported, "and at least it would come out being a cake."

This willingness to focus on results—"at least it would come out being a cake"—was precisely the attitude the food industry hoped to foster among home cooks and was a harbinger of many such victories in the realm of gustatory revisionism. The difference between a real cake and a cake-mix cake was apparent to most women baking for their families in the '50s, but as generation followed generation, the number of home cooks recognizing that difference dwindled. Middle-class girls growing up after the war were more likely to spend their time after school with piano lessons, television, and phone calls than hanging around the kitchen absorbing the sensory lessons of home cooking. Decade by decade, as the proponents of packaged-food cuisine worked tirelessly to make it the center of American cookery, they met less resistance from women who lacked the taste memory and the skills their mothers or grandmothers had brought to the kitchen. Home economics classes, which were widespread in the public school system, generally made the situation worse. Early in the '50s, for example, many home ec teachers decided that the best way for students to learn baking was to use mixes, since they ensured that the young cooks would never have the discouraging experience of meeting with failure. (The food industry, which supplied copious teaching materials including syllabi to home economics classrooms around the country, was the not-so-invisible hand behind this approach.) "These mixes eliminate much of the tedious, uninteresting part of the work for the students," explained a 1955 article in *Forecast*. "Then, too, mixes are in keeping with our speed era. But the sure, quick, glamorous results that bloom forth from each package of mix still depend largely upon good technique." Here the concept of technique melted quietly into what the author called "the personal element" that would transform a box of mix into "an individual product." Such an attitude, which downplayed the acquiring of skills and ignored the whole concept of flavor, summed up everything James Beard and his colleagues despised about the "home ec gal" and her pernicious influence.

But Beard and some of the other cooking teachers and writers who had been the standard-bearers for good food were starting to promote shortcuts themselves. The industry's repeated assertion that American women were enthralled by instant cookery had become the conventional wisdom on the subject. Few commentators questioned it, and the professional gastronomes in the food world feared their high standards were making them irrelevant. In his writing and teaching, Beard continued to emphasize the importance of fine, fresh ingredients and the glories of regional cuisine; but he was always anxious about maintaining his income, and he thought he could see the grim future of home cooking. Maybe he could do some good, for himself and for American food, by working for the enemy.

Over the years Beard turned up on one industry payroll after another—Green Giant, Nestlé, French's, and more—creating recipes and acting as a spokesman. "I know damned well we'll make money if we can make the easy things taste better than the others can, and I think that is probably our mission in life," he told Helen Evans Brown in a 1955 letter that was at once rueful and ambitious. Five years later he was no longer even rueful. "There are some good mixes on the market," he reported as he was working on a book of baking-mix recipes for *House and Garden.* "I like the hot roll mix of Pillsbury and the buttermilk pancake mix of Duncan Hines, and their cake mixes aren't so bad either." The worst thing about the mixes was the "poison" taste that came from artificial vanilla, he added. "I have managed to smother it in a couple of cases with rum and cognac." His colleagues, too, were climbing on board, including many with lofty reputations in the food world. Some of these converts may have been reluctant, but they all had a healthy respect for their own careers. Dione Lucas of the Cordon Bleu cooking school in New York once received a request for a "quick" meat recipe. "How simply horrid," she said with a grimace. A year later she had come out with a full line of canned soups. Lillian Langseth-Christensen, the sophisticated food writer who contributed classic Viennese recipes to *Gourmet,* produced a book called *The Instant Epicure Cookbook,* dedicated to good food at high speed. Her recipes tended to be quick because they were simple (steak au poivre, cheese fondue, zabaglione), but she didn't hesitate to heat slices of delicatessen turkey in canned cream of chicken soup or fill her salads with canned vegetables.

Such gestures of support for packaged-food cuisine, coming as they did from some of the best professional cooks in the country, helped erode the foundations of traditional home cooking just as teaching cake mixes to schoolchildren did. But an even more insidious attack on home cooking was carried out by Pillsbury, the very company that boldly launched the Bake-Off in 1949 as an unabashed celebration of women's skills in the kitchen. During the first ten or fifteen years of the Bake-Off, relatively few packaged foods showed up in the recipes, though none were explicitly forbidden except mixes. Many contestants used canned soups or tomato sauce in their main dish recipes, and caramels, chocolates, and marshmallows swarmed through the cakes and cookies, but for the most part the contestants cooked from scratch. What's more, their recipes displayed a wide range of culinary influences. The homemaker who baked Crusty French Bread at the first Bake-Off said she had "coaxed" the recipe from the chef at a little café outside Paris; other winners credited their mothers, grandmothers, and great-aunts. And, of course, many created recipes that would have been perfectly at home in any of the popular women's magazines—Chicken Salad Pie, for example, a 1954 winner for which a pie shell was filled with chicken salad that was dressed up with shredded cheese, crushed pineapple, and slivered almonds; then covered with mayonnaise and whipped cream, and decorated with carrot curls.

Tasty or terrifying, it was all home cooking. Then Pillsbury began to inject a different sensibility into the Bake-Off, one that was more compatible with the company's shortcut products. In 1958 a special supplement appeared at the end of the Bake-Off recipe booklet. After the one hundred winning recipes, the editors offered seventeen "Busy Day" recipes that had been created in the company's test kitchens with Pillsbury's new refrigerated biscuits, cookies, and sweet rolls. "In these busy days there are times when the fun of baking from a recipe isn't possible because you lack the time," Ann Pillsbury explained in an introductory note addressed to "Busy Women." The next big move was a complete overhaul: Pillsbury came up with a new name and a new format, both now entirely dedicated to being busy. The 1966 recipe booklet identified the contest as The Pillsbury Busy Lady Bake-Off, and the company all but begged contestants to think in terms of packaged-food cuisine. "Ease and simplicity of preparation, recipe shortcuts, streamlined methods and use of few utensils will count heavily," the rules promised. Pillsbury went so far as to offer a Special $1,000 Bonus Award for any winning recipes made with mixes. A year later the prize cake had a box of buttercream-caramel frosting mix stirred right into the batter, and the Bake-Off never recovered. From then on the contest honored nothing at all, save perhaps American ingenuity in the service of store-bought products.

Despite such triumphs, however, the long march of packaged-food cuisine did not lay waste to American cookery. There was indeed a war in the '50s between the food industry and the defenders of hands-on cookery, a war in which professionals were shoulder to shoulder with home cooks on the front lines of both sides. But this was a war characterized most strongly by its truces, not its battles. Traditional and high-speed recipes invariably showed up in the same cookbook, the same magazine story, the same household, even the same meal. The home cooks who contributed their favorite recipes to the *June Fete Cookbook,* which was published in 1955 to benefit a Pennsylvania hospital, liked to make cream of almond soup, oysters Rockefeller, and coq au vin from scratch. They were accustomed to cooking with wine and herbs, could turn out a by-the-book Caesar salad as well as an old-fashioned cole slaw, and took pride in the pies and cakes they made by hand. They also prepared pot roast with canned tomato sauce mixed with soy sauce. They made Gourmet Pâté de Foie

Gras out of cream cheese, liverwurst, and a can of bouillon; they added sherry and Cheez Whiz to broccoli; and they put curry powder, canned grated Parmesan, and bacon into a dish called Zucchini Creole. To these women the ricochet between culinary opposites wasn't dizzying, it was desirable. As they explained in the introduction, they enjoyed real cooking for the "gracious living" it symbolized, but they wanted their book to acknowledge "the busy tempo of modern times" as well.

Chapter 3

Don't Check Your Brains
at the Kitchen Door

Poppy Cannon, in a 1954 picture that appeared on the back of The Bride's Cookbook. *When she assembled this, her second cookbook, she included recipes for shashlik and scalloped oysters from scratch; she scattered edible flowers across a May Day salad—yet she couldn't resist making steak and kidney pie out of cans or starting her recipe for mint jelly with lime gelatin. Her whole approach contradicted itself and she knew it, but she was determined to make it the foundation of a great, twentieth-century cuisine designed for a new Everywoman.* (Photo: Ewing Galloway.)

Poppy Cannon was standing nervously inside the house when the camera found her. She looked the very picture of domestic glamour in a shirtwaist dress with a tightly wrapped top, her hair pulled back in a sleek coronet, her makeup deftly applied. But her voice betrayed her: It came out rushed and breathy as she greeted Edward R. Murrow and welcomed a national television audience into her home. Murrow wasn't really there, of course; he relaxed in a chair in the studio during *Person to Person* and chatted with his guests via live hookup as they talked eagerly into the air. That particular evening in October 1954 he had started the program by visiting with Sid Caesar and his wife. Now Murrow was introducing his audience to another prominent family, civil rights leader Walter White and his wife, the cookbook author Poppy Cannon.

Although she had appeared often on television, her experience was chiefly on daytime TV, demonstrating recipes to housewives. This was prime time, this was the famed newscaster Edward R. Murrow, and Cannon had plainly rehearsed how she was going to launch a discussion of her favorite subject. "Both of us feel that food is rather more than something to eat, though that is the most important thing that it is," she said graciously, if rapidly. "We feel that food is a kind of universal bringer-together of people. There's no better way to get people to talking about what they like and who they are and what their grandma used to make and what their wife cooks. It's the most wonderful icebreaker in the world, just talking about food."

Maybe so, but not for Murrow. While the camera followed Cannon, the distinguished newsman asked culinary questions so tentative that even she looked surprised. "I'm in strange territory," he announced at the outset of the interview. "Could you show us around your kitchen a little?" "I'd love to," Cannon responded promptly and gestured toward a lazy Susan covered with small jars. "This is a lazy Susan, as you can see, and it's full of flavoring extracts—I have them arranged alphabetically," she remarked and turned away. But before she could move on, Murrow interrupted her. "Wait a minute, Poppy—how can you find the right bottle in a hurry?" "Well, you start with A," said Cannon, carefully maintaining her gracious tone. She hadn't anticipated having to explain the alphabet to Edward R. Murrow. "If you're looking for, ah, apple blossom flavoring, then you have A. And if you're looking for vanilla, you turn around and find V. It's all from A to V. I have no Z's." The tour of the kitchen continued: Cannon pointed out Puerto Rican icons representing the patron saints of cookery, Chinese kitchen gods, strings of dried herbs and okra, a ravioli cutter, a Cape Cod cranberry scoop, and a huge perforated spoon she described as a "Hungarian noodle strainer." "It looks big enough to feed an army," Murrow interjected. "I guess it would be," Cannon agreed, then added even more agreeably, "if they liked noodles, especially." After they had examined every inch of the kitchen, Murrow finally asked her if she could make something as ordinary as scrambled eggs in it. "Oh yes, you could do scrambled eggs," she said, looking a bit unsure as to whether she was supposed to produce a plateful on the spot. At this, her husband stepped in. "Ed, you obviously haven't read Poppy's book, *The Bride's Cookbook*," he said smoothly. "There's a whole section on eggs. I'll send you a copy tomorrow." With some relief, Murrow turned his attention to civil rights and to the more properly newsworthy half of the family.

Poppy Cannon's moment in nationwide prime time was brief, but she had used it to talk about food in a manner quite unlike the way most cooking experts took up the subject. No recipes were discussed, no cooking took place, no packaged products were displayed; instead, she put food in the context of anthropology, religion, and world travel. If James Beard was watching, he must have blinked in astonishment. As we have seen, he and his friends considered Cannon the very personification of the food industry, a woman who made her career shilling for shortcuts and cared nothing about gastronomic tradition. Yet Cannon was a far more complex figure than this view, or indeed much of her own work, suggested. Her career swept across the whole rambunctious spectacle of midcentury American cooking—from the greatness to the inanity, from the promise to the curse. As a person, moreover, she was virtually a time capsule of the issues that made the '50s a turning point for American women, especially the increasingly complicated relationship between the housewife and the house. Her story sums up that anxiety-filled moment in American culinary history when it first became possible for ordinary women, not just the rich, to decide whether or not to cook for their families.

As it happened, Poppy Cannon knew fine food as well as Beard did. They were both professionals in the New York food world, and they had easy access to the city's best restaurants. Like Beard, she traveled through Europe tasting the cuisine of famous chefs as well as traditional dishes from the countryside, and like Beard she visited wineries and vineyards. At home she kept a food library of some six hundred volumes and made constant use of it. Cannon ate with gusto and curiosity, and she loved to map culinary research trails across centuries and continents. If she was in thrall to the miracles promised by the food industry, it certainly wasn't because she disdained the cuisine of the real world. But she saw the kitchen very differently from the way Beard did. At the center of Beard's culinary life was a glorious heap of fresh ingredients—the meats, fish, vegetables, and herbs that needed only his talented hands to release their goodness. At the center of Poppy Cannon's culinary life was an American housewife, and she just got home from work.

All Cannon's thinking about food was inspired by that particular Everywoman, a creature who cheerfully tied an apron over her stylish dress each evening and went striding into the second half of the twentieth century as if she owned it. Education, ambition, love, creativity, and a firm grip on her own financial destiny were her birthrights, and so was the honor of making a home for her family. At a time when almost nobody discussed women and work without framing the subject as a debate, Cannon took it for granted that having a job was as natural and necessary to a woman as it was to a man. She also believed that domestic life was perfectly manageable alongside a career, as long as a woman was adept with automatic appliances and knew her way up and down the grocery aisles. In the course of a relaxed hour between work and dinnertime, a fine meal would materialize from boxes and jars—Cannon evoked that meal many, many times in her writing—and family members would flock to the table with delighted exclamations.

Cannon's faith in this vision sprang from her own need to work, a financial need but also a visceral one. She loved having a career and wouldn't have lived any other way. But she conjured that magical banquet of canned and frozen products for another reason as well, a reason that went far beyond her duty to the advertising industry where she worked for years. A stubborn allegiance to food technology ran across her career like a fault line in its very foundation. It was as if she cooked with a willing suspension of disbelief, moving about the kitchen swathed in the illusion that garlic powder tasted exactly like garlic and a canned string bean was the same as a fresh one. The truth, which she never publicly acknowledged, was that she had to believe in miracles because she couldn't cook. She did cook, of course, for hours and hours every week, testing and developing recipes. But it came hard to her, and she wouldn't have chosen to spend all that time in the kitchen if there had been any other way to support herself in the food world. She lacked the instincts that enable good cooks to create by taste and imagination alone; she had no interest in perfecting the more finicky skills, many of the tasks she found tedious; and on the whole, she'd rather have been reading.

Not many eras in culinary history would have permitted someone with such an unwieldy combination of appetite and infelicity to create for herself a profession in cookery, but it could happen in midcentury America. Thanks to the food industry's commitment to innovation at any gastronomic price, the kitchen had become a realm of many possibilities, only one of which was traditional cooking. Cannon understood to the core what a comfort it would be to have dinnertime made manageable by instant vichyssoise. To work hard all day and then go home to loving companionship and a splendid meal—surely women as well as men deserved the full benefits of this contemporary paradise. At the heart of all her efforts was the conviction that modern women had the right to make new domestic choices as they followed their stars. She lived in a remarkable moment for American cookery: Many of its futures were already present and jostling for space. Poppy Cannon could see what was going on. She set up shop at the crossroads of commerce and cuisine, and there she flourished.

First, however, she had to become Poppy Cannon, a transformation she made with care and determination. Most food writers plumb their early years often for taste memories and inspiration; Cannon never did. She rarely spoke of her childhood, and she even quit her name as soon as she could assemble a new one. She was born Lillian Gruskin, in Capetown, South Africa, in 1905. Her parents were Jews from Lithuania who were making their way from the old country to America, where they had relatives. After Lillian's birth they took up their journey once more and settled in Pennsylvania. Her father worked as a merchant and tried his hand at photography, but he was an elusive figure in the family, spending weeks at a time away from home. Finally, he walked out on his wife and three children for good. Lillian was fourteen when her parents divorced. Her mother could do little to help the children through the trauma; she suffered for years from mental illness and eventually had to be institutionalized. The three children finished growing up largely on their own, and each won a scholarship—Lillian to Vassar, her brother to Amherst, and her sister (who became the award-winning fashion designer Anne Fogarty) to Carnegie Mellon. One summer during college Lillian, whose goal was to be a writer, took a job at the New York Public Library, where she met a librarian and bibliographer named Carl Cannon. They married as soon as she graduated, and although she stayed in touch with her mother and siblings over the years, the extended family would never be a close one. "Poppy" had been a longtime nickname, and it went nicely with her husband's surname. Within a few years only the Vassar alumnae office still knew her as Lillian Gruskin.

Cannon had plenty of ambition to fuel her career, but what drew her into the professional food world for the first time was romance. In 1928 when she was a new bride living in New York, she went to a party and met the man who would become the love of her life. An interracial crowd of artists, writers, and political activists, many of them associated with the Harlem Renaissance, were dancing and drinking that night at the home of a lawyer who worked with the National Association for the Advancement of Colored People. Cannon knew a number of the guests already, including James Weldon Johnson, the black writer and musicologist who headed the NAACP, but she had never been introduced to his famous assistant, Walter White. They met in the kitchen. Cannon was busy making sandwiches, and it didn't occur to her that this new acquaintance might be Johnson's second-in-command; after all, the gregarious stranger was fair-skinned, blond, and blue-eyed. But White—who loved the irony of his name—was born to an Atlanta family classified as black despite its skin color. (White's great-grandfather was William Henry Harrison, who had six children with a slave named Dilsia before deciding to run for president. Dilsia's daughter Marie was herself taken up by a white man, with whom she had four children. Her daughter Madeline was White's mother.)

At the time he met Cannon, White had just spent ten years on a series of dangerous assignments for the NAACP, posing as a white man and infiltrating himself into small towns in the South to investigate lynchings. The horrifying evidence he gathered—he reported in detail on forty-one lynchings and eight race riots—forced white Americans to confront the violent face of racism for the first time, and made White a hero among many blacks. During the 1920s he wrote two impassioned novels about race relations and racial identity, and also published a nonfiction book about lynching. In 1930 he succeeded Johnson at the NAACP and ran the organization for the next quarter century.

That night in the kitchen he and Cannon straightaway fell into a conversation about food. Both were fascinated by the subject, and by the end of the evening they were fascinated by each other as well. There was no question that a love affair would mean trouble, especially for White, who was highly visible in the black community. His wife, Gladys, had been a secretary at the NAACP, and they had two small children. Whatever ensued from that party, therefore, ensued quietly. And very quickly. Within a year White and Cannon were agonizing about whether to leave their families and marry. White knew the indignities and dangers that were in store for a white woman married to a black man, and he feared for her life. His own family, too, would be vulnerable; and his career would probably collapse under the scandal. When Cannon and her husband had a daughter, Cynthia, the stakes got higher still. Years later, in a letter to Cannon, White described himself as a "coward" during that time of indecision, as well as "unwilling to subject you to nameless terrors and persecutions."

But in the midst of all this passion, drama, and guilt, they kept talking about food, and finally they dreamed up a project they could work on together. It would be a book about "Negro" cookery, with social and cultural research as well as recipes. "We would collect precious recipes, reconstruct ancient methods, delve deep into the reasons why the Negro had developed a true American cuisine," as Cannon recalled it later. White was the one with the well-known name and the publishing connections, so he was the one to sign the contract with Knopf. They received an advance of $250, and in 1934, Cannon set out on a research trip through the South, following a route she and White had planned over long lunches at the Brevoort in Greenwich Village. She traveled with Hope Spingarn, the daughter of a prominent white NAACP official, meeting up with White's family, friends, and acquaintances everywhere. As a couple of white women seeking black cooks to interview, they encountered prejudice at times, but chiefly it was from those friendly whites who were taken aback when Cannon and Spingarn shook the hand of the family cook or called her "Mrs." "It was a subtle thing, but the distinction was clear," wrote Cannon later. "Not even the so-called liberals were free of it." She amassed quite a bit of material, but soon after their return to New York, White made the decision that he had to stop seeing her; and the book project came to nothing. It resurfaced, awkwardly, fourteen years later when *The New Yorker* published a two-part profile of White. By that time Cannon and White were enmeshed all over again and planning to marry, but neither one was divorced yet; and White was an internationally known activist lobbying hard for racial justice in a heavily segregated nation. This was no time for their long, secret relationship to be made public. So a carefully bowdlerized version of the cookbook episode appeared in *The New Yorker*: "White got an advance on the cookbook, and he also got himself a researcher, a young colored woman who conscientiously toured the South accumulating little-known recipes and kitchen lore. She ultimately used her experiences profitably by becoming a consultant for General Foods and for H. J. Heinz, but White never quite got around to tackling his end."

The reference to General Foods and Heinz, at least, was accurate. After White broke off their relationship, Cannon took a job with an advertising agency and began working with these and other food companies, amassing publicity for her clients and writing ad copy. She spent the next fifteen years in advertising even while building a simultaneous career in journalism. Under the notably relaxed standards that had long governed food writing, there was never any need to choose between the two professions; Cannon's journalism and her commercial work overlapped so consistently that they were often indistinguishable. Cannon loved writing, but she was also determined to support herself, which meant slanting her career toward the marketplace. Despite or perhaps because of the fact that she married four times in just over two decades, she could never look upon marriage as a safe harbor. Nothing in her childhood gave her any reason to believe that having a husband constituted a good investment strategy.

Cannon landed her first regular writing job in 1940 when she became a food columnist at *Mademoiselle*. Five years old and highly successful, *Mademoiselle* called itself "The Magazine for Smart Young Women." As one of the first publications to target a newly identified consumer market of women in their late teens and twenties, *Mademoiselle* unabashedly invited its readers to think of themselves as working women, not just premarried women. Of course they would walk down the aisle in splendor someday—love and romance were recurring themes—but the magazine exuded an airy certainty that today's smart young women were delighted with their single lives and took their jobs seriously. Cannon was just the right person to tell them about food. Until she took over, the magazine had no consistent approach to the subject, though it ran an occasional shopping column on the latest in cheese crackers and canned turtle soups. The last food story to be published before Cannon's debut was a feature called "Cocktails for Two," which instructed readers on how to entertain a male friend at drinks. "After taking his hat . . . you say, 'I hope you won't have to leave before quarter-of-seven. I'm not dining until seven-thirty.' . . . If you don't keep a maid, ask him to bring in the tray. . . . A girl may wear a hostess gown, but not a negligee. . . . Conversation? You'll toss him little cues about the things he's interested in. He'll talk. And you'll listen." Nothing could have been farther from this antimacassar wisdom than the lighthearted voice that was introduced a month later in Cannon's column. She, too, was instructing readers on social rituals; she, too, was pitching brand-name products; but first and foremost she wanted her readers to see exactly who they were—free-spirited young moderns, living at top speed and in high style. "Fair reader, sometime or other you have to eat," she began briskly. "Granted you haven't the time or the space or even the mood to dream up an angel food cake. Nevertheless, you can serve food—good food, too—exciting, interesting victuals. A smooth cocktail party, a buffet supper, an evening snack, intimate little dinners for two. . . . It's all out of tins—but with verve, my dear, with dash."

This bright, lively hostess in the high heels and apron, the girl too smart to cook the way her mother did, was Cannon's brain-child. She nurtured it in columns that were titled "Eat and Run" until the war years, when the name shifted to a more practical "Food for Fun and Fitness." The heroines of her column were constantly inviting men to brunch or throwing together a sponta-neous after-theater supper or staging a wedding breakfast for ten in a one-room apartment—even though they were working girls and had never cooked in their lives. "This is a true story with a practical moral—several of them," she started one typical tale in 1940. "It's about Vivi—the girl who always said that 'whipping around in the kitchen gives me the gleeps.' However, that was a long time ago—way back last summer, before she met Tommy and went off into her starry-eyed dither. Imagine our astonish-ment when Vivi asked us to dinner and tossed off an all-time high in feeds—with never so much as a flicker of a well-curled eye-lash." Vivi's secret was canned foods, which supplied the entire lavish meal, from Underwood's puree mongole to La Touraine's baba au rhum.

Cannon's prose style in these columns was relentless, but it had a great deal of work to do. She was trying to transform a cen-tury's worth of domestic imagery and shift the nature of culinary authority from tradition to the back of the box. Mothers and home economists had no place in the kitchens she created, and neither did the nation's most treasured convictions about good food. At the same time she wanted to retain all the positive associ-ations clustered around home cooking. These demands, as well as her background in writing ad copy, inspired her to adopt a voice and vocabulary that would be impossible to confuse with the old kitchen manuals. When she wanted to liven up a dish, she called for "a splotch of wine, a fleck of spice or a flutter of herbs," "a drift of caraway seeds," "a flurry of fresh coconut," "a great swish of sour cream," "a generous flutter of chopped chives," or "a fleck of allspice for the *touch unusual.*" Sometimes she simply in-vented words: "At one of the snorkier dinner-parties of the year, cranberry sherbet was brought in with the chicken. And why not?" She advised readers to "mix furiously" or "stir like crazy" or "fling" ingredients together; once she referred to tossing a salad as "salad-flinging." These mannerisms scattered through her para-graphs evoked a kind of screwball comedy set in the kitchen, with the cook as the madcap heroine. "When up a tree for a quick dessert, you can rassle a lemon pie in a jiff. Haven't you heard of the new wonderstuff called Clovernook . . . ?" What counted here was a brilliant splash of activity and a happy ending. Readers weren't supposed to question the quality of the food any more than they would have puzzled over the plot in a funny movie.

But the quality of the food kept buzzing around Cannon's imagination like a fly she couldn't swat away. Often she reassured readers that packaged foods were as good if not better than their homemade equivalents, and to back up this assertion she defined any shortfalls in flavor as seasoning problems. Factory-made prod-ucts had to be formulated so that they would be widely accept-able, she explained. They tended to be bland, but smart cooks knew how to pep them up and make them release their full po-tential. "Those as yearn for food with personality plus must work on it," she counseled. To "work on it" meant dousing Libby's Vienna sausages with brandy and setting them on fire. It meant adding a spoonful of sherry to Cresca Bisque of Shrimp ("Any haughty Creole cook would be proud of the result"), and simmer-ing a jar of sweet-and-sour cabbage with salami, onions, and canned potatoes until it became "Hungarian salami goulash." It's impossible to know whether Cannon herself was fully persuaded by such dishes, but she defended them in public when necessary. Once she published a recipe that started with a few slices of Spam placed in the bottom of a casserole, then a layer of canned macaroni and cheese, then a layer of canned asparagus, and finally a layer of grated cheese and bread crumbs. This one got a response: George Frazier, a Boston journalist who reviewed record albums for *Mademoiselle,* wrote a letter to the editor. "Honest to God, it was terrible," he complained. "Not quaint or ineffable or anything, but just terrible. It tasted very much as I imagine that a piece of carpet would taste if I were to run my tongue over it when I have one of my inimitable hangovers. . . . Eat and Run? Good God, I'm not even able to walk. I'm in bed." An editor's note followed. "It must be that heavy masculine hand," someone retorted, probably Cannon. "A staff member (*two* staff members, in fact) tried the same recipe and report that it was *divine.*"

Most of Cannon's work in *Mademoiselle* was published under pseudonyms: she used "Snack" and "Blair Jennings" at first, then settled on "Fillip." This was a version of her latest married name: Poppy Cannon Philippe. After her first marriage ended in divorce and her affair with White collapsed, she was married for a short time to an engineer named Alf Askland. Their son, Alf, was born in 1938, and six months later Askland died. She married Claude Philippe soon thereafter. They met through friends in the food world—not the advertisers' food world where she worked but the haute cuisine world of the city's gastronomes, who gathered often to enjoy fine dinners and wines in French restaurants or their own homes. Philippe had the name and expertise to cut a swaggering figure in this circle. Trained in Europe, he was a rising power at the Waldorf-Astoria. Soon he would be placed in charge of all meals and banquets at the great hotel and start signing his name with regal simplicity as Philippe of the Waldorf. He traveled often to Europe to buy wine and energetically cultivated the social, theatrical, and literary stars who came and went at the Waldorf. Philippe was tyrannical in his business dealings and too coldly ambitious to maintain most personal relationships, but for New

Yorkers he made a perfect symbol of the French high culinary tradition at its most exclusive.

Despite the differences in their professional approaches to food, Cannon was an avid student of the lofty cuisine that Philippe represented. To her, shortcut cooking was a branch of great traditional cuisine, not a departure from it, and she wanted to see and taste everything that went on in the best kitchens. She also had useful business contacts throughout the food industry and all the social skills Philippe lacked. The marriage started hopefully and in short order produced their daughter, Claudia, but the couple disintegrated fast. Philippe continued having the affairs for which he was notorious, and Cannon moved to an apartment of her own. Even so, Philippe balked at the idea of a divorce, and the marriage dragged on until 1949, when Cannon slipped off to the Virgin Islands and obtained a quick but legal divorce there. Three years later, speaking to a conference of newspaper food editors, Philippe said bluntly that no woman could become a good cook if she was "a robot to a can opener."

One reason this difficult marriage lasted so long was that Cannon was trying desperately to end it without scandal. In 1944, when Claudia was three years old, Cannon and Walter White resumed their affair; and this time they decided they would marry no matter what the public consequences might be. But they had to proceed cautiously. Philippe had a famous temper and was likely to be so appalled by the relationship that he would fight for custody of Claudia. White's children were grown, but he dreaded the thought of putting his wife through the agony and humiliation of a separation that was sure to be in the papers. By now he was one of the most widely respected black men of his time. In a 1946 feature story on White, *Ebony* magazine called him "the No. 1 champion of Negro rights in the land," pointedly described him as a "model husband and father," and quoted his wife calling him "an ideal family man."

For the next five years the two of them staged rapturous meetings whenever they could and corresponded ardently between rendezvous, gripped by the operatic intensity of their plight. "Darling, were ever two people so diabolically plagued by people and circumstance?" White wrote to her early in 1949. Some of their friends and coworkers knew about the relationship, but Philippe was resisting divorce, Gladys was miserable, and White's colleagues were making it clear that they despised interracial marriage. One friend at the NAACP suggested that if he married Cannon, he should leave the organization and take a diplomatic post overseas. But, as White noted, such an appointment would need confirmation by the Senate. "Our marriage—that of a much-hated 'Negro' agitator to a 'white' woman would provide a field day for the Dixiecrats," he wrote to Cannon. "Whatever happens, I won't let you, my Beloved, be subjected to that slime."

Cannon wrote back that she was simply grateful for "what so few people ever get—a second chance at happiness." Their love was a great wine, she told him, "silken upon the lips, fiery-soft upon the heart." In July 1949 the two were married at last in a judge's chambers in New Jersey—a location chosen for its obscurity, though Cannon suspected her husband was a little disappointed that nobody recognized him. She herself was in bliss as more than two decades of stress and sorrow dropped away. The next day she was back at work writing ad copy for frozen vegetables: "quick-frozen peas fresh as a day in June, tender as love."

White had hoped that his years of dedicated service would speak for themselves, but even he wasn't able to marry a white woman and get away with it, at least at first. Mixed marriage was hardly unheard of, but it was still illegal in twenty states. "No interracial marriage of the past half-century has aroused as much bitter controversy as the recent action of NAACP Secretary Walter White in taking a white magazine editor, Poppy Cannon, as his bride," reported *Ebony* in a cover story. The issue was the biggest seller in the magazine's first five years. Gladys and his son and daughter would have nothing to do with White after he left them, and only after much debate did the NAACP decide to keep him in his position. Cannon, too, felt the effects. She was still working in advertising, but she had run into problems with some of her accounts that led White to wonder if her association with him was hindering her career. Not long after the wedding, she quit advertising entirely. As for Philippe, he was outraged when he heard of the marriage; he had finally agreed to the divorce and to shared custody of Claudia, but now he begged Cannon to let Claudia stay with him permanently so that she would not have to live "in one household with you and your negro husband." (Later, he relented.) Meanwhile, they were trying to buy a small house on East Sixty-eighth Street—on Manhattan's Upper East Side. Twenty-one banks turned them down for a mortgage. Ultimately, they arranged private financing, but after White's death, Cannon wrote to the Community Church of New York, offering to make the top floor of the house available to any students or teachers who were having trouble finding housing in her neighborhood. She expressed a special wish to open her home to Africans, Indians, and Pakistanis.

But the public frenzy didn't last long. As a reader of *Ebony* wrote to the magazine, "I found myself wondering what would have happened had either one of them been *black*!" White was indeed an unusual black, and not just because of his skin color. He moved in far more glamorous circles than Cannon did, and once they were married, her world was populated with the headline-making names of the time. White knew heads of state around the globe; in Washington he had good friends on the Supreme Court and in the White House; and at home he socialized with New York's leading artists, writers, and political figures. It is unlikely, absent White in her life, that Cannon would have sent President Dwight D. Eisenhower a copy of *The Can-Opener Cookbook* with her warm regards or dashed off an "entirely personal" letter to the president of the Republic of Haiti urging Haiti to take a stand "on the side of human rights" and reverse its U.N. vote in favor of returning Somaliland to Italy. White's extraordinary roster of friends and acquaintances was legendary, and one of the greatest pleasures he and Cannon had in common was name-dropping, especially because they really did know every person whose name they dropped. One day she accompanied him on a typical round of engagements, which included conferring with Ralphe Bunche on U.N. business, a meeting with Nelson Rockefeller, tea with Eleanor Roosevelt, and dinner with Lena Horne. That evening Sugar Ray Robinson dropped by.

Cannon and White had a wonderful time being married to each other. They loved the romance, they loved the social life, and they loved taking a hand in each other's work. For years White was deeply involved in the Caribbean, lobbying hard against U.S. financial control of Haiti and promoting locally controlled development in the Virgin Islands, where he believed "genuine racial democracy" was possible. Cannon did everything she could to promote his work: She rounded up her friends in the press for junkets to the Caribbean, wrote constantly about the food of the islands, and organized press briefings and cocktail parties. For his part, White found Cannon the best writer and editor, finest TV performer, and greatest cook he knew, and he said so often. Perhaps only a husband as worshipful as White would have gone so far as to invite his famous friends home for Cannon's experiments with what she called "the quick gourmet meal." Vijaya Lakshmi

Pandit, for instance, the Indian diplomat and sister of Prime Minister Nehru, joined them in the kitchen one evening for a long chat about the problems in Kashmir, pausing frequently to taste and discuss five kinds of frozen chicken. On another occasion Senator Estes Kefauver fell into a profound discussion of the South with Cannon and White but found himself "diverted," as Cannon put it, by her shortcut version of a pâté maison.

Cannon started planning *The Bride's Cookbook* right around the time she became a bride herself for the last time. Her original idea was to call it "Enchantment on Our Lips" and fill it with the love poetry she had written to White for years, attaching just a few "treasured recipes" to each cluster of poems. By the time the book appeared in 1954, she had been forced to adopt a more conventional structure, with several hundred recipes organized in the usual categories; but she managed to rescue half a dozen poems and dot the text with them. Here is one:

Domestic Villanella

How can I say I love you
   as I do
save through this liturgy of common things
save through the simple, ordinary things
   I do

The way I pull the curtain to the side
so that the sunlight may more featly pour
   for your delight

. . . the loaves I shape with these two hands for you
   the pies I bake,
the apples that I slice . . .
and dash with spice.

How can I say I love you
   as I do
just by the foods (seasoned with joy) that I cook for you,
just by the way, at dusk, I look for you . . .
   "I do."

Cannon took a great deal of pride in her poetry. Like the rest of her writing, it both conceals and exposes its author by constantly evoking a persona, often the woman who cooks for her beloved. "Yolks must be whipped / with rapture / Whites folded in with tenderness," she wrote in "Rule for a Cake." Or, from "To Make a Salad":

Now take a front lawn by a small, white house
a yard where myriad, tiny, savage teeth
of dandelions dare to show their spears
and lift them, one by one, with a sharp knife
then wash and whirl and lay them in a bowl
well rubbed with garlic . . . bless with olive oil
like sunshaft molten . . .

Her *Mademoiselle* columns, too, evoked the woman in the kitchen, but that flighty young thing was out to dazzle her sweetheart, not just feed him. Here, by contrast, was a woman who cooked like a grown-up—by hand, from scratch. Cannon had a palate for sentiment as forgiving as her palate for canned gravy, and some of this poetry could pass for greeting-card verse. To sustain an authentic voice of her own at any length was beyond her. But she knew what feelings were, and she knew they didn't come in cans.

For this reason the poetry in *The Bride's Cookbook* vied uncomfortably with the prose. Cannon believed profoundly in work, in marriage, and in good food—a faith that for women might just as well have represented three points of a compass, sending them in irreconcilably different directions. She was able to embrace all three at once only by virtue of her expertise in wishful thinking. Thus, the poetry is about cooking that takes time, that revels in fresh ingredients, that gets the cook's hands dirty. "Time is a savor," she wrote in one poem. "Time is a mellowing, / wizard's device. / Time is the X-thing that marries a stew." But with the prose she swerved in a different direction and tried not to look back. "Time is the X-thing that marries a stew," she conceded. "But in this day and age, it needn't be *your* time. All the really fine prepared stews, soups, sauces, and quick-frozen specialties have been made from the same ingredients that you would use, and with the addition of time, art, and skill. All that remains for you is to translate them into your own idiom, to serve them in your own inimitable fashion, and with your sweetest smile."

These warring allegiences to fine food and convenience fought their way across Cannon's working life for decades, and the battle grew even more intense in 1953 when she moved into one of the most prestigious jobs in her field: food editor of *House Beautiful* magazine. Sumptuous and sophisticated, *House Beautiful* aimed to be the arbiter of taste in a period when, for the first time, a critical mass of Americans had money to spend on comfort and culture. Its dashing editor, Elizabeth Gordon, liked to burst forth with extravagant campaigns based on her philosophy of style—"A Report to the World on How Americans Live" or "The Meaning of Colonial Williamsburg for Us Today"—and she persistently trumpeted the work of her favorite architect, Frank Lloyd Wright. Every issue was a demonstration project illustrating her mandate: to show readers how to conduct their domestic lives the intelligent, graceful, and above all modern way.

The modern way with food was very much a preoccupation of Gordon's even before she hired Cannon to preside over the magazine's extensive food pages. Since 1944, *House Beautiful* had been running artful musings on gastronomy by M.F.K. Fisher and other knowledgeable food writers; typically, these were interspersed with ad-friendly features on the rationale for using new appliances and convenience products. Gordon herself contributed some of the latter stories. "Have you discovered the new freedom in homemaking?" she asked readers in 1951. "Eating well no longer means drudgery in the kitchen, though millions of people have not yet discovered this fact. . . . We have been slow to coordinate into our lives all the new homemaking inventions and food improvements of the last 20 years." This editorial environment, much classier than *Mademoiselle*'s, offered the food industry all the support it required but gave ample space as well to a refined, moneyed view of cooking, an approach that didn't aspire to gracious living so much as take it for granted.

These new surroundings encouraged a fresh and genuinely progressive note in Cannon's thinking about food. She had always considered herself far above the marshmallow-salad school of quick cooking, because her business was imitating great cuisine. Now she started revising her approach to greatness, trying to understand its substance rather than focusing on its surface. The modern epicure, she wrote in one of her early stories for the magazine, was a different creature from a Lucullus or a Madame du Pompadour. They had the luxury of being able to exercise their refined tastes on food prepared by experts. But a 1950s epicure was on her own. "If you want to dine well today, you have to know how to cook a good meal yourself," she wrote—an admission she had never made before. "But if you don't want to make cooking a full-time occupation, you have to know all the short-cuts and how to harness all the modern foodstuffs and equipment born in our times." Without reducing her commitment to packaged foods, Cannon was trying to look at them from a different perspective, for the help they could offer a woman who was already fully competent in the kitchen, not for the pretend banquets they could produce for a girl who'd rather go dancing. "To be a modern epicure," she went on, "means having a sensitive appreciation for the foodstuff you are working with, regardless of whether it is fresh, frozen, canned, dried, bottled, or whatever. It means being lovingly aware of the intrinsic flavor, so you know how to bring it out." For the first time in her career, Cannon was putting the food first.

Suppose you buy strawberries. *Taste* them before you decide what to do with them, she emphasized. "If they are perfect, you serve them plain with sugar. If they are not so fine, you make them into a shortcake. If they are hardly acceptable, you stew them with rhubarb. . . . In short, the modern epicure lets the quality of the food itself dictate the recipe." Again and again she wrote about the importance of tasting, attentively and with an open mind—"not just with your tongue, but with your eyes and your nose, your sense of touch, your imagination, memories, and your intellect." The true gourmet would appreciate a truffle, of course, but a radish right out of the garden or a handful of fiddlehead ferns in spring could be just as soul-stirring. And the garden, she stressed, was the only place where epicures could be sure of finding delicious fruits and vegetables, for they had all but disappeared from grocery stores. City dwellers should expect to search all over town for good produce: "Not the quickest-maturing, the fine shippers, the longest keepers, the best lookers, but those whose one and only claim to distinction is flavor, and more flavor."

Yet when she turned her attention to convenience foods, she lost her palate or perhaps her nerve. Occasionally, she voiced a criticism of one or another packaged product ("Canned chicken fricassee may be good, but often it is terrible"), but the category as a whole remained fundamental to her faith and her cooking. A silent contradiction between her senses and her convictions, between what she ate and what she insisted she believed about it, ran unimpeded through her *House Beautiful* stories. "Why, oh why, can't we have real stock, rich, cooked-down beef as well as chicken, quick-frozen, perhaps, in cubes?" she lamented once, decrying the usual bouillon cubes. In the same column she suggested that a bowl of Campbell's tomato soup "garnished" with canned Norwegian fish cakes would make an elegant first course for a dinner party. She wrote a detailed, cross-cultural study of pancakes, including chapatis, tortillas, and Chinese pancakes; she also advised substituting a little Cherry Heering for the liquid in black cherry Jell-O, for a "new and sophisticated" dessert. Drawing on her extensive knowledge of the Caribbean, she wrote a culinary geography of the region, tracing many specialties back to their roots around the world. Then she offered an easy way to recreate a West Indian stew by mixing canned sausage with canned rice. Packaged foods, to her, were symbols; all it took to make them real was a cook with brains. Espagnole sauce? "Franco-American beef gravy darkened with Kitchen Bouquet, thinned slightly with a little wine or brandy," she explained.

Cannon never apologized, and the contradictions she embraced never gave her pause. She was proud of her work, especially when she could take food writing beyond recipes into literature, history, anthropology, and culture. The writers with whom she identified were the acknowledged artists in the field, and whether or not they would have accepted her into their ranks, she didn't hesitate to place herself there. Assembling a list titled "Our Fifty Favorite Books About Food," she went right to the books of her time that would continue to be praised half a century later, including Buwei Yang Chao's *How to Cook and Eat in Chinese,* James Beard's *Fish Cookery,* Helen Evans Brown's *West Coast Cookery,* and the one she called her favorite of all food books, M.F.K. Fisher's *The Art of Eating,* published in 1954. Alongside such classics-in-the-making she put *The Can-Opener Cookbook* and *The Bride's Cookbook.*

As far as she was concerned, this wasn't hubris but common cause. She, too, was in search of the finest food, was willing to find it in the humblest places, was entranced by its lineage and its stories. She, too, wanted to help American homemakers cook with imagination and pleasure. So when famous writers contributed stories and recipes to *House Beautiful,* she didn't hesitate to add her own touches to their work. M.F.K. Fisher, for example, wrote a piece about bouillabaisse for the magazine in her characteristically evocative style, emphasizing that this legendary fish soup varied from place to place but always featured very fresh fish. She included several recipes, and Cannon, too, appended a recipe—for a shortcut bouillabaisse. "Every single one of the ingredients can be kept on hand in your kitchen or in the freezer," she noted helpfully, specifying frozen flounder, canned tomatoes, frozen shrimp, wine, and saffron. And for a dramatic presentation, she added, why not add Pernod at the end and set the whole thing on fire?

Of all the culinary gods Cannon studied and worshiped, the most exalted was Alice B. Toklas, formidable companion of Gertrude Stein until Stein's death in 1946. During their thirty-nine years together in Paris, Toklas had steeped herself in classic French culinary techniques and traditions, and the dinners she prepared for their famous friends were as fabled as the Picassos hanging on the walls of the flat in rue de Fleurus. It would have seemed inconceivable to anyone who knew her that Toklas, who shopped at dawn at Les Halles and refused to let a packaged mix into her kitchen, had a kindred spirit in Poppy Cannon. Yet when the two women met in Venice in 1954—brought together by *House Beautiful*—they hit it off immediately. For the next few years they corresponded, visited, exchanged gifts, discussed food endlessly, and even published a cookbook together.

Making friends with Toklas ranked as one of the highlights of Cannon's career, for Toklas personified with tremendous cachet that combination of brains and cookery that Cannon had been trying to promote for years. Here was a brilliant woman with access to everything notable in French avant-garde culture, and she chose food as her medium. What a triumph it was for Cannon to know that such a woman existed, and to drop her name as a friend! At the same time, Cannon was confident that she, too, had something to offer. After all, she was "the original 'gourmet in a hurry,'" as a magazine once termed her, and she was proud of it. None of the other food writers of the '50s would have had the temerity to send Alice B. Toklas a blender, but Cannon did. Toklas adored it.

Toklas was seventy-seven when they met and very much the widow since Stein's death eight years earlier. Like Cannon, Toklas had made an unconventional marriage, but unlike Cannon, she was content to be an entirely conventional wife. She had dedicated her life to supporting Stein and her art—running the household as Stein liked it, getting up early to pick tiny strawberries for Stein's breakfast, reverently typing Stein's manuscripts, and entertaining the wives of the artists and writers who came to visit, lest the women irritate Stein by hanging around listening for witticisms. After Stein's death, Toklas's commitment only deepened. She became the legal guardian of Stein's work, but more important, she became the keeper of a sacred trust, polishing and repolishing the icon and crafting the mythology. When she granted interviews, the subject had to be Stein and not herself; when she read articles and books about Stein, she went into a rage if they didn't seem laudatory enough. Meanwhile, she had started to write about food in order to make some money, but what she conjured most often in her tales and recipes was Stein and the world they had shared. "I am nothing but the memory of her," she told a friend. Nonetheless, Toklas turned out to be such a captivating writer—dry, witty, and graceful—that she quite supplanted Stein for most of the reading public.

Stein and Toklas nearly always had a cook, but soon after they began living together, Stein asked her companion to prepare meals on occasion, and before long Toklas had unearthed her own passion. She started collecting cookbooks and studying them for history as well as recipes; she gathered recipes whenever they traveled or visited friends; her appetite was always primed, and her curiosity was incessant. In her first magazine article, written for *Vogue* in 1950, she described how she prepared a striped bass one day when Picasso was coming for lunch. She poached the fish and spread it all over with mayonnaise, then used a pastry bag to pipe designs in red mayonnaise ("not made with catsup, horror of horrors, but with concentrated tomato juice") over the white. She continued decorating with pieces of hard-boiled egg, truffles, and herbs, and then served her masterpiece to a very appreciative Picasso. He did say, she reported, that he thought it looked more like a Matisse.

Anecdotes like this ran all through *The Alice B. Toklas Cook Book,* which appeared in 1954 and made Toklas the belle of the food world. She welcomed the income, but assembling the book had been nightmarish for her. She called the job "miserable" and "tormenting," barely met the deadline, and had to beg her friends for a chapter's worth of recipes just to make the manuscript long enough. She sent all the recipes to Harper & Bros. without bothering to test them, nor did she proofread the manuscript, which was probably why she overlooked the recipe called Haschich Fudge, contributed by her friend Brion Gysin, a painter. Harper discreetly left it out of the American edition, but when the book was published in Britain, Gysin's high-flying fudge quickly became notorious. Toklas was furious: Fans and skeptics alike had been wondering for years whether Stein was on drugs when she wrote, and now they thought they knew.

Even without the marijuana recipe, Americans were entranced by her book. Few of them were about to soak, pound, and strain pistachio nuts to make a nut butter to add to a cream sauce to pour over poached eggs that were sitting in puff paste that had been baked beforehand, but that didn't interfere with their delight in Toklas's writing. In wise, worldly tones edged with gentle amusement, she recounted wartime experiences, tales of friends, servants, cars, and pets, and visits to homes and restaurants where she and Stein had been served wondrous meals or, occasionally, dreadful ones. Readers who adored France or the idea of France, who subscribed to *Gourmet,* and who fondly remembered their youthful efforts to absorb Gertrude Stein called it their favorite cookbook.

Once Toklas was a celebrity in her own right, Elizabeth Gordon became fascinated by her. "What do you think is going to happen to me," Toklas wrote jubilantly to a friend in 1954. "I am going to fly to Italy on April Fool's Day—for ten days. Rome, Florence and Italy—with a fat fee by the editor of *House Beautiful*—she wishes to *consult* with me! blah blah!" Gordon had decided Toklas would be a good source to advise on a story about American domestic architecture in 1900 ("Do you suppose there isn't anyone else alive whose memory goes so far back," Toklas wondered) and arranged for this extended meeting at a time when

Gordon would be in Europe working on other stories. Cannon was on the trip as well, and when they all arrived in Venice, she was introduced to Toklas.

"Alice Toklas by the way isn't at all as I had imagined," she wrote to White. "She is a sweet, gentle little darling with a black mustache and short-cut hair with bangs which also look like a mustache. All of which sounds very strange but in ten minutes you have forgotten all that and hear only the kind, warm, wise things she says." That day the two of them wandered around town looking for a certain Jesuit church, which they never found, but discovering food shops and fish stalls and wine stores and a fine place for espresso. Toklas was just the sort of epicure that Cannon admired, and she lost no time corraling her for *House Beautiful*'s food section. For her part, Toklas found Cannon a flattering audience as well as a generous and warmhearted friend. After Cannon returned to New York, she sent Toklas a package of tea, and Toklas promptly sent her a Holland cheese. Cannon sent Toklas a kitchen knife; Toklas sent Cannon recipes and offered walnut oil if it was unavailable in New York. When Cannon published a memoir of Walter White in 1956, she sent a copy to Toklas, who wrote back that she "devoured it at once." She added that she had "lingered over five or six readings since." Over the next few years the two of them exchanged affectionate letters, and for *House Beautiful* they traveled together to the Cognac and Champagne regions of France.

They also argued a lot in the course of their friendship, for Toklas's cooking was about as far from Cannon's as cooking could get. The food that emerged from that Paris kitchen was pristine. Every ingredient was the finest and freshest she could obtain; no procedure was deemed too much trouble. If she admitted the concept of "convenience" to her consciousness at all, it was reserved for a dish that could be prepared ahead and didn't need last-minute touches. "I have a new trick for jellied eggs," she wrote to a friend in 1956, and gave directions for soft-boiling the eggs, covering them with gelatin and wine, and garnishing with chives and shrimp. "Takes ½ hour for a dozen eggs and is made hours in advance," she added. "You see my preparations are modern—no real troubles—though mixer hasn't yet seduced me—no chicken à la king—no readymade piecrusts biscuits cakes or muffins—not yet nor likely in the future."

But Toklas was skirting the truth here, as she often did when Stein's image or her own was at issue. The cookbook had charmed Americans in part because Toklas's culinary world seemed so different from their own and vastly more desirable. Toklas wasn't about to hint that she had long ago fallen for one of the best-known symbols of American efficiency in the kitchen. Back in 1940, while Stein and Toklas were living in the country house where they spent the war years, a package had arrived from Chicago. Samuel Steward, an American writer they had befriended, had decided to send them a Mixmaster. "Gertrude had said she liked things that went around—gramophone records, whirling grouse, eggbeaters, and the world," he wrote later in a memoir. "The Mixmaster seemed like the perfect gift, and useful to Alice as well."

Stein and Toklas were ecstatic. "The Mix master came Easter Sunday, and we have not had time to more than read the literature put it together and gloat, oh so beautiful is the Mix master, so beautiful and the literature so beautiful, and the shoe button potatoes that same day so beautiful and everything so beautiful," wrote Stein. She ended her letter, "Alice all smiles and murmurs in her dreams, Mix Master." Ten days later she wrote again: "Day and night Mix master is a delight. . . . Now Alice works it all alone and it saves her hours and effort, she can write a whole advertisement for Mix master she is so pleased." Toklas was using it for everything she could think of, including spoon bread and mashed potatoes. Then disaster—Toklas dropped the bowl, and it shattered. Stein begged Steward to send a replacement: ". . . you see you can use other bowls but they do not twirl around in that lovely green mix master way and when they do not twirl their contents instead of staying down rise up and spill and therefore the mix master will have to be a mix master still." Steward couldn't send a new bowl until 1945. He also sent new beaters, for Stein reported that the originals "got busted."

Of course the Mixmaster didn't change the nature of the food that Toklas was preparing; it simply saved her time and labor. Her vigilance against convenience foods and ersatz ingredients remained severe. Although it had been many years since she tasted anything made from mixes, she told Cannon, she remembered poor flavor, synthetic ingredients, and too much salt. With this, Cannon saw an opening for missionary work, and on her next trip to France she carried a suitcase full of packaged mixes. A month later Toklas reported back: She had had "huge success" with the yellow and devil's food cakes. It's possible that cake mixes had improved significantly since she first tried them; it's also likely that even the manufacturers never dreamed their cake-mix cakes would turn out the way Toklas turned them out. She made curaçao-flavored buttercream filling and a Drambuie icing for one cake, filled and iced another with rum-flavored cream, and filled another with crystallized fruits and kirsch-flavored cream, then frosted it with a kirsch icing. She made praline cream and icing for one of the devil's food cakes and later tried mocha cream. "Delicious!" she wrote.

Cannon was so buoyed by this response that she mailed off a Waring Blendor, which proved another huge success. "It has revolutionized kitchen work and has been a life saver," Toklas wrote, adding that it was "very beautiful" as well. "The blendor is kept on the dining room table and is a perfect center piece for the Tuscan Renaissance table. How can I ever thank you enough for its magic, its beauty." Cannon knew just how Toklas could thank her: by writing an appreciative article about the blender for *House Beautiful*. There could be no more dramatic endorsement. Toklas responded with a manuscript so full of praise that even Cannon was startled. Everyone knew the Blendor could not be used for whipping cream or beating egg whites, but Toklas did both and reported excellent results. And why, queried Cannon, was Toklas so excited about the tomatoes she put in the blender? "The blended tomatoes are ineffably delicious," Toklas wrote back. "Have gone completely haywire on blended tomatoes. Try them poured on lettuce. Heavenly." She still had an image to protect, but she knew a great quenelle when she tasted one, and the Blendor deserved the credit.

Harper & Bros. had an option on Toklas's second book, but neither she nor Harper wanted to struggle through another cookbook. What Harper wanted was her reminiscences, and by 1956 she was finally willing to write them. But she refused to work with anyone except Robert Lescher, an editor at Holt, Rinehart and Winston whom she liked and trusted. After much negotiating, Harper agreed to let the reminiscences go to Holt, and Toklas was permitted to fulfill her contract with a second cookbook. Toklas turned to this project with resentment. All she wanted to do now was start her memoir; she had no interest in telling more food stories or gathering more recipes. The manuscript she submitted was little more than a pile of complicated French recipes, none of them formally tested or put into standard cookbook format, and it bore scant evidence of Toklas's personality. The publisher was enraged.

At this point Poppy Cannon was called in to intercede. The book had to be rescued, and Harper's editors were finding it impossible to work with Toklas. Cannon was an experienced food editor, and she understood that Harper wanted to publish an accessible and usable book. Most important, Toklas trusted her. Cannon had edited their *House Beautiful* stories, and Toklas hadn't objected—or at least she hadn't ended the relationship—when a "Note from Poppy Cannon" appeared with the blender story, telling readers they could substitute a doctored-up can of soup for Toklas's shrimp sauce. In other words, when she accepted Cannon's help on the new cookbook, Toklas knew what was coming. Even so, they battled for months over the manuscript, by mail and in person. "How should I know how many it serves?" Toklas railed at one question. "It depends—on their appetites—what else they have for dinner—whether they like it or not." She refused to let Harper substitute the word *beat* where she had put *stir*—"Stirring is a round-and-round motion, beating is up, down and around. Experience has shown that the end result, the taste and the texture, are quite different." The questions she was being forced to answer were "typically home economics," she complained. "They are so finicky, but not thorough. There's a difference."

In the end, Toklas hated the book and told friends she did not want to be associated with it. Many of them, especially her friends in the food world, assumed it was the recipes that incensed her, and to this day fans of Toklas revile the book for the damage they say it did to Toklas's cooking. It's true that Cannon added numerous suggestions for making the recipes easier, including the use of frozen artichokes, biscuit mix, canned soup, and other shortcut products. But these suggestions were confined to the headnotes, and they were printed in a different typeface from the recipes. Just as she had done in *House Beautiful,* Cannon left the recipes alone. They ran exactly as Toklas had wished, with all the ingredients and procedures just as she specified and every *stir* in place.

Toklas's antipathy may have stemmed less from what Cannon

did to the food than what Cannon did to Toklas's image. By the time the book came out, Toklas was deep in a close and mutually adoring friendship with James Beard, who visited her whenever he was in Paris. She told her literary agent she had "completely lost my heart" to him and that he was an expert in "sensuous living" equal only to Picasso. His opinion about the book would have mattered enormously to her; and though it's not known what Beard said to her on the subject, he made it clear to other friends that he thought Cannon's participation had been disastrous. ("There is about as much Alice in it as there is Elizabeth Barrett Browning," he fumed to Helen Evans Brown.) The review in *The New York Times* could only have made matters worse, enthusiastic though it was. Charlotte Turgeon, who was making a respected name for herself translating and adapting classic French cookbooks, liked *Aromas and Flavors* very much and made it clear that she admired both authors for their different strengths. "What makes this book fun is seeing these two ladies get together," she wrote. "Miss Cannon keeps the busy housewife in mind, and the result is a book that is refreshing to read and a promise of exciting eating."

Toklas was far too fierce a caretaker of Stein's reputation and her own to be pleased with this implication that she and Cannon were equal partners, working as a team. In this regard, the introduction to the book, which Turgeon urged readers not to miss, was even more offensive. Cannon had written a long, worshipful essay drenched in artificial intimacy—virtually a trumpet blast heralding Cannon's public presence in Toklas's life. She lavished admiration on Toklas's clothes, her perfume, her energy, and her brilliance; described working with her in the flat in Paris, with its dazzling art and "headachy" kerosene heater, and portrayed Toklas and herself arguing affectionately all through their work on the cookbook. Toklas was appalled. She told a friend it was "overlaudatory" and "embarrassingly untrue." Nobody had ever written about her in such a blatantly commercial manner—nobody would have dared. Her public persona was unrelentingly formal and dignified. Toklas had always refused to be pulled into the empty spotlight after Stein's death, and in narrating her first cookbook she had carefully positioned herself to one side, keeping the story about Stein. Even her own memoir was going to focus on Stein. Now, for the first time, she had forfeited control. Cannon placed her front and center, wrote about her with all kinds of flourishes that Toklas would never have permitted in her own dry and nuanced prose, and even told the world what happened when Toklas encountered the cake mix. This was not how Toklas wanted to go public.

Despite this clash, Toklas and Cannon managed to remain cordial, if not close. Three years later Cannon published a collection of recipes demonstrating the use of all the latest electrical appliances, *The Electric Epicure's Cookbook,* and decided it made an appropriate vehicle for honoring Toklas as well as an irresistible way to drop her name to resounding effect. "This book is for my treasured friend Alice B. Toklas, one of this century's most accomplished gourmets, whose imaginative experiments with the electric blender opened my eyes to a new world of cooking," ran the dedication. Toklas's reaction to this bouquet has not been recorded.

Aromas and Flavors of Past and Present was one of five books that Cannon published between 1956 and 1961—an amazing burst of productivity and the only way she knew to absorb the most terrible loss she had ever suffered. In 1955, Walter White died of a heart attack. Thousands turned out for his funeral; presidents and heads of state sent tributes; and notes and telegrams poured in from all over the world, including the small towns in the South where people remembered his work. Cannon was engulfed in the job of being his widow, but when quieter days descended, she went straight back to writing. She survived her grief by working through it and not looking up. A year after White's death she brought out a memoir of him and their marriage, which she called *A Gentle Knight,* after Chaucer: "He was a verray parfit gentil knight." It was a selective and heavily romanticized account of their time together, but it gave her a chance to let loose her emotions on the page, depicting herself and White in the thrillingly operatic terms they had both cherished. Then came a year of top-speed work on *Aromas and Flavors,* and while she was busy with Toklas, she was simultaneously assembling 150 recipes for a book on low-calorie desserts based on artificial sweeteners, which she called *Unforbidden Sweets.* Her book on electrical appliance cooking came out in 1961, and that same year she published *Poppy Cannon's Eating European Abroad and at Home.*

This extraordinary output, spinning across a wide range of postwar ambitions and appetites, was pure Cannon. One minute she was making a pain bagna; another she was turning out a "fruitcake" with diet gelatin and diet fruit cocktail. A classic salmon soufflé appeared, and so did a blender Hollandaise. And there was a love poem to White called "Enchanted Breakfast" ("How do you add the honey and the dew / to unripe melon / As, my love, you do!"). But what was most remarkable about the cookbooks in this mélange is how strongly they tilted toward fresh ingredients and traditional methods. The low-calorie collection was the only one that featured inordinate amounts of packaged foods; even *The Electric Epicure* was full of recipes calling for fresh ingredients, though electric griddles, rotisseries, fryers, and the like did the actual cooking. It was as if her years of happiness with White had inspired or perhaps freed her, allowing her to step away from a strict focus on convenience and revel in the flavors and textures of food as she had never done before. Food had been her obsession; it had been her work, her income, her identity. Now she was beginning to understand the way it fed people. Some of her writing in *House Beautiful* was imbued with this new awareness, but the books she wrote after living with White for six years were flooded with it. She never disavowed her previous work—on the contrary, she continued creating shortcut "gourmet" recipes all her life and believed in them—but it took more than quick-and-easy to satisfy her hunger now.

During these years of intense productivity, Cannon was also traveling a great deal, which always brought out the best in her culinary sensibilities. Her palate may have been unreliable in her own kitchen, but it worked beautifully when she was touring foreign countries. She loved prowling the shops and markets, eagerly trying the specialties at grand restaurants and just as happily making a meal of street food. Then once she got home, she would try to re-create those experiences using cans and boxes—an effort that was as damaging to the imagination as it was to the food. But with *Eating European Abroad and at Home,* she broke away from this pattern and came up with the best book she would ever write.

Eating European was based on a series of articles that Cannon wrote for *Town & Country,* the high-society magazine where she took a new job in 1961. Thanks to the boom in jet travel, Americans—especially well-off Americans, such as the readers of *Town & Country*—had started pouring into Europe in ever-increasing planeloads. The idea of the series was to encourage these sightseers to be food travelers, to hunt down the great flavors of Europe as well as the great cathedrals and paintings. Cannon turned out to be a wonderful guide. "Even though you have visited Buckingham Palace and heard the orators in Hyde Park, don't think of leaving London till you have stood at a stall and eaten jellied eels from a thick, small china cup, spooning up aspic jelly that glitters like sea-water jade," she urged her readers. On a ramble through Marseilles she scooped sea urchins from their shells with her thumbnail and ate them with bread and wine; in Switzerland she tasted shavings of air-dried beef with pickles and onions; on the banks of the Rhine she buttered pumpernickel bread and laid slices of Westphalian ham on it, then ate the sandwich—as instructed—with a knife and fork; in Lisbon she celebrated the spotted, misshapen, and incomparably delicious peaches, apricots, berries, and figs. For the first time in any of her books Cannon was elbow-deep in the glorious food she was describing.

There were more than three hundred recipes in *Eating European,* nearly all of them based on fresh ingredients. Sometimes Cannon listed a canned vegetable as an alternative to fresh, and here and there she dropped in a suggestion for pastry cream made with vanilla pudding mix, or a pancake starting with popover mix. But for the most part she jettisoned her fixation on speed and ease. To summon the flavors of Europe, she seemed to be saying, you start with fresh food. Alfredo's Fettuccine needed sweet butter and Parmesan that was grated right at the table. A spring soup from northern Germany had to be made with tiny green beans, young peas, and fresh asparagus. She admitted that canned broth could substitute for homemade stock in her French onion soup recipe, but she sounded downright reluctant to have to say so. And although she offered a list of French delicacies that were available in cans at American gourmet shops, for once she didn't claim they were equal to the originals.

Eating European earned good reviews, but it didn't make Cannon famous. She was already famous: She was the author of *The Can-Opener Cookbook,* which was selling very well in its second, revised edition even as *Eating European* quietly disappeared. Her reputation was assured, though it was not the reputation she would have chosen. She liked to think of herself as progressive, but as the '60s picked up speed, new ideas in the food world were racing past her.

Mastering the Art of French Cooking, the book that introduced Julia Child to the American kitchen, appeared in 1961 and became indispensable for the nation's most ambitious home cooks. Child's approach, which emphasized the teaching of fundamental technical skills, was far beyond the abilities of Poppy Cannon either as a cook or a writer. Nor could Cannon work up much enthusiasm for the other trend dawning in the '60s: a drab cuisine featuring brown rice and granola, imbued with politics instead of romance. Meanwhile, her specialty, quick cooking, was plummeting to a level that dismayed her. She had always believed that convenience cookery should be seen simply as the modern face of traditional cookery, sharing with its predecessor the goal of delicious food or at least an imitation of delicious food. Even if her Coupe Royale was nothing but frozen mixed fruit, it did sport a little Cointreau, and it was most certainly served in champagne glasses. Now she was worried that convenience was becoming an end in itself, that "casual" just meant slapdash. "Perhaps it is retribution that I should be the one to wail: Please world, you've gone too far!" she wrote in 1964. "Couldn't-care-less has become a cult. Not for what it achieves, but for its own sake, the shortcut is king."

Cannon was still able to find work at the top of her profession: She was writing a syndicated column called "The Fast Gourmet" and in 1965 became food editor of the *Ladies' Home Journal.* But toward the end of the decade her productivity flagged as she sank into an overwhelming clinical depression that may have been related to her mother's mental illness. The condition did not respond to any therapy she tried, including shock treatments and lithium. Medication made it impossible for her to work and then brought on hallucinations, and her lifelong dread of not being able to support herself grew to terrifying proportions. In 1970 she made her first attempt at suicide; five years later she made her last, jumping from the balcony of her apartment. She was sixty-nine.

Poppy Cannon rarely published a recipe without describing in detail how to show off the dish to greatest advantage. "Much of the difference between just cooking and epicurean cooking is the *difference in the way the food is served*," she stressed in *The Can-Opener Cookbook*. Cannon wanted the moment of presentation to be a spectacle, a kind of theater-at-the-table she liked to call "drama." Her favorite recipes were the ones that threw a spotlight on the hostess and made her a star. "Drama incarnate for your most elegant entertaining!" she exclaimed over a recipe for whole chicken baked in modeling clay. At serving time the hostess picked up a little hammer and daintily demolished the hardened clay. For even greater drama she could cook the entire dish in front of an audience, a feat Cannon loved to conjure. For salmon mousse the hostess sat smiling at the table with a blender in front of her and dropped in each ingredient—the canned salmon, the cream, the red food coloring, the crushed ice. Then she ran the blender for forty seconds and triumphantly dished out the mousse. Or she might sit at her place and prepare fillets of sole amandine, sautéing the fish in an electric skillet and then fixing the sauce while the fish stayed warm on an electric hot tray. Or she could broil shrimp with garlic "in full view on an infra-red broiler," then pass them around to the admiring dinner guests. Perhaps the most dazzling tour de force Cannon created along these lines was a dessert she called Dinner Table Soufflé, which called for the hostess to sit within easy reach of a blender, a portable electric mixer, and a rotisserie oven. First she ran the blender, which had egg yolks, sugar, and rum in it. Then she preheated the oven, switched on the electric mixer, beat the egg whites right in the baking dish until stiff, and folded the whites and the yolk mixture together. The soufflé took twenty minutes in the oven: "Great drama for the guests to watch! If the bell rings before you are ready for your dessert, simply turn the oven down to 300."

The ultimate in sheer spectacle, of course, was fire. During the '50s many hostesses tried their hands at crêpes suzettes served en flambé; but to Cannon, flaming pancakes were just the beginning. As she saw it, there was hardly a meal that couldn't be improved by setting one dish or another on fire, not excluding the breakfast kippers (warmed in rum, then set ablaze). Canned mushrooms would never be called pedestrian after being heated in cream, piled on toast, and baked, then carried to the table blazing. "Consider the drama of a whole canned ham, richly glazed with honey, and at the table set ablaze with brandy," she suggested one Christmas. She liked the idea of carrying London broil to the table, then heating cognac "in a tiny saucepan or ramekin" and pouring it aflame over the beef. And she loved Flaming Cabbage, in which toothpicks holding a bit of sausage or frankfurter were stuck all over a big cabbage. A can of Sterno was placed in the center of the cabbage, and as the fire blazed, the guests stood around the cabbage toasting their own miniature snacks.

Most elaborate of all was the ritual known as Café Diable. First the hostess heated brandy in a chafing dish, along with orange and lemon peels, sugar, cloves, and cinnamon. Then she picked up a ladle and warmed it slightly over a candle flame. She dipped it into the brandy mixture, placed two sugar lumps in the ladleful of brandy, and set them on fire. Carefully she poured the blazing ladleful back into the chafing dish, where the original brandy mixture promptly burst into flames. While the flames leaped, she added two measuring cups filled with powdered demitasse to the chafing dish. She waited for the flames to die down, then poured coffee all around. For maximum effect, Cannon recommended conducting the entire ceremony in a darkened room. And for that last touch, while the guests were lingering over the charred remains of dinner, Cannon suggested putting out a heat-proof platter covered with bunches of sultana raisins on stems. "Pour on warmed rum or brandy. Set the liquor afire and you have The Snapdragon of Merrie Old England," she informed her readers. "The idea is to snatch as many raisins as you can. 'Who gets the most is luckiest.'"

Cannon wasn't always luckiest, but she managed to snatch a good many raisins from the fire. Every day she insisted on living front and center on the stage she claimed for her own life. She used to whirl into press parties late, making an entrance nobody could miss, and in print she projected an image she spent her whole career trying to realize. She would be the American woman in full bloom—working, traveling, loving, and dreaming, and serving food that blazed, literally, with postwar confidence. "'I' stands for Intelligence," she wrote once in an alphabet for cooks. "Don't check your brains at the kitchen door. The kind of thinking that gets you a raise or an A in English or Economics will stand you in very good stead when you cook." Her ambition was to map the way home for smart, energetic women like herself who wanted to live in both worlds—man's and woman's—and make it one. In this she was genuinely modern, with a more radical message about domesticity than many of her peers with better recipes. But the only aspect of her work that would survive her was the dogged faith in packaged foods that would be enshrined forever in *The Can-Opener Cookbook*. A decade later when she wrote *Eating European,* she came up with a perfectly honorable version of onion soup: onions sautéed until golden, beef stock with a bit of wine, toasted French bread in the bowl, grated Gruyère on top. It was too late. And maybe it was too little as well. One of the very last recipes she published was for a fake vichyssoise—as if she couldn't bear to turn her back on it. Like the '50s themselves, Poppy Cannon left the wrong legacy.

Chapter 4

I Hate to Cook

The homemaker at her wit's end, pictured here in the frontispiece for Jean Kerr's best-selling book, Please Don't Eat the Daisies, *was an archetype who frequently appeared in women's nonfiction throughout the postwar period. Like a Greek chorus in a housedress, she commented on the domestic chaos around her, and then, most important, she laughed.* (Illustration by Carl Rose, copyright © 1957 by Carl Rose from PLEASE DON'T EAT THE DAISIES by Jean Kerr. Used by permission of Doubleday, a division of Random House Inc.)

ONE OF THE most famous women in America at midcentury was the peripatetic journalist Dorothy Thompson, who spent decades filing dispatches from war zones and other trouble spots in Europe, the Soviet Union, and the Middle East. She published books on Hitler and Russia, wrote frequently for such widely read magazines as *The Saturday Evening Post,* and produced a syndicated political column that ran in scores of newspapers. She had a second, equally successful career on the lecture circuit, and a third as a regular broadcaster on NBC radio. Thompson also turned out a monthly column for the *Ladies' Home Journal,* but here she liked to put aside foreign affairs and address humbler subjects. In one of her *Journal* pieces, published in 1949, she described the dilemma of a woman friend who was filling out an official questionnaire when she was forced to stop short at the space marked "Occupation." "I've never made *anything* out of my life," the friend confessed mournfully to Thompson. "I'm just a housewife." Hearing this, Thompson just laughed. Her friend's problem wasn't the lack of a career, it was simply the lack of a word, a job title, capable of summing up all the myriad aspects of her expertise. What she ought to put down in that questionnaire, Thompson advised, was "business manager, cook, nurse, chauffeur, dressmaker, interior decorator, accountant, caterer, teacher, private secretary. . . ."

Thompson's description of domestic work was typical of a litany that became as familiar as the Pledge of Allegiance in the postwar years: the grand unfurling of the professions that defined the career of housewife. "The businessman or industrial worker has one job. The housewife has a dozen," declared Lillian Gilbreth in a manual called *Management in the Home.* "She is nurse, cook, housemaid, laundress, shopper. She attends to mending, discipline, entertaining, and interior decoration." Such efforts to raise the status of housekeeping and make it resemble a desirable life's work were hardly new: Half a century earlier, the founders of home economics were determined to recast the American home into what they called a "center for right living," to be headed by a wife and mother trained in chemistry, biology, bacteriology, economics, and the principles of art. Thompson's version brought these skills smartly up to date by adding "chauffeur" and "private secretary"; and a few years later the editors of *Living* promoted the modern housewife to an office they called "Vice President in Charge of Home," with a portfolio that included health, travel, purchasing, and public relations.

But no matter how enthusiastically journalists and other commentators in the '50s touted such a résumé for professional domesticity, its day had passed. Far too much had happened during the war years for anyone to accept a declaration like Thompson's ("The homemaker . . . is the constant re-creator of culture, civilization, and virtue") as a genuine call to single-minded homemaking. Thompson herself, married three times and a mother, was engaged in a prominent public career that plainly diminished her credibility on the subject of full-time domesticity. Similarly, most of the other women writing so admiringly about homemaking as a career were writers, teachers, home economists, or businesswomen, and many had household help. (Gilbreth, best known as the mother of the family immortalized in *Cheaper by the Dozen,* was an industrial engineer whose inability to cook was a standing joke among her children.) Housewives themselves tended to be fairly skeptical about the glory of housework, and they had never cherished any illusions about its social status. When home economists in the early 1900s tried to encourage women's clubs to devote their meetings to a study of the modern housewife, the club women made it clear they preferred to discuss music appreciation or the art of ancient Rome. In 1938 the writer Margaret Halsey recalled how years earlier, arriving in Britain with her husband shortly after their marriage, she was handed a form to fill out and quickly came to the notorious space marked "Occupation." First she put down "none," but the official rejected it; then she tried "parasite," which was also rejected. Finally, the official himself wrote "housewife." " 'Be a prince,' I said. 'Make it typhoid carrier.' "

During the postwar years there was no unanimous conviction throughout American society that a woman's place was in the home, although present-day sentiment invariably recalls the '50s in those terms. It's true that most women were still closely woven into a society and an economy that depended on them to carry out traditionally feminine roles. But the war instigated fresh thinking, and by the late '40s a woman's place was in dispute. The notion of paid employment for wives and mothers was filtering into middle-class houses like early sun, throwing pale new streaks of light on this room or that corner. Rosie the Riveter had gotten fired at war's end; a few years later, she was married and living in a brand-new suburb. But for the rest of her life she remembered what it was like to work for pay. In one way or another, that memory changed everything.

An upheaval in the culture of domesticity was not, of course, part of the plan. The plan had been to encourage women to take wartime jobs so that both war production and the home-front economy would keep humming. When the war was over, women would return home, and life would get back to normal. But as it turned out, it just wasn't possible to inject 6 million women into the workforce and then pretend it never happened. Women who had never been employed before loved collecting their pay envelopes once a week. And others, particularly black women who were accustomed to life in the labor force, found wartime factory jobs a great deal more to their liking than their previous work, typically in domestic service. The number of working women soared by 50 percent during the war, and by 1945 well over a third of all women were employed, including a quarter of all married women. Around that time business and labor leaders were assuring the public that women were eager to get back home where they belonged, and women themselves seemed to back up the claim. Two years earlier, poll takers had asked women under thirty-five—single and married, employed and at home—what sort of work they would like to do. The majority in all categories chose marriage and homemaking. In 1945 a mere 18 percent of those surveyed in a Gallup poll said it was acceptable for married women to work if their husbands could support them. But faced with the real-life choice of giving up their jobs or keeping them, most employed women decided that work suited them very well. A survey conducted by the Women's Bureau of the Department of Labor in 1944 turned up the fact that 80 percent of women employed in war-related industries had no wish to stop working after the war. A year later, even with peace at hand and husbands or boyfriends on the way home, a survey of women throughout the workforce found that 61 percent wanted to keep right on going at their jobs.

Although many did return home—more than 3 million left the workforce between 1945 and 1946—the downward trend lasted only until 1947. At that point women began making their way into factories, shops, and offices again, and by 1953 the number of working women was over 18 million, just under its wartime high. This time there was no turning back. In the mid-'50s, the very heart of the era best known for enshrining motherhood as a career, more than one-third of all women with children under eighteen had jobs. Among black families the prevailing image of what it meant to be a married woman with children had always encompassed work, and now this image was spreading more widely, well beyond the city streets where employed women were a familiar sight. A study published in 1956 found that about three-quarters of the eighth- and twelfth-grade boys surveyed in a Georgia county expected their wives to stay home, but more than half the girls expected to work after marriage. That same year a study of women seniors at Purdue University appeared, and these women, too, expected to work. Researchers found that most of them hoped to combine marriage with employment or further education in their first years out of college. Nearly 90 percent hoped to be full-time homemakers when their children were young, but once their children were grown, about a third planned to return to work. These were small studies, but they fit into larger trends that researchers were noticing in the course of the decade. Because women were marrying so young—the median age for first-time brides in 1956 was twenty, an all-time low—the most demanding period of child care was over by the time they reached thirty-five or forty. They had half their lives ahead of them. In 1955, Eli Ginzberg, the Columbia University economist, saw a pattern emerging and concluded that the time was near when women would work all their adult lives except for the years when their children were small.

In 1957, Ph.D. student Hortense Glenn interviewed 247 married white homemakers in a small southern community—all of them from the middle and lower economic classes and about a third of them employed—to find out their attitudes toward married women who took jobs. Most of them, employed or not, tended to approve of the idea unless there were small children at home or the husbands were opposed. There was greater support for women who worked for clear financial reasons and relatively little support for women who worked because they were bored keeping house. In other words, these wives felt that women had to justify the decision to work; it was not yet a birthright. Nevertheless, the attitudes expressed by the small-town subjects of Glenn's study were far from the domestic imperative with which the '50s would be identified in the future.

If these changes in women's lives made news, and they did, it was because the women starting work in such unprecedented numbers tended to be white and increasingly from the middle class. Until the war years, the majority of America's working women were poor; most were single, and most of the others had husbands who couldn't support them. A disproportionate number were black, clustered at the bottom of the job ladder in terms of both status and pay. In 1940 a third of all black women were working, and about 60 percent of them were in domestic service. But ten years later that figure had dropped to 42 percent as black women gained access to factory and white-collar jobs. Segregation and discrimination kept black women's earnings the lowest of all workers, but the rising number of skilled female workers contributed significantly to the expansion of the black middle class after the war. By 1960 nearly half of the nation's black married women were employed, and so were nearly a third of the nation's white married women. The female workforce had been a reality for centuries; during the '50s it finally, and disconcertingly, became visible.

Educators, psychologists, sociologists, and government officials, who had apparently never noticed that their offices were cleaned every night by women, suddenly discovered women workers and launched a national debate. Psychiatrists attributed female ambition to various debilitating sexual neuroses, while social scientists tried to ascertain whether children were harmed by having mothers who worked. (No matter how they framed the research, it turned out to be nearly impossible to distinguish among maladjusted children solely on the basis of the mother's employment status.) But the discussion emanating from economists and government officials took a different tone. What interested them was the mounting evidence that working women were crucial to America's postwar boom times. By the early '50s more than half of the nation's families owned their own homes, thanks in part to women's paychecks, and many of the families out shopping on Saturdays for new refrigerators, cars, television sets, and lawn mowers could afford them precisely because there were two wage earners in the house. Nobody with an eye on consumer spending really wanted to turn off that spigot. "Working wives are one of the great factors in making Americans the most prosperous people on earth," proclaimed Sinclair Weeks, Secretary of Commerce, in 1954. This distinctly pragmatic view of the female workforce spurred an enormous amount of research, much of it undertaken by the Women's Bureau of the Department of Labor, which issued reports on such topics as the opportunities for women in various fields and industries, how best to educate women for work, and how to help older women join or rejoin the workforce. The National Manpower Council, established by the Ford Foundation in 1951 to study the nation's current and potential labor force, discovered to its surprise that the question of women's employment was no longer a question. The revolution had happened already; from then on the Council began addressing what it called "womanpower" and generated volumes of data and analyses that were widely circulated.

It was clear to experts throughout government and academia that women's employment was an undeniable fact of American life, that it showed no signs of letting up—quite the contrary—and that it was crucial to the nation's economic well-being. Even Congress could read the numbers and relaxed its usual oratory on the subject of traditional femininity long enough to pass a tax deduction for child care expenses in 1954. Working mothers with a family income below the median of $4,500 were eligible, and the measure was backed by numerous organizations including unions and professional associations as well as the General Federation of Women's Clubs. But few other substantive changes in law or policy emerged in the '50s. Despite the fact that myriad forms of sex discrimination, including glaring inequalities in pay, existed in most industries and professions, protest was sparse. The anti-Communist witch hunt under way in Congress was silencing many feminists and progressive organizations while inspiring vast waves of public rhetoric to cement the association between female domesticity and American values. But a great deal more than McCarthyism lay behind the nation's long, stubborn refusal to support women's work lives in any meaningful way. It was as if nobody in a position to influence policy or popular culture wanted to believe what was happening in plain sight: One of the central myths of American life was being torn to shreds.

The image of an ideal middle-class home had hovered over the nation since the industrial revolution, invariably starring a father who worked hard to support the family and a mother who lovingly tended her brood. This iconography never constituted an accurate description of women's contributions, either to their families or to the economy. But the belief in a natural and unbridgeable divide between man's world and woman's world ran very deep. Men dealt in money, women dealt in emotion. Men made deals, women made cakes. Men were independent, women needed men. Women simply were not supposed to constitute freestanding entities with no economic links to a father or a husband. Those who were forced to support themselves on account of poverty or who were economically independent on account of wealth could most comfortably be understood as aberrations, occasional bumps in the normal scheme of things.

What's more, though the teaching and preaching about

woman's place never stressed this point, working women had long been a cheap source of labor. Traditionally, they came from the margins of society, and their second-class status made it possible for employers to exploit them with relative impunity. Hence, from the point of view of many in business and government, there was little to be gained by encouraging women to take themselves seriously as wage earners. "When a woman comes to be viewed first as a source of manpower, second as a mother, then I think we are losing much that supposedly separates us from the Communist world," proclaimed James O'Connel, Undersecretary of Labor, in 1960. This was a time when one out of three married women was employed and two-thirds of working wives had school-age children.

A dazzling degree of contradiction became one of the hallmarks of the postwar years as Americans tried to shoehorn present-day realities into a context marked by wishful thinking. Despite the clear boost to the economy provided by two-earner households, corporations and advertisers clung hard to their longtime conviction that women made their most important contribution to prosperity by going shopping. The more obvious it became that many women were backing away from a lifelong commitment to homemaking, the more enthusiastically women's magazines hailed a renaissance in the home arts. "*House Beautiful* has watched the clear emergence, since the war, of a new attitude among women toward homemaking," the magazine's editors insisted in 1956. "They are finding that housekeeping and family management are fascinating, enjoyable pursuits, offering the fullest opportunities to express themselves and their capabilities." Ads for new kitchen appliances tried to have it both ways. They emphasized how fast and easy housekeeping would become, with the implication that women would be free to spend more time elsewhere, yet the pictures often showed mothers and daughters dressed in matching outfits, as if nothing but size separated the girl from her domestic future. Even companies that stood to benefit from women entering the workforce hesitated to celebrate the trend outright. The frozen-food industry, for example, rejoiced at the ever-increasing rate of women's employment, since working women appeared to constitute an obvious market for convenience foods. Story after story in *Quick Frozen Foods* recited the statistics and reveled in them. But images of working women rarely showed up in ads for frozen foods. Instead, the advertising tended to portray homemakers who were so busy attending to their families and other activities that they had no time to cook from scratch. "How to Be a Volunteer Worker . . . and a Good Wife, Too" was the headline for a 1959 Swanson's TV dinner ad. An industry convinced that its very future depended on a steady increase in the number of working women still couldn't bring itself to target them directly.

At the same time a number of editors and advertisers plainly took for granted the fact that employment had changed the landscape of women's lives. Many references to working women showed up without fanfare in women's magazines and newspaper women's sections, and the matter-of-fact tone of such references suggests that women with jobs were considered just another segment of the readership. Food stories featuring quickly prepared recipes were published for "the bread-winner and homemaker," as *The Boston Globe* called her, or "career wives," as they were termed in the *Chicago Tribune*. The *Tribune*'s women's pages included a regular column for office workers called "White Collar Girl," which sat squarely amid the recipes and housekeeping features. An ad for Betty Crocker's new Answer Cake—a smaller-than-usual box of cake mix packaged with its own aluminium pan—explained that the product was created in part to answer the cake needs of "27 million working women, the majority of them married." (This particular ad ran in *Forecast,* whose readers were themselves working women. Unlike much of the frozen-food industry, General Mills, the company behind Answer Cake, had long made a point of keeping in close touch with its customers.) Stories and ads in *Mademoiselle,* "The Magazine for Smart Young Women," and *Charm,* "The Magazine for Women Who Work," were directed specifically at women with jobs; and such classic women's magazines as the *Woman's Home Companion* and the *Ladies' Home Journal* interspersed their tireless coverage of domestic life and civic responsibilities with articles that examined employment issues and championed working women. "Woman's hard-won right to work outside the home has developed into a powerful urge to work," announced the *Woman's Home Companion* in 1956. "Their drive to work is exceeded only by their employers' delight in having them aboard." Even *Woman's Day,* which ran a regular column called "How to Be a Girl" ("Now is the time to master the mechanics of a home, the ways of smoothing the lives of your own family"), also published features in which working women showed up regularly, and not as pariahs. "A woman, like a man, has a right to the world she feels most comfortable in, whether it's in the home, outside, or both," concluded the author of a 1954 story.

One popular way for the media to acknowledge the new world of work while maintaining the primacy of domestic life was to assign them different values, making sure that work didn't take up too much moral space. Singer Sue Bennett "rates her other careers as wife of a busy doctor and mother of a year-old son as more important even than her job," *The Boston Globe* assured readers in 1954, using a rhetorical formula that turned up constantly in profiles of famous women (and would persist into the twenty-first century). Penny and Pete, real-life newlyweds who were featured in *Living,* were described as having two sources of income: Pete's salary and the "driblets" Penny earned as an illustrator. Even *Ebony,* published for readers who needed no introduction to the concept of working wives and mothers, frequently applied standard middle-class rhetoric to the subject. Dorothy Dandridge was "a busy career girl ... . who is also a perfect mother and a good housewife," and as far as movie star Maidie Norman was concerned, "being a homemaker is as important as her career." A 1952 photo feature in *Ebony* demonstrated how a black professional ballerina combined home duties with a career: Wearing leotard, tights, and pointe shoes, she practiced her *grand jetés* as she hung out the laundry, and she balanced on pointe as she peered into a pot on the stove.

Not every woman had a job—the majority, in fact, did not—but everybody knew somebody who did. Many were contemplating or wondering about the idea even if they never went ahead with it; and most women raising families in the '50s knew that their daughters were likely to work. What had long been true for women on the margins was starting to come true for women in the mainstream: that growing up female meant growing up and earning a living. For all the talk about creativity in homemaking, women's culture in the '50s was not limited to the passionate defenses of domesticity that turned up repeatedly in magazines. Rather, it was a culture of struggle, negotiation, and nuance as new values permeated everyday life and became part of the way women saw the world.

Contributors to the "Confidential Chat"—women who were so involved in domesticity that they kept up with the *Globe*'s housekeeping pages on a daily basis—wrote letter after letter about work. For the most part they said they were happy being wives and mothers, but they wanted more—more money, more challenges, more self-respect. When they tried to figure out how to incorporate paid employment into their lives, they encountered all sorts of logistical problems including child care and house-work; but they were equally beset by psychological concerns. They could see they had to reorient themselves, to figure out where they wanted to be positioned in a domestic world they no longer accepted as the whole of life. "I am twenty-four, have two children, six and four, who are in school. . . . I would like to take a job, but I hear so much criticism of 'working mothers,' that they're neglecting their children, etc. . . . If I could get a job, I could contribute something extra to the family budget, get myself a new perspective on my own usefulness, and I'm sure be less edgy when my family and I sit down to dinner," a Chatter mused in 1952. A few days later she heard from "Working Mother" (all Chat contributors used pseudonyms) who had taken a part-time job three years earlier when her children were six, four, and three. "I've come to the conclusion that we overindulge and overprotect our own children," she stated firmly. "Mine are now more helpful and more resourceful because I work."

Some Chatters admitted they loved full-time domesticity, oth-ers argued for careers, and many were looking for work they could do at home, such as baking or typing. But by 1961 the day-to-day reality of holding down a job was so well entrenched even among these committed homemakers that a newlywed signing herself "Cuddles" included it automatically when she asked for advice about setting up her new household. "I've so many ques-tions it's difficult to decide where to begin," she wrote. "I adore my homemaker's role and have a full-time secretary's job besides. Most of all I want to please my brand-new husband. I would like some casseroles which can be made the night before . . . and a fruitcake for the holiday." Home, a job, love, convenience, dinner at six, and family tradition—Cuddles wondered a little desperately how she could contain these multitudes. Whether they went out to work each day or just puzzled over the possibilities, many homemakers were casting about for independent identities that would somehow, perhaps through sheer longing, fit smoothly into their domestic lives.

During this period, as middle-class homemakers uneasily began to renegotiate a domestic contract they had signed and sealed years earlier, many turned for support to a distinctive new genre of women's inspirational literature. To be sure, much of the wisdom-laden nonfiction aimed at women in the '50s took the same form it had been taking for centuries: intimate volumes of spiritual and emotional guidance. One book in particular from that tradition, published in 1955, rang so true to so many that it became a best-seller and remains in print to this day. Anne Morrow Lindbergh's *Gift from the Sea* is a series of meditations on being a woman in the modern world—on being, in effect, Cuddles. The seashells Lindbergh finds on the beach, each one prompting a chapter's worth of reflections, are metaphors meant to ease readers toward contemplation and calm. "The problem is not merely one of *Woman and Career, Woman and the Home, Woman and Independence,*" she writes. "It is more basically: how to remain whole in the midst of the distractions of life; how to remain balanced, no matter what centrifugal forces tend to pull one off center; how to remain strong, no matter what shocks come in at the periphery and tend to crack the hub of the wheel." Women liked Lindbergh's clarity of perspective and were stirred by the spiritual renewal exemplified by her thoughtful walks along the shore. Rebellion is not in the picture, but sanity is.

Gift from the Sea, however, was not the only sort of guidance available in the '50s. A very different brand of moral restorative was flourishing alongside it, a literary genre that careened through the postwar era without so much as a nod to the art of poetic rumination. The authors at work in this mode had no time for woman's soul and spirit; instead, they were absorbed in her sticky linoleum (did the new puppy have an accident?) and the cereal spilled behind the sofa cushions and the balky car and the finger-paint smeared all over the kids' faces. Their genre might be called the literature of domestic chaos. Created and sustained by women writers and readers, it spoke knowledgeably about the psychic mess at the heart of the home, and then, most important, it laughed.

Writing humorously about the home was a new venture for women. For hundreds of years they had been publishing on domestic topics, but most often with instruction or uplift as their purpose: recipes, housekeeping manuals, moral tracts, sentimental tributes. As for being funny, it was rare to encounter a woman's voice anywhere in that literary domain until the 1920s, when a market for sophisticated wit opened up in the pages of *The New Yorker* and a few other magazines. In these venues such personable authors as Dorothy Parker, Ruth McKenney, and Hildegarde Dolson made their names, turning out sketches and memoirs notable for their brainy, well-tuned humor. But very little of this work touched on homemaking, perhaps because the writers themselves tended not to do much of it—many were single, and most had maids.

Not until the 1940s did a different persona for women humor writers start to appear: the ordinary, hapless homemaker pitted against her own life. Betty MacDonald's *The Egg and I,* while not strictly in this mode, undoubtedly warmed up the audience. Published in 1945, *The Egg and I* was a wonderfully caustic account of what happened when MacDonald obediently followed her new husband to his dream job: running a chicken ranch in the godforsaken wilds of the Pacific Northwest. Her adventures in misery became a best-seller and later a movie, starring Claudette Colbert and Fred MacMurray. Although it wasn't typical of the household chaos literature that would follow—domestic matters per se were not at the heart of MacDonald's work—*The Egg and I* did show that it was possible to be funny about home life, at least in extreme circumstances.

The most influential examples of the literature of domestic chaos, stories that would define the genre and inspire legions of imitators, started to appear shortly after the war, when fiction writer Shirley Jackson decided to make some extra money by selling nonfiction pieces to women's magazines. Editors loved her funny essays about family life, and so did readers. Eventually she had so many of the pieces in print that she was able to publish two collections: *Life Among the Savages* (1953) and *Raising Demons* (1957). The savages and demons were her children, and that was the point. "I won't write love stories and junk about gay young married couples, and they won't take ordinary children stories, and this sort of thing is a compromise between their notions and mine," she explained in a letter to her parents. Her particular approach to writing about domestic subjects, she added, "is unusual enough so that I am the only person I know of who is doing it." Jackson was right: Nobody was addressing homemaking quite the way she did, as if she were making beds and cooking meals for a family of Keystone Kops.

One sleepy summer Sunday, for instance, her son races in to announce that six foreign visitors are about to show up at the door. They're in town on a goodwill tour and have been sent to see a typical American home. Jackson hadn't realized her house was on the itinerary.

Serve them coffee, I thought frantically, or perhaps something typically American—hot dogs? No, no, not in the middle of a hot afternoon. Iced coffee; iced coffee, and there was a box of doughnuts in the breadbox if the children hadn't gotten to it; cookies? I wish I had some ice cream, I thought; can't serve company popsicles from the deep freeze, and I took the three bottom steps in one leap. I was plugging in the electric coffeepot when Jannie and Sally came through the back door; I threw their dresses at them and said, "Company, wash your faces." They disappeared, murmuring, and I moved swiftly in to Barry, who was amused at the idea of wearing the sunsuit, since it was the first article of formal attire he had seen since summer's start. I tied Sally's sash, took a swipe at each head with the hairbrush, heard voices outside, emptied an ashtray on my way to the door, ducked my mystery out of sight and opened the door. "Good afternoon," I said, only slightly out of breath.

Jackson regarded her family sketches primarily as moneymakers, not serious writing, but one reason they soared to the top of their genre was that she was a skillful and distinctive stylist in every format. Her fiction, including scores of short stories and six novels, was an eerie admixture of the psychological and the quotidian, written in an even, often companionable tone of voice that rides implacably on top of vast, unspoken fears and tensions. (Her most famous story, "The Lottery," describes a pleasant little village that undertakes a special ritual each year: One person is selected to be stoned to death.) Often, an element of the supernatural seeps through the plot or the characters are touched by otherworldly powers in ways they barely comprehend. When she wrote family sketches, she balanced the tales in similar fashion between ordinary life and its mysterious underpinnings, though she changed the pitch of her narrative voice. No supernatural forces as such come into play, but the narrator has a constant sense—familiar to every homemaker—that she is barely fending off disaster. She can do laundry, wash dishes, and make sandwiches, but essentially these are helpless offerings to a force that operates according to its own impenetrable laws, transforming cleaned-out closets into bursting-full closets within minutes and depositing gray scum all over the just-scrubbed bathtub. Here is breakfast on the day she's going to the hospital to have her third baby:

> I went into the kitchen and proceeded methodically to work, humming cheerfully and stopping occasionally to grab the back of a chair and hold my breath. My husband told me later that he found his cup and saucer (the one with FATHER written on it) in the oven, but I am inclined to believe that he was too upset to be a completely reliable informant. . . . My single immediate objective was a cup of coffee, and I decided to heat it in the frying pan because anyone knows that a broad shallow container will heat liquid faster than a tall narrow one like the coffee-pot. . . .
>
> By the time the children came down everything seemed to be moving along handsomely; Laurie grimly got two glasses and filled them with fruit juice for Jannie and himself. He offered me one, but I had no desire to eat, or in fact to do anything which might upset my precarious balance between two and three children, or to interrupt my morning's work for more than coffee, which I was still doggedly making in the frying pan. . . .
>
> My husband asked politely, "May I help you with breakfast?"
>
> "No, indeed," I said. I stopped to catch my breath and smiled reassuringly. "I feel *so* well," I said.
>
> "Would you be offended," he said, still very politely, "if I took this egg out of my glass?"
>
> "Certainly not," I said. "I'm sorry; I can't think how it got there."
>
> "It's nothing at all," my husband said. "I was just thirsty."

The life Jackson was living every day was very different from the one she was typing. Just as the sketches have it, she made her home in Vermont with four children and a bookish husband who teaches at a nearby women's college, but once these basics were in place, she concentrated on storytelling, not factual accuracy. Although the children are given their real names, both the narrator and her husband are nameless, and Jackson keeps the two of them well camouflaged in other ways as well. She rarely lets on that she is a successful fiction writer; on the contrary, she tends to present herself as a full-time homemaker forever turning out batches of brownies and rounding up lost library books, all but invisible in social situations. In reality she was an enormous and unmistakable physical presence. Overweight, sloppily dressed, a chronic smoker, heavy drinker, and terrible housekeeper, she suffered from agoraphobia and for many years was addicted to diet pills. She served steak dyed blue and mashed potatoes dyed red, practiced a little witchcraft, read and wrote voraciously, and didn't mind giving the kids a smack when they acted up. Her husband—depicted as a passive if genial presence in many of the family stories—was the critic and teacher Stanley Edgar Hyman. Egotistical and overbearing, he maintained a relentless self-absorption that kept everyone else in the family at his service, and he had a tiresome habit of chasing women, although he didn't do much when he caught them. Jackson was devoted to him, albeit with a loyalty shot through with irritation and exasperation.

None of this would have made very amusing material for *Good Housekeeping,* and Jackson was careful to keep the family stories wry and winning. But one of the persistent themes of her serious fiction was the runaway female, a woman who calmly packs up and leaves to assemble a fresh life for herself in another town. She rents a room, finds a job, chooses a new name. Plainly the narrator of the family stories would never do such a thing. But once—just once—Jackson permitted her a timid and temporary escape. In a story that ran in *Woman's Day,* the narrator hesitantly plans to leave her husband and children so she can spend a weekend away, visiting with old friends. She makes painstaking arrangements—organizes playdates for the children, fixes a casserole and leaves it in the refrigerator, even puts out the peanut butter and jelly for the children's lunch. Then she departs for what turns out to be a tepid couple of days ("everyone seemed to have aged noticeably") and returns to an empty house. The family is at the movies, they appear to have eaten most of their meals at a hamburger stand, and her long list of detailed instructions has been largely ignored. It's as if the homemaker's presence or absence is immaterial, as if all the work she pours into family life is destined to evaporate when day is done. That, of course, is the nature of housework: It evaporates and leaves no trace. Jackson knew how easy it was for women to feel the same way about themselves, to fear that they, too, might disappear from their own lives without anybody's noticing. The nameless narrator of her family stories uses humor to keep daily life pinned to its moorings, and herself secured within it.

Both of Jackson's collections of family stories received good reviews, especially *Life Among the Savages*. ("Never, in this reviewer's opinion, has the state of domestic chaos been so perfectly illuminated," wrote freelance critic Jane Cobb in *The New York Times*. The *Christian Science Monitor* called it "wholesome," a nice tribute considering Jackson's fondness for witchcraft.) But her imitators didn't wait for the reviews to come out. As soon as Jackson had published enough magazine stories to establish the hallmarks of the new literary mode—rambunctious but witty children, laconic but witty husbands, and beset but witty housewives—women writers rushed to their typewriters. Midcentury magazines had a vast appetite for these tales, and readers found them addictive. Despite her habit of self-deprecation, the typical narrator made for an admirable heroine, successfully bushwhacking a trail across the murky landscape of woman's world. Often she worked—she was, after all, a writer—but there was no doubt about her commitment to housekeeping and mothering. Career woman or not, her identity was inextricably attached to the emotional web of family life. Yet by virtue of her role as the narrator, she was able to stand apart from the disasters roiling about her and comment on them, like a Greek chorus in a housedress. That ability to remain ever so slightly above the fray, thanks to a sharp sense of humor, gave her a great deal of charm and far more charisma than just about any other housewife in literature.

Cynthia Lindsay's essays in *Home Is Where You Hang Yourself*, published in 1962, were narrated in the recognizable voice of this new domestic sensibility. "I have met the caterpillar's challenge in a way you may find useful," she remarks in the gardening chapter of her book, which she says is about "the art of being a woman." Since children adore caterpillars and will never allow you to step on one ("Stop! It's my friend!"), she instructs the struggling gardener to get the child to collect all his or her fuzzy friends and put them in a coffee can. The coffee can goes into the trunk of the car, along with an identical coffee can that has a toy in it. Then you take the child for an ice-cream cone, wait until the ice cream drips on the seat of the car, and exclaim that you must immediately get a towel from the trunk to clean up the spill. "At this point speed is essential," Lindsay writes. "Stop the car, leap out, open the trunk, grab the can of caterpillars (you *have* been careful to make sure the lid was *tight*?), drop the can quietly into one of the refuse tins lined up for city pickup. . . . Once home, mop up, remove the lid from the second can, and say, '*Look!* They've all run away, but they've left you a *present!*' As I say, it's elaborate, but it works."

Like Lindsay's narrator, the woman at the center of many tales of domestic delirium is a professional writer, constantly trying to get her work done amid the tumult of family life. Clearly, one reason women writers adopted this genre was that it really did offer a solution to the problem of how to combine home and work: Anything that happened in the course of a day could be mined for material. But the genre was fueled as well by the enthusiastic participation of beginners: women at home, with a sinkful of dishes and a vague yen to write. This subsection of homemakers has always constituted a large and restless population, and in the literature of domestic chaos they discovered a format that seemed ideally suited to them. "I would like to know if little incidents from family life [are] saleable material if written as such and not in book form," wondered "Blue Jeans," writing to the Confidential Chat in 1956. "Perhaps something along the idea of 'Diary of a Mother'—the things that can happen in a family of four children (all extroverts)!!!" Sometimes women like Blue Jeans really did break into print. Adeline Daley, a housewife with seven children in Millbrae, California, spent the three years before her marriage covering high school sports for the San Francisco Call-Bulletin. Fifteen years later she decided to try reclaiming her career as a writer, this time with home as her subject. "Please! Will everybody stop writing and talking about 'trapped housewives'!" began her first piece. It went on to complain cheerfully that neighbors on their way to a glassblowing class or some other fulfilling activity were always dropping off their children at her house, figuring one or two more wouldn't make any difference. The editors of Coronet snapped up her story and featured it with a short profile in which the new contributor chattily described her long-postponed return to writing. "Finally, last fall . . . I hustled through breakfast dishes, put clothes in the washer, and with the two-year-old draped around my neck and the baby in her bassinet next to my typewriter, started to write," Daley told Coronet's readers. "Often laughed when I thought, while writing with TV on, all the neighborhood kids underfoot, phones ringing to ask if I'd serve at the Brownie dinner or make cupcakes for the P.T.A., that the article would come back with the comment, 'This lacks authenticity.'"

Adeline Daley didn't see herself as a "trapped housewife," she saw herself as a trapped writer. Amateur or professional, the writers who chose home as their subject matter were creating a solution for themselves to a psychological problem that would resonate for everyone else into the next century. These women found they could reconcile—at least at the level of imagination—the clash of identities endemic to working mothers. To rig up a sense of self large and resilient enough to encompass both mother and professional, wife and money earner, homemaker and intellectual was an unwieldy emotional project, especially for a middle-class woman who could have afforded to stay home if she chose. When children clamored for her time or her husband glowered or a thousand interruptions plagued her writing, she could feel guilt and fury leap up and grab their swords. Working in the literature of domesic chaos didn't stop the kids from getting measles, but it enabled her to put her experience in perspective and gain a measure of control over the dueling sides of a harsh conflict. After all, her job was to make it funny.

This perpetual jostling between the narrator's housewife identity and her writer identity became an accepted feature of the genre. Jackson was unusual in keeping her work as a fiction writer largely muted in the family stories; more often, authors made a point of describing the conflict. "I've always wanted to be the kind of mother whose kids come in at 3:30 from school, cold and wet and hungry, and find cups of hot chocolate waiting, and freshly baked cookies, and the house smelling of cinnamon and love," lamented Lesley Conger in *Love and Peanut Butter*. "The trouble is I also want to be a writer, so they're just as likely to come home and find nothing at all but the sound of the typewriter and my snarling voice, 'Fix yourself a peanut-butter sandwich and *wash the knife afterwards!*' " Even after her first book was published, Conger depicted herself as a woman in a state of struggle, someone who never quite believes she is a successful writer. What's most pressing to her narrator is always domestic life; writing trails along behind. This posture echoes the familiar rhetoric of '50s journalism on the subject of women with careers: Nothing they did professionally could be more rewarding than homemaking.

Among writers in the genre of domestic chaos, it was the best known who took the greatest care to be dismissive about their professions. Jean Kerr was a successful playwright in 1957 when she published her first book of family stories, *Please Don't Eat the Daisies,* but the woman presiding over the stories is chiefly a homemaker. Whenever she does characterize herself as a writer, it's in strictly jovial fashion. "I will read *anything* rather than work," she remarks in the book's introduction. "The truth is that, rather than put a word on paper, I will spend a whole half hour reading the label of a milk-of-magnesia bottle. 'Phillips' Milk of Magnesia,' I read with the absolute absorption of someone just stumbling on Congreve, 'is prepared only by the Charles H. Phillips Co. division of Sterling Drug, Inc. Not to be used when abdominal pain, nausea, vomiting, or other symptoms of appendicitis are present,' etc.

"For this reason, and because I have four boys, I do about half of my 'work' in the family car, parked alongside a sign that says 'Littering Is Punishable by a $50 Fine.' . . . The few things there are to read in the front-seat area (Chevrolet, E-gasoline-F, 100-temp-200) I have long since committed to memory. So there is nothing to do but write, after I have the glove compartment tidied up."

Kerr, whose husband was the *New York Herald-Tribune* theater critic Walter Kerr, always had a maid to run the house so she could spend most evenings at the theater. Jackson's fiction was full of wives who found refuge in new lives or altered worlds. Betty MacDonald was so wretched on the chicken ranch and so hopeless about her marriage that one bleak day she wrote her husband a note and left for good with the children. But no such jarring contradictions bothered the narrators who stood in for these writers. Although MacDonald acknowledged the failure of her marriage in a later memoir, she ended *The Egg and I* on an artificially optimistic note by hinting that she and her husband eventually sold the ranch and moved back to the city. Similarly, Hilda Cole Espy produced a cheerful memoir in 1958 about raising five children (*Quiet, Yelled Mrs. Rabbit*), and four years later a second, more reflective book about how the family changed as the children left home and she got a part-time job (*Look Both Ways*). What she never mentioned was that during this period she and her husband were divorced. These writers were in the humor business, not the truth-telling business, and their particular branch of humor could not bear very much reality.

One of the writers who struggled hardest over how to package her professional ambition to make it fit her domestic life was Ernestine Gilbreth Carey, coauthor with her brother of the wildly successful family memoirs *Cheaper by the Dozen* (1948) and *Belles on Their Toes* (1950). These were not, strictly speaking, books in the mode of domestic chaos, since they are told from the children's point of view rather than the homemaker's. But as pitch-perfect narratives of improbable family life they reign splendidly over a field crowded with classics, from Clarence Day's *Life with Father* to the family tales of James Thurber. Carey and her brother had writing careers independent of each other, but although both were successful, neither one of them ever topped their Gilbreth books.

The Gilbreths were a family of eleven children (the second-born died at age six) headed by remarkable parents: Frank B. Gilbreth, founder of a discipline in industrial engineering he called "motion study," which aims to discern the most efficient way to undertake any kind of work, and his wife and colleague, Lillian Moller Gilbreth. After Frank's death in 1924, Lillian Gilbreth carried on their joint career by herself, writing and consulting and speaking while she raised their children and put each one through college. Although she hadn't a shred of interest in housework, she found a receptive market for efficiency studies in the field of home economics and turned out two books on the subject, *The Home-Maker and Her Job* and *Management in the Home*. As a working mother, Lillian Gilbreth was not only a role model for her daughters but something close to an idol. "For years I really believed that my mother worked only because she had to," wrote Carey's younger sister, Martha, in an essay that was published in *Scribner's* in 1936. "I know now that I was wrong. She did have to work, but she loved the work. . . . To see your own mother able to work all day, and then come home at night and suddenly snap from a 'business man' into a most understanding and sympathetic mother, makes one feel that it would be possible for more people to do the same."

At the time Martha Gilbreth wrote this essay, Carey was twenty-eight and herself a working woman, well launched into a career she relished as a buyer for several departments of Macy's. She and her husband, Charles Carey, a fledgling businessman, were stretching their salaries around a tiny apartment in Greenwich Village. They both wanted children, but they were nervous about starting a family on such a tight budget. What's more, Carey had no desire to leave her job. Reading a typed copy of Martha's article before it was published, she picked up a pencil and underscored the phrase "She did have to work, but she loved the work."

That passion for work was Carey's closest bond with her mother. "Mother and I found each other a very special source of strength," Carey reflected once in her diary, looking back on the years when she was trying to hold a job and care for her family at the same time. " 'You understand,' we would tell each other pausing midway in a sentence. . . . What did we understand? . . . First beyond home and family ties the joy, the blessedness of interesting work." Ultimately, Carey and her husband went ahead and had two children, Jill in 1938 and Charles in 1942, and after taking a short maternity leave for each one, Carey went right back to her job, leaving the domestic front to a succession of nursemaids and housekeepers. When Jill was six and Charles was two, the family moved to Long Island, and Carey announced her formal retirement from Macy's. Staying home lasted two years, and then she accepted an offer from another Manhattan department store, McCreery's, and went back to work. Finally, in 1948, she retired once more, this time for good.

Each time she quit working, Carey's intention was to focus on home and family without distractions; nevertheless, she couldn't make that focus her whole world. She had long been interested in writing, and even before leaving Macy's in 1944, she was deep into the planning stages of what she hoped would be her first book. She wanted to write about working mothers. As she saw it, the book would give detailed, practical advice to married women who knew their lives would feel incomplete without children but who loved working far too much to give it up. Her outline for the book, which she proposed to title *A Mother's Place Can Be in Business,* included chapters on planning a leave of absence, preparing for the baby and having it on schedule (this chapter would be written "from the business woman's angle," she noted), setting up domestic life so it "functions automatically" after the return to work, and solving various problems bound to emerge both on the job and at home. She also drafted chapter 1, which she called "Ready—Get Set—Go!" "Everyone will tell you that a mother's place is in the home and that this is a full-time job in itself," she warned. "Don't expect anyone to clap you on the back and urge you to take a plunge at the combination of family and job. . . . And don't expect your husband to cheer you on toward making this decision. . . . He will want you to follow the pattern of his boyhood and do just as his mother did."

Despite the efforts of Carey's agent to find a publisher for *A Mother's Place Can Be in Business,* there were no takers. Officially, women's employment was purely a wartime phenomenon, and most people assumed it would disappear when peace returned and the G.I.s came home. So Carey, who was still eager to write a book, started thinking about the Gilbreth family. She contacted her siblings and gathered their stories and memories, and eventually pulled in her brother, a journalist, to collaborate with her. From 1946 until the publication of *Cheaper by the Dozen* in 1948, she was holding down her job at McCreery's, writing the book with her brother, and running a household. By the time she and Frank were writing *Belles on Their Toes,* she had quit the business world, but with a best-seller to her credit, she was able to launch a new career as a speaker on the lecture circuit. For years she traveled to colleges and women's clubs to give talks about family life, the Gilbreths, and the books she was continuing to turn out, which included *Jumping Jupiter* and *Giddy Moment,* both novels, and *Rings Around Us,* a memoir in the genre of domestic chaos. In 1956, when *Rings Around Us* was published, Carey was interviewed by a columnist for the *Chicago Tribune* who asked her what it had been like to leave her business career and become a housewife. It was a "really serious challenge," Carey responded, adding that it had been "so great an adjustment" that she hadn't been able to write about it in the memoir. In truth, she hadn't written about it because she never did make the adjustment.

Carey's notes for her book on working mothers, jotted down during her first effort to be a full-time housewife, hint at considerable stress and suggest how very determined she was to convince herself that running the house was a worthwhile career. Planning a chapter called "The Business Mother Decides to Retire and Keep House," she decided to explain just why she herself had retired ("pull between home and job") and describe her struggles with housework and childcare ("frustrations of housekeeping"). She might even have to confess that the challenges of homemaking just couldn't compare with the challenges of business ("lack of personal thrill and satisfaction from accomplishing a tough job"). Here she added a warning note to herself: "Look out this is dangerous ground, I know!"

It was indeed dangerous ground, and Carey tread carefully on it for many years. Homemaking had its rewards, but for her they just didn't add up to a whole life. Yet it seemed impossible to tackle a business career and still meet all the demands of her family. The extraordinary example set by her mother was the gold standard for Carey: As an industrial engineer, a loving mother, and an author, Lillian Gilbreth balanced the male world of work and the female world of family life, and by all accounts did so with grace and wisdom. "Mother is a miracle," Carey wrote once in her diary. Her own life was made of more ordinary stuff: two children, not twelve; a businessman husband, not a charismatic inventor and trailblazer; and herself full of strains, frustrations, and unrealized ambitions. No miracles here. She wrote *Rings Around Us,* about the jolly goings-on in the home of a supremely contented housewife, the way devotees in many religions write their wishes on pieces of paper and tie them to trees—to make it all come true.

Rings Around Us starts in 1929, on the day she met her husband-to-be at a party in Greenwich Village, and ends around 1953, with their family of four joking and hugging in a Manhasset, Long Island, kitchen. As the narrator, Carey drops not a single hint about her writing career, despite the fact that by the time the family was hugging in the kitchen she had coauthored two immensely popular memoirs and written a well-received first novel. As for her department store career, it plays an uneasy role in the book. She and her husband grew up in very different families: hers a democracy headed by a husband and wife who were equal partners, his a traditional hierarchy headed by the husband. Carey's cautionary note in her outline for the book on working mothers—warning readers that their husbands would resist any deviation from the pattern set by their mothers—was clearly borne of experience.

Tensions over her career start early and keep recurring, like a broken key on a piano, throughout the bright tones of *Rings Around Us*. Returning to work after her daughter is born, for example, seems "right," for this is how her parents ran their lives. Six years later, however, with the job increasingly demanding and household help getting ever harder to find, she reluctantly agrees with her husband that it's time to quit. Staying home offers a certain amount of reassurance: "Mother, dad, son and daughter, I thought, aware of a new closeness, a new simplicity. The backbone of America." But whenever her husband talks about his job, she feels all her energy and ambition rushing back. "Like an old fire horse, I'd itch to be back in this world of his," she admits, then quickly adds, "Yet I knew that we and the children shared something more important now." Finally, she accepts an offer to return to work, but she is careful to explain that she does so only because they've located a wonderful housekeeper, her son is starting school, and the job will be a nice way for her to "keep busy." Two years later she's back home for reasons she never spells out, although she takes pains to emphasize how pleased she is with the decision. "Thank goodness I've retired from retailing forever," she tells herself as children swarm through her kitchen after school. "Who'd want to miss these goings-on now?" And when the family gathers around the dinner table on her birthday, she describes her husband, happily carving the roast. "Thank goodness we're back to normal, with no outside help underfoot," he says, beaming with satisfaction. "This is the way it *should* be."

What's "normal" to the husband and what's "right" to the wife never do jibe very persuasively in *Rings Around Us*. Yet writing the book offered Carey a chance to bring the disparate forces in her life together for the first time. To have been the coauthor of *Cheaper by the Dozen*—a book so appealing that more than half a century after publication it still sells about thirty-five thousand copies a year—was a different sort of triumph, one that was tangential to the career she was trying to shape around herself. With *Rings Around Us* she was a writer on her own, fully professional and deeply committed, and at the same time she was the homemaker at the heart of the story. This was what the literature of domestic chaos did best: It was a genre of reconciliation and acceptance. It helped writers tame their household demons and helped readers exorcise theirs.

Very few of the writers spawned by this genre had the style or imagination to outlive their moment. Apart from Erma Bombeck, who started writing a newspaper column in 1964 and maintained the spirit of domestic chaos in articles and books for more than thirty years, most of its practitioners quickly faded from the marketplace. But one of them—the only writer in the literature of domestic chaos who set her sights on the kitchen—flourished handily even while literary and culinary trends sped right past her.

Peg Bracken's *The I Hate to Cook Book,* published in 1960, sold more than 3 million copies and became the most fondly remembered cookbook of its time.

As her recipes and culinary tips make clear, Bracken didn't hate to cook at all; but she took a lot of pleasure in claiming she did, and her readers were overjoyed to hear it. Whether or not they hated making dinner, they did hate the endless silent tyranny of cooking—the pressure to meet its emotional demands and master its technical demands, to accomplish it day after day to the standards set by their mothers, husbands, friends, and every magazine they flipped open. Bracken wrote her book from a fresh stance and a welcome one. She made no demands whatsoever and firmly dismissed all but the most practical kitchen wisdom. Any culinary ideas that were circulating in the 1950s solely by virtue of fashion or ambition she booted from the premises. The point was to put a good-enough dinner on the table without tormenting the cook. Indeed, it was Bracken's unfailing commitment to the latter half of this goal—never torment the cook—that made her book distinctive. Women for whom guilt was as fundamental to cooking as their pots and pans loved meeting an expert who believed that "flair" and "creativity" made no contributions that couldn't be equaled by a nice cheese sauce. Bracken understood the social and emotional baggage that many women dragged into the kitchen with them, and she was a master at setting them free. "This chapter contains recipes for thirty everyday main dishes," she explains in a chapter she subtitles "The Rock Pile." "Some of them aren't very exciting. In fact, some are pretty dull—just as a lot of recipes are in the other cookbooks, but the other cookbooks don't admit it. . . . The thing about these recipes is this: they're *here!* You don't have to ferret them out of your huge, jolly, encyclopedic cookbook. *And they'll get you through the month!*"

Like many of her colleagues in the genre, Bracken had been a writer in search of a specialty when she struck gold with domestic chaos. During the 1940s and 1950s she worked as an advertising copywriter and then a freelance writer. Her stories and poems appeared in most of the major magazines, but not until 1958 did she come up with the persona that would turn into a lifelong career. "My Husband Ought to Fire Me" was a brisk little sketch that appeared in the *Saturday Evening Post*; years later Bracken said that with this story her "true voice" finally emerged. Domestic chaos was a well-established theme by the time Bracken tried her hand at it, but she took up a position slightly to one side of the usual hapless housewife. She began by tackling the familiar litany of professions said to define homemaking: "*business manager, practical nurse, house cleaner, child psychologist, home decorator, chauffeur, laundress, cook, hostess*—all this, besides being a gay, well-groomed companion." Then she pointed out that according to the numerous authorities, often male, who loved holding forth on this subject, a homemaker's worth "at prevailing wage rates" was about $20,000 a year. But women themselves didn't believe in any such arithmetic, and why should they? "From my own computations one salient fact emerges loud and clear: all my household skills together wouldn't earn enough to maintain one small-sized guppy." In this bold stroke, Bracken carved out an approach to homemaking that would become her trademark. If you can't do something well, don't try, pretty much sums up her general wisdom on domestic challenges. You can probably yank a reasonably credible solution out of thin air, and paprika will handle the rest. Or, as she once put it, "Let's get real."

With the title *I Hate to Cook,* Bracken placed herself firmly in the opposite camp from Irma Rombauer's *Joy of Cooking,* yet the two books shared certain qualities that endeared them to home cooks—especially nervous home cooks. Each writer had a warm, unaffected voice that seemed genuinely her own, each conveyed a sense of authority that never spilled over into superiority, and each could make readers feel that she was right there beside them at the kitchen counter, advising and rescuing and, most of all, keeping them excellent company. "Never believe the people who tell you that pricking potatoes with a fork keeps them fresh and flaky if you're going to let the potatoes sit around for a while after they've baked," Bracken counsels. "These people are dreamers, for the potatoes will be only *slightly* less soggy if pricked than if un-pricked. . . . However, all this is a minor matter; and if a some-what soggy potato is the worst thing that ever happens to you, you are Lady Luck's own tot. The butter and salt and pepper will make them taste good anyway."

Unlike Rombauer, Bracken was not writing the sort of cook-book that starts with food or even the sort of cookbook that has food as a central preoccupation. In *I Hate to Cook,* food plays a different and somewhat humbler role. Most often it shows up as the solution to a stated problem, with the implication that while there are certainly better meals around, they aren't likely to solve your problem as efficiently as this meal does. The terms *good* or *quite good* appear once in a while; "tastes rather exotic and looks quite beautiful" is her appraisal for a beef stew with basil and tar-ragon, but on the whole Bracken pays as little attention to the pleasure of eating as she does to the joy of cooking. For the cooks in Bracken's world, pleasure lies mostly in the painless execution of the task. *I Hate to Cook* starts with the woman in the kitchen; the recipes are her servants, and they do what they're supposed to do without stalling or arguing. "When you hate to cook, you ask a lot of a cooky recipe," she says in her dessert chapter. "It must call for *no exotic ingredients.* It must be *easy.* It must not, above all, call for any *rolling out and cutting.* It must produce *extremely good cookies.* And quite a lot of them. The following cooky recipes meet these stern requirements."

Bracken writes that she has no idea who originated most of the recipes in *I Hate to Cook,* for she copied them "from batter-spattered file cards belonging to people who had copied them from other batter-spattered file cards." And, indeed, these recipes exude the ordinary; they seem as comfortable to prepare as an old sweater is to pull on. Canned soup is a staple. A party means wild rice. Leave out the herbs and spices if you don't like them. Keep a bottle of cooking sherry around. But although speed and simplicity are Bracken's guiding principles, and she urges her readers to embrace every convenience product they can find in the supermarket, the recipes are by no means confined to packaged-food cuisine. A large handful of them list all fresh ingredients, a smaller handful rely on packaged ingredients almost exclusively, and the greatest number call for both. That is, most of the recipes reflect the way millions of women were cooking in the '50s: They used one or two shortcut ingredients in otherwise standard preparations.

For many American cooks, to be sure, a standard preparation was one that had been simplified generations earlier. Bracken was hardly the first to throw cubes of beef, peas, carrots, and some liquid into a casserole, slap the cover on, and a few hours later call it a stew; the browning and flavoring and seasonal vegetables had disappeared from this procedure long ago. To substitute a can of soup for the liquid was just a variation on the theme. In many instances she follows this yellow brick road straight to culinary Oz, baking frozen fish sticks doused with cream of celery soup or heating up mayonnaise mixed with milk for a "fake hollandaise." But she also offers a number of recipes based on relatively traditional ingredients and methods, including chicken livers, lasagna, cheese strata, and various potato dishes; she is vehement when it comes to classic vinaigrette; and although she warmly endorses baking mixes, her cakes and cookies are made from scratch. It's home cooking.

James Beard summed up Bracken as "the enemy camp" in a memo he scribbled to himself in 1954. Her complete disregard for the freshness or quality of the ingredients, not to mention the hair-raising nature of some of the recipes, horrified him. Yet Bracken knew very well that cookery in her time did not begin and end with jars of processed cheese spread. *I Hate to Cook* is full of jocular references to more refined cuisine, many hinting at women's postwar struggles with new ideals and new identities in the kitchen. "We live in a cooking-happy age," she writes in a chapter on leftovers. "You watch your friends redoing their kitchens and hoarding their pennies for glamorous cooking equipment and new cookbooks called *Eggplant Comes to the Party* or *Let's Waltz into the Kitchen,* and presently you begin to feel un-American." In this frame of mind, she goes on, you may feel duty-bound to use up the leftover creamed corn by creatively putting it in, say, stuffed tomatoes; but this is a big mistake. Creativity on that order is for cooks who know their way around herbs and spices. All others are going to end up with leftover creamed corn ruining a perfectly good tomato. Throughout the book, the craft and imagination that her stylish colleagues put into their cooking serve as a widely recognized benchmark against which Bracken's recipes proudly fall short.

Stick with what you can handle, she tells readers over and over. Yet she also assumes that they're going to cook with wine (and serve it with dinner), that they like garlic and will hunt around town for "honest, true, genuine, tough-crusted, sour-dough French bread," and that they'll find homemade croutons better than store-bought. A substratum of very tasty food supports *I Hate to Cook* or at least lurks in the vicinity. It's most noticeable in a chapter called "Good Cooksmanship," where Bracken lists a dozen of her favorite ways to liven up a simple dish. A little savory in the scrambled eggs, oregano on the garlic bread, grated orange peel in the cranberry sauce, red wine in the onion soup—these are unsurprising, but they're very specifically about flavor, and more so than some of the recipes, they hint at the presence of a hands-on cook in the kitchen.

Just as important, they hint at the presence—somewhere behind all those cans and boxes—of an honest cook who can't stand pretension. In the same chapter Bracken explains how it's possible for even a novice to discuss cooking with a food expert and not embarrass herself. First, always remember to use the word *crispy* instead of *crisp*. Be sure that you describe cold dishes as *chilled* and hot dishes as *piping hot*. Instead of remarking that something tastes good with something else, always say, "It's a good foil for . . ." Nothing is ever *light brown* if it can possibly be termed *golden,* and hamburger has to be *ground round* or *ground sirloin*. "Never say hamburger," Bracken emphasizes, "even if you mean *hamburger*."

Her deft disparaging of the lingo made it plain to readers that Bracken stood outside the culinary establishment—a place they knew by heart from magazines and newspapers, a place of flawless meals and bright innovations. Bracken would have nothing to do with it. In her company they could rest within safe boundaries and regain their bearings. *I Hate to Cook* was a proclamation of freedom that didn't demand too much, one that restored comfort while doling out challenges only upon request, like a Statue of Liberty dozing quietly in a chair. The kitchen has always been the place where housewives who feel inadequate must confront their own failings day after day, where guilt runs like tap water and the possibility of disappointing the family burns endlessly. Hence the longevity of Bracken's cookbook while many other works in the literature of domestic chaos lost their savor over time. These narratives were rooted in a single postwar moment, that turning point when new female futures were hovering but none of the maps had been redrawn yet. Bracken's book was rooted in the kitchen, where the maps for women change very slowly—far more slowly than the food.

Chapter 5

Is She Real?

The first in a succession of portraits of Betty Crocker was this one, painted by Neysa McMein in 1936 and ubiquitous through the mid-'50s. The nation's most famous and trustworthy authority on cooking was no Happy Housewife; on the contrary, her portrait conveyed a dignity and professionalism meant to conjure management, not meat loaf. (Courtesy of the General Mills Archives.)

JANE WAS A young bride, madly in love and eager to learn to cook. She was still working as a secretary—"to help our finances for the time being," as she wrote in her diary—but a job certainly wasn't going to prevent her from living up to the culinary resolutions she had made after the honeymoon. She would plan each meal with care, she vowed. She would write down every menu, try unusual recipes, and experiment with herbs and spices. Above all she would serve "the best food I can" while striving daily to become "the best wife anyone could be."

Jane's "diary" was in fact a cookbook, written by the prolific food and travel writer Myra Waldo. She called it *The Bride's Cookbook,* and as soon as it appeared in 1958, it joined a throng of similar books, articles, and advertisements, all aimed at novice cooks. (Poppy Cannon had used the same title for her own contribution to this genre, published four years earlier.) Newlyweds had long been identified as an excellent market for cookbooks, and after the war there were more young wives than ever. But brides were by no means the only homemakers looking for advice during these years. As we've seen, the culinary terrain was vast in the '50s, and much of it was uncharted. Simply to open a package of frozen broccoli for the first time or to experiment with a cream puff mix was to go where few cooks had gone before. And if visionary home cooks aimed to try some of the sumptuous dishes they read about in *Life* (Salmis of Pheasant, Pompano Claudet) or one of the unfamiliar menu items encountered in restaurants, even they might need help. "Does anyone have a recipe for shrimps in brown gravy as served at our Chinese restaurants?" a reader of the "Confidential Chat" inquired in 1959. Other Chatters who had been tasting dishes new to them were wondering how to make chicken cacciatore, sabayon, café au lait, and "those nice Italian cookies that are a biscuit type."

As Jane set out to become a fine and adventurous cook, she had no trouble finding authoritative sources for tips and recipes; and soon she was able to serve her husband everything from frank-furter casseroles to sole amandine. But a moral imperative beyond dinner was lurking in this culinary bildungsroman. Tucked into many of the recipes was a firm reminder of the gender hierarchy that governed food and cooking in the '50s. Waldo made certain there were clear distinctions between the help Jane received from other women and the help she received from men. Jane called her mother-in-law, for instance, when she wanted advice on how to cook cheap cuts of meat. A woman she met in the supermarket offered tips on corned beef and cabbage. Her friend Dorothy gave her the recipe for a foolproof chocolate soufflé made with a box of pudding mix. That is, as she set about mastering the more pedestrian accomplishments of day-to-day cooking, her teachers were women—either women she knew personally or the home economists who were producing recipes for the food industry. When she ventured toward higher levels of expertise, however, the teachers were male. It was a visiting Frenchman who advised her to serve a chilled Pouilly-Fumé with her sole amandine, and it was a male friend from California who introduced her to grilled spareribs and Caesar salad. "He was almost professional in his competence, and I watched him carefully and took notes all day long," Jane wrote admiringly in her diary.

True, her source for an exotic supper of sukiyaki was a woman—a Japanese war bride named Peach Blossom—but the dish turned out to be so "quick and easy" to prepare that Jane made no mention at all in her diary of Peach Blossom's cooking skills. She was far more impressed by the Japanese woman's skill at being a wife, in particular her submissive and adoring attitude toward her husband, which was quite unlike the way Jane treated Peter. "I realize now that P.B. did everything she could to build up her husband's male ego, whereas I did nothing but tear it down," she mused. As her diary makes clear, the distinction between male glory and female subservience deserved to be honored wherever it appeared, in the kitchen or anyplace else.

It was certainly no accident that a man was making dinner the night Jane discovered grilled spareribs. During the '50s the food most powerfully identified with men was that of the outdoors: slabs of meat sizzling over hot coals. Long popular on the West Coast, barbecuing in the backyard was an idyll that raced across the nation in the years following World War II as millions of families moved into burgeoning suburbs and excitedly took possession of their own small portions of land. By 1952, makers of charcoal briquettes were reporting that sales had doubled, tripled, or jumped 500 percent in the last two years. Kingsford increased production by 35 percent and added thousands of retail outlets, typically gas stations, but was restricting its advertising for fear of not being able to meet the demand. In fact, relatively little advertising accompanied the barbecue boom in its early years. "Possibly it is the closest thing to a natural, national phenomenon since baseball," reported a business magazine.

There was a good deal of resemblance between the two national pastimes. Both were so wholeheartedly American that to enjoy them was a form of patriotism; both were associated with warm weather and easy living; and both were as ardently masculine as the Boy Scouts. Women could cheer the players and fix the cole slaw, but they were quite tangential to the full glory of the imagery. Here was plain, hefty food with big, vigorous flavors. A pan of instant scalloped potatoes or a plate of cupcakes made from a mix might show up, but the main event was protein and fire. Never mind that the electric range was only a few steps from the yard; never mind that Mom sometimes happened to be the one who turned the hamburgers. When a barbecue was under way, mythology took charge, and there was no bridging the divide between woman's place and man's dominion.

Packaged-food cuisine, by contrast, was widely understood to be women's cuisine. In part, this identification sprang from the way the food actually came about. As we have seen, it was invented for housewives and proliferated in the magazines and newspaper pages aimed at women. But even more definitively, this cuisine was feminine by virtue of its artifice. Thanks to a legacy dating back to the turn of the century, the appropriate food for women was still considered nonfood. Women could vote by the 1950s, and they could drive cars and work for wages, but they weren't supposed to eat like men, much less look as though they did. Canned and frozen products, food that had been stripped, sanitized, and rendered lifeless, was perfectly suited to the kind of women shown in the ads for refrigerators and ranges, all smiles in their aprons and high heels. Their personal touch, the element that made the meal visibly feminine, came in dollops of pure sentimentality that had long been associated with ladies at table. Whipped cream, maraschino cherries, quivering gelatin salads— by midcentury the link between femaleness and weird, gaudy dishes of no recognizable provenance was a culinary assumption as inevitable as the pairing of salt and pepper.

When '50s cooking moved beyond packaged foods and entered the realm of haute cuisine, however, women were left behind. Gastronomy was for men. Most of the Americans who practiced an allegiance to the higher culinary arts during the '50s modeled their behavior on the French, who had long insisted that refined and expensive cuisine was a male preserve. Women didn't cook in the great restaurants of France, and they didn't belong to the various societies for gourmets, or attend their sumptuous banquets. Hence, on the American side of the Atlantic there were no women in the Lucullan Circle, which gathered at the Waldorf-Astoria for black-tie dinners showcasing themes in classic French cuisine. Although the New York branch of the Wine and Food Society was open to female members, women were barred from the branches in Los Angeles and San Francisco. *Gourmet* magazine had plenty of women on staff and in the readership; even so, for years the magazine deliberately projected the air of an exclusive men's club where members entertained themselves by reminiscing about a certain splendid foie gras or an especially delightful vermouth. A cartoon in the second issue nicely captured the magazine's view of the culinary gender divide by depicting a stout woman in a fancy restaurant speaking eagerly to the waiter: "If the Chef will give me his recipe for Biscuit Tortoni, I'll give him mine for apple jelly!"

In reality, of course, most home cooks were women no matter where on the gender spectrum they fixed dinner. Everybody knew women who turned out splendid meals and had no interest in Mock Jambalaya or Cheez Whiz hors d'oeuvres. But the image of an American housewife cooking a fine, sophisticated meal couldn't compete with the prevailing stereotype, any more than the fact that millions of mothers had jobs could compete with the stereotype of contented moms at home. Magazine food stories aimed at women often included recipes for quick, artificial versions of beef Stroganoff or coq au vin; but when the story featured a man in the kitchen, he was making his famous chili or his authentic coquilles St. Jacques from scratch. Women might be depicted pouring a can of soup over the suppertime chops or having just a dab of cottage cheese for lunch; men swabbed the salad bowl with garlic and tended gigantic steaks on the grill. *Living*, which often reported on how couples managed the culinary side of wedded bliss, once described life in the kitchen with a twosome named Paul and Ginny. Paul could pan-broil, roast, and fry; he experimented with pineapple vinegar in the salad; he hunted down ripe Camembert and carefully selected the wine. Ginny heated a can of shoestring potatoes now and then ("very cautiously") and bought pastries at the bakery. When a woman wrote to Irma Rombauer in 1953 to say how much she liked the *Joy of Cooking,* she included the highest praise she could think of—that every recipe belonged on the male side of the culinary divide. "Nothing, not even salads or cakes, have that peculiar female quality that a man so often detests and objects to," she assured Rombauer.

This notion of a "peculiar female quality" clung hard to women's cuisine, often for good reason. "At [a wedding shower] we were served *tuna fish* chow mein with rancid noodles," Betty MacDonald once complained. She went on to describe other local banquets that left her in shock, all of them prepared by and for women. "A garden club meeting, creamed tuna fish and peanuts over canned asparagus. A hospital group dredged up a salad of elbow macaroni, pineapple chunks, Spanish peanuts, chopped cabbage, chopped marshmallows, ripe olives and salad dressing. . . . I don't know what is happening to the women of America but it ought to be stopped." Yet she also stated emphatically that she, her daughters, and her mother were all fine cooks. In the making of the stereotype, it was the food associated with ladies' luncheons and women's club meetings that became definitive—the food women ate when they gathered in the name of femininity.

Good cooks of both sexes derided women's culinary follies, and even Jane could see the dangers of taking too much advice from female experts. One day when she was planning her menu, she happened to turn on the radio. There was "Harriet Hepplewhite, the Happy Housewife," making her daily broadcast. "She was giving a recipe for a new salad, made with marshmallows, cherries, nuts, figs, dates, apples, mayonnaise, candied orange peel, chopped egg, and whipped cream," Jane reported. "It sounded horrible, but I was mentally trapped (like a bird is supposed to be when confronted by a cobra) and I just listened, getting weaker and weaker while [she] recited her nauseating list of ingredients." In the book, Jane escaped by spinning the radio dial. In real kitchens across America, housewives put their faith in a food expert very different from Harriet, someone who wasn't herself a joke and who never, ever insulted women for being women. This expert had good ideas and reliable advice; she lived in very pleasant surroundings, she had a great job, and she didn't answer to a man. Her name was Betty Crocker.

Betty Crocker was one of many women widely known for their culinary expertise at midcentury who did not in fact exist. There were some who did exist, of course, but it was often hard to tell the difference. When Irma Rombauer published her book on convenience foods, *Streamlined Cooking,* she thanked by name all the home economists who had shared their ideas and recipes with her, but she made no effort to distinguish between, say, Jeanette Kelley (real) and Martha Logan (fictional). It was an understandable lapse, especially if her only contact with these women had been by letter. Kelley worked for Lever Brothers at that time, dealing with the public under her own name; but Logan was a pen-and-ink portrait created by Swift and Company to be its spokeswoman. A team of Swift's home economists wrote her advice and signed her mail; when she made a personal appearance, it was one of them who showed up. At Carnation, home economists did the same for Mary Blake; at Quaker Oats, they supported Mary Alden; and at Libby's, their boss was Mary Hale Martin. Dole's chief cookery expert on pineapple was called Patricia

Collier; Ann Pillsbury presided over Pillsbury's tips and recipes; and a bespectacled woman known as Aunt Jenny cooked everything with Spry and loved to explain why. Marie Gifford of Armour was one of the longest-lived in this sorority; born in 1920, she never grew old. Others had more turbulent careers. Kellogg dismissed Barbara B. Brooks, then summoned her back and gave her a new name: Kay Kellogg. General Foods was grooming Frances Barton for major public appearances—"She'll be dropping into your kitchen like a next-door neighbor pretty soon," promised the ads—but the big moment never came, and she faded away. Even so, she lasted longer than Marcia Camp, who worked only briefly before she disappeared, leaving barely a trace of her exemplary enthusiasm for Campfire marshmallows.

The real women who stood behind each name enjoyed far more authority as fictional figures than most of their colleagues did as living, breathing home economists. For pen-and-ink portraits, authority was a mandate. Known in the business world as "live trademarks," they were designed to put a human face on food corporations bidding for the attention of female shoppers. Unfamiliar new products were arriving every day on supermarket shelves; somehow, homemakers had to be persuaded that a box of powder really would produce mashed potatoes. The kind female faces appearing in the advertising were there to forge a crucial link between old habits and modern foods. "Ideally, the corporate character is a woman, between the ages of 32 and 40, attractive, but not competitively so, mature but youthful-looking, competent yet warm, understanding but not sentimental, interested in the consumer but not involved with her," explained a business publication in 1957. In person and in print a range of figures created according to these guidelines taught women how to use new electric stoves, mixers, and blenders; how to cook blocks of frozen

peas; how to garnish canned ham with pears dipped in food coloring; and how to make crêpes suzettes with pancake mix.

These authorities worked in a surreal universe that left purely
optional the distinction between fiction and reality. In the pages
of *Forecast*, real and invented home economists mingled especially
comfortably. Mary Alden of Quaker Oats lent her byline to an article on nutritious oatmeal breakfasts, and the magazine's real-life
editor reported on a charming luncheon given by Frances Barton
of General Foods. On one occasion Mary Barber, a real-life
spokeswoman for Kellogg, took a press junket to Honduras courtesy of United Fruit. Describing the trip later, in an ad touting the
virtues of cereal and bananas, she singled out one of her colleagues for special praise: the noted home economist Chiquita Banana. "I came home with a new understanding of what makes
Chiquita Banana the successful teacher she is!" exclaimed Mary
Barber. "It's Chiquita's warmth, her sympathy, her *showmanship*."

For all the cordial relations among these figures and their real-
life counterparts, there was one whose name was never mentioned
by the others, despite her fame and longevity. That was Aunt
Jemima, oldest of them all, the "mammy" character who first appeared in public at the 1893 World's Fair promoting pancake mix.
Portrayed in person over the years by a succession of black
women, Aunt Jemima spent decades traveling the nation, first for
the small company that created the mix, and then for Quaker
Oats, which bought Aunt Jemima Pancake Mix in 1925. She appeared at trade fairs, pancake breakfasts, supermarket openings,
and other promotional events; and in 1955 she took up residence
at Disneyland, launching a restaurant in Frontierland known as
Aunt Jemima's Pancake House. There she flipped thousands of
pancakes for delighted visitors. Even Nehru stopped by. But she
never showed up in the pages of *Forecast* or shared an ad with

another spokeswoman. In their ever-pleasant universe, none of the real or fictional home economists who visited cheerily back and forth acknowledged their black colleague. They were proud to spend time with Chiquita Banana, but as far as they were concerned, Aunt Jemima could eat in the kitchen.

Among those personalities, the one who made the biggest name for herself was Betty Crocker, to this day the most successful culinary authority ever invented. During her glory years in the 1940s and 1950s, ninety-nine out of one hundred homemakers knew Betty Crocker's name as well as their own. They knew her face from the picture on ads and packages, they knew her firm, unembellished signature, they knew her voice from innumerable radio broadcasts, and they knew her *Picture Cook Book,* which made publishing history in 1950 with a first printing of 950,000 copies. Today she is more symbolic than genuinely authoritative, but Betty Crocker still watches over home cooking from a unique perch in the nation's collective imagination, a figure so familiar that she renders all but unanswerable the question most frequently asked about her: "Is she real?"

The Betty Crocker whose voice reached millions of homemakers via print and radio for decades was in large part the creation of Marjorie Child Husted. A graduate of the University of Minnesota, where she majored in home economics and German, Husted went to work in 1924 for Washburn Crosby, the Minneapolis flour company that produced Gold Medal flour and would later become General Mills. The company made a practice even then of fostering strong ties with consumers, notably by setting up short-term cooking schools around the nation and sending specially trained women to run them. Sponsored by local newspapers and businesses, the schools were held in stores, churches, and clubs. In 1925 thousands of women attended a Gold Medal cooking school at the convention center in Tulsa, Oklahoma, sponsored by the *Tulsa Tribune*. Prizes were handed out for the best angel food cakes made with Gold Medal flour, and hostesses at the cooking demonstrations showed up in paper dresses assembled from *Tulsa Tribune* want-ad pages. The school was a local sensation, and according to the teacher, it sold "loads of flour" in a city that had never before paid much attention to Gold Medal.

That teacher was Husted. She made such a success of the Gold Medal cooking schools that after a year on the road she was summoned back to Minneapolis and put in charge of Washburn Crosby's Home Service Department. There were five home economists on the staff at the time, but Husted took special interest in a sixth, a woman who existed in name only. Betty Crocker had been created back in 1921, in the wake of a promotional campaign for Gold Medal. The company had run a magazine ad with a jigsaw puzzle in it, and readers who put the puzzle together and sent it to Washburn Crosby were promised a prize: a pincushion in the shape of a Gold Medal flour sack. This offer drew a much bigger response than the ad department had expected, with thirty thousand completed puzzles pouring in; but what startled the executives even more were the letters that arrived with the puzzles. Women had snatched at the chance to contact someone who might be able to solve their baking problems. "What makes my cake crack on top?" "What made my bread go sour?" "How do you make a one-crust cherry pie?" The company's home economists set about answering each letter personally, and at first an executive signed the letters with his own name. Eventually it occurred to the ad department that perhaps a businessman wasn't the most credible source for advice on cooking, and they decided to create a spokeswoman. They chose "Betty" for its homey qualities, and "Crocker" in honor of a former company executive. Then they asked all the women in the company to write "Betty Crocker," and using features from the different handwriting samples, they designed a signature for the company's newest employee.

Betty Crocker was still spending a great deal of time as a signature when Husted arrived at the Home Service Department five years later. Over the next few decades she built up the Betty Crocker name and expanded its functions until what was once a prop for selling flour became a virtually independent empire in American homemaking, encompassing radio, TV, newspaper columns, books, pamphlets, and food products, not to mention hopeful forays into silverware and small appliances. In a story about Husted that was published in the General Mills in-house newsletter, the author made an effort to describe Husted's office in warm, feminine terms. "Comfortable chairs, attractive lamps, interesting pictures take away that 'strictly business' atmosphere," the story exclaimed. "A quiet, cozy place to work!" But quiet and cozy wasn't Husted's style. She was an ambitious, inventive businesswoman—not unlike her younger contemporary, Poppy Cannon—and although she liked cooking at home for her husband, what she loved was her career.

Many of Husted's convictions about Betty Crocker's role came from what she had learned when she was running the Gold Medal cooking schools. Whenever she landed in a new city, she made a habit of rounding up high school girls and sending them about town to investigate the way local women cooked. In this way she gathered an enormous trove of information about homemakers' habits in the kitchen, and she kept up the practice when she returned to Minneapolis. Recipes created in the company's test kitchens would be given to local homemakers, and Husted would visit their kitchens to watch them cook. "I could see, for instance, when they measured flour and they measured sugar they would tap down the cup," she told an interviewer years later—a bad habit that led to flour or sugar being packed down into the cup until it held more than a standard one-cup measure. The cake would be disappointing, and the woman would feel that she had failed. Betty Crocker's recipes had to be more than reliable, Husted could see; they had to be foolproof against the casual errors of ordinary home cooks. Her observations went directly to the company's research department, where they were factored into recipes, advice, and instructions emanating from Betty Crocker. Eventually, General Mills developed a three-stage testing process for every product that came out of its laboratories: First the company's own home economists worked with it in their test kitchens, then a group of specially selected homemakers in the Minneapolis area tried it, and finally it was tested by a battalion of home cooks throughout the country. It was a process that reduced each dish to its bare elements and made the woman herself virtually an onlooker of her own cooking; but when she picked up a Betty Crocker recipe she could proclaim, with Susan B. Anthony, "Failure is impossible."

As Husted started her work at the Home Service Department, the Gold Medal cooking schools were being phased out in favor of an exciting and efficient new selling medium: radio. Washburn Crosby had acquired its own radio station, WCCO, which became famous for introducing the first singing commercial. (To the tune of "She's a Jazz Baby": "Have you tried Wheaties? / They're whole wheat with all of the bran. / Won't you try Wheaties? / For wheat is the best food of man.") In 1924 the company inaugurated the "Betty Crocker Cooking School of the Air," with Blanche Ingersoll of the Home Service Department speaking to American women as Betty Crocker. Those who managed to tune her in—WCCO had a relatively limited range in the Midwest—learned that they could enroll in the "Betty Crocker Cooking School of the Air" simply by sending for printed recipes. They were instructed to prepare all the recipes, write reports on how each one came out, and mail them to Betty Crocker. If they completed the entire course, they were invited to attend a graduation ceremony at the WCCO studio. At the end of the first year, 238 women showed up for graduation and received diplomas. The company quickly began training other Betty Crockers to broadcast from different regions of the country, and although efforts were made to impose uniform standards, inevitably the voices varied. Not until 1936 did it finally become possible for women in every city and town to listen to the same Betty Crocker.

As Betty Crocker's name circulated ever more widely, millions of women wrote to her with their homemaking problems, requested her recipe booklets, and encountered her in newspaper and magazine ads. But she had her greatest impact on the public through radio. "The radio made Betty," declared *Fortune* magazine in 1945, adding, "It is fair to say that it did for her career in commerce what it did for Franklin D. Roosevelt's in politics." Not only did radio have a national reach that no other medium could match, it was also a peculiarly appropriate home for a figure whose relation to the real world was so intangible. To hear her voice was to add a dimension to her persona that print could not provide, but for a listener to complete the picture required imagination—itself a good medium for someone who was, in fact, imaginary. Betty Crocker's radio career grew steadily through the 1930s and then ballooned during the war years. Thanks to the War Food Administration, which commissioned a radio series from General Mills called "Our Nation's Rations," she became a coast-to-coast personification of patriotic home cooking. Advising homemakers on how to deal with shortages and make good use of available foods, she won huge new audiences. Her free pamphlet of wartime recipes and cooking tips, "Your Share," reached 7 million households, and by 1945 she was receiving some four thousand letters a day asking for recipes and help with kitchen problems.

Husted wrote all the scripts for Betty Crocker's cooking school, did some of the broadcasting, and dreamed up unexpected and immensely popular elements to add to Betty Crocker's radio personality. During the early 1930s, Betty Crocker interviewed "eligible bachelors," asking them what they were looking for in prospective brides. She visited Hollywood movie stars—Cary Grant, Norma Shearer, Dolores Del Rio, and others—to ask about their home lives and what home meant to them. She conducted interviews with husbands and wives, she made up games and quizzes, she created short dramas inspired by the letters she received, and she instituted the Betty Crocker Home Legion, a wartime promotion centered on recognizing women's contribution to the war effort. After the war she helped create a new radio program, "The Betty Crocker Magazine of the Air," which was aired in addition to a five-minute food show called "Time for Betty Crocker." All this took Home Service into areas nobody foresaw back when the company was first mailing out recipes and answering cooking questions, as Husted acknowledged in a 1952 speech to advertising executives: "But as I came to know more about women's lives we added service more deeply needed—service built on increased understanding of the fundamental needs of women. And then we received much greater response."

Husted went home every night with a briefcase full of letters written to Betty Crocker. Those queries and complaints gave her direct access to women's lives, just as her visits to local homes had done; and the more she learned, the more she was convinced that American homemakers felt left out. Their work made no money, it often went unnoticed, and it certainly carried no status. "Women needed a champion," Husted recalled to an interviewer years later. "Here were millions of them staying at home alone, doing a job with children, cooking, cleaning on minimal budgets—the whole depressing mess of it. They needed someone to remind them they had value." Under her direction, Betty Crocker became a figure of dignity who treated homemakers with respect.

If issues of value and respect were paramount for Husted, one reason was that they were her own issues, not just the inferences she pulled from the mail each night. Even though she was instrumental in establishing every facet of the Betty Crocker enterprise and even though company executives told her that she had done more for sales at General Mills than any other single person, the company paid its star salesman four times what it paid Husted. "Management is dominated by men and there is no indication of interest on the part of employers for change," she charged at a conference of the American Association of University Women in 1951. "Let's discuss the problem frankly. Do women get equal recognition with men in business? Do they get equal pay for jobs of commensurate value?" She was livid—but she wasn't about to forget those women trapped with "the whole depressing mess of it" at home. "Let's help every woman recognize that true homemaking is still the most important career of all for women," she appealed, right after she demanded recognition for women in business and just before insisting on equal pay. "No matter how many housekeeping duties modern conveniences take out of the home, the chief function of the homemaker still remains: To give the love and security—the training for character and attitudes which make for successful living." As a home economist, she struggled to put a value on women's work that made it equal in status to men's. As a businesswoman, she just wanted to be taken seriously.

As soon as Husted took over the Home Service Department, she started being confused with Betty Crocker herself. If she went out in public in an official capacity or greeted visitors at the General Mills test kitchens, people assumed they were meeting the company's most famous representative. "At first, I'd hedge and say, 'Well, I'm director of the Home Service Department, I do the broadcasting, and I prepare the talks, but we all work under the firm name of 'Betty Crocker,'" she recalled later. Finally, the president of the company advised her that she should always be introduced as Betty Crocker, and from then on she was. It wasn't entirely a fiction. Husted not only put the words in Betty Crocker's mouth—and frequently spoke them herself—but behind the scenes she was instrumental in creating the personality that presided over correspondence, recipe booklets, advertising, and newspaper columns. Perhaps not surprisingly, that personality owed a great deal to Husted's own, especially her defiant stance between man's world and woman's place. Husted believed that work belonged as naturally in women's lives as it did in men's, and that domestic work—the most important of all, as she never missed an opportunity to emphasize—was far from being the only appropriate choice for women. "The trend in American life today is for the girl to work before she is married—then stop for a few years while she is bringing up a family—then to go back to work to improve their standard of living," she told the AAUW in her 1951 speech, well before such a trend had settled into place. If Husted was jumping the gun, it was because she wanted so desperately for it to be so. Within the constraints of General Mills's purpose for her, Betty Crocker was living the dream.

Husted was determined, for instance, to convey the impression that as the nation's home-economist-in-chief, Betty Crocker's vast knowledge of cooking and baking was derived from professional experience, rather than private life as a homemaker. Betty Crocker was always depicted working in the offices and kitchens of General Mills, the only people close to her were her colleagues, and if she picked up a spoon or a sifter, she was pursuing knowledge, not dessert. "Daily Betty Crocker and her staff critically test Gold Medal flour, by actually baking bread and cakes in the General Mills Kitchen," explained a behind-the-scenes introduction to the *Betty Crocker Cook Book of All-Purpose Baking,* a 25-cent booklet published in 1942 and distributed to more than 800,000 households. A full-page color illustration shows four women working in a pleasant kitchen. The walls are yellow, and blue plaid curtains hang at the windows; there's a matching ruffle on the mantel over the stove, a copper kettle on one shelf, and a red watering pail on another. It's home. And yet the women are dressed in white uniforms; their expressions are solemn; and they're poring over baked goods. So it's not home after all; this is a workplace. But as a workplace, it's Betty Crocker's home—a friendly kitchen where sober, disciplined professionals strive tirelessly to make baking easier and more foolproof.

Unlike Betty Crocker herself, the women on her staff—whom she constantly evoked by name in her writing—all had satisfying family lives at home. "Our Mildred has a son who plays on his high school football team. To celebrate the big game of the year, she plans a 'football cake,'" Betty Crocker wrote in a column-length newspaper ad, before giving directions for the cake. Or, in another column, "Our Vicky, who is off for a European tour, writes from her plane on Sabena Belgian Air Lines: 'Never again will I hesitate to give a large dinner party with my tiny kitchen. The Belgian Air Lines take pride in doing their cooking aloft.'" She may have been a consummate professional with no private life, but Betty Crocker was always flanked by emblems of a comfortable and prosperous middle-class life. Home and work, love and business—those intractable opponents forever dueling—joined hands at last in Betty Crocker's kitchen.

By the time the artist Neysa McMein was commissioned to

paint an official portrait of Betty Crocker in 1936, she had such well-defined character traits that McMein was able to come up with a face that was recognizably the outward expression of an inner truth. The portrait showed a quiet, unsmiling woman with a bright red mouth firmly closed. Her nose was long and dignified, the planes of the cheeks were flat. Her hair waved tidily off her face, and a white ruffled collar stood up around her neck—emblems of charm held firmly in check. Competence and self-assurance radiated from those features, and the bit of red dress visible at her shoulders suggested a modest accumulation of power. All the details said feminine, and the overall impression just as clearly said masculine.

This was the image of Betty Crocker that hovered over the radio whenever it was tuned to one of her shows. "And here she is, America's first lady of food—your Betty Crocker!" the announcer used to say, underscoring the fact that Betty Crocker belonged to her public and could be precisely what people wanted her to be. These shows, which were developed before broadcasting enforced any important distinction between editorial content and advertising, conveyed a remarkably fluid version of reality. They seemed to emanate from a world without boundaries, where real people conversed easily with made-up colleagues and genuine discussions melted into commercial fantasies. "Time for Betty Crocker," for instance, was a five-minute show that played nine times a week during the '50s and reached more than 8 million homes. The real-life Win Elliot—Betty Crocker's longtime announcer and interlocutor—always introduced the fictional Betty Crocker. "Hello, everybody," Betty Crocker would say cordially. Her voice was pleasant and confident, never intimate and never coy. "You know we've found that noodle casseroles are popular with most families," she informed her listeners on a typical show. "But they can become pretty humdrum unless we're careful to vary them. And our Noodles Cantonese recipe from my new *Good and Easy Cookbook* does just that." Win Elliot, by contrast, spoke in far more casual tones. "Hey, from all I gather, Betty Crocker, the gals are really going for *all* the recipes in that new cookbook of yours." When the talk turned to 4-Square Fudge Cake, the vehicle for discussing Gold Medal flour, it was Win Elliot who created the domestic context. His wife, Rita, he said, had just made the cake for company. "The women all wanted the recipe, and the men—well, they wanted second and third helpings. What a success! The crunchy nuts in that moist, chocolatey, rich, tender . . . *de*licious cake . . . ummmm mmmmmm." Betty Crocker then chuckled and told him, "Win, you've just been describing what we like to call 'that good Gold Medal texture!' " And she went on explaining the merits of Gold Medal until Win Elliot said, "Well, Betty Crocker. It looks like time's up." "So it is, Win," she agreed.

Strikingly, while she calls him Win, he invariably addresses her as Betty Crocker. There's an implicit hierarchy in Betty Crocker's radio world, one that subtly reverses traditional sex roles. It's Win who's a little silly, who curries favor with the audience and always tries to please, while Betty Crocker's presence needs no such bolstering. She presides; Win merely helps out. She's the professional; Win is the homebody. She's the authority and the source of information; Win is the wide-eyed enthusiast. In print, Betty Crocker often praised the housewife's importance, and on the radio she conveyed the same message indirectly. Her praise went undercover, in a sense, and thereby gained considerable power. Rather than overtly patting homemakers on the back, she simply ran the show with ease, described her work and travels, and emphasized that good cooking was an achievement in which women could take pride. Nobody in Betty Crocker's vicinity was in danger of being identified as "just a housewife," certainly not

Rita, whose chocolate cake—"What a success!"—was applauded prominently by all. In any home where Betty Crocker reigns, her radio shows promised, the woman in the kitchen finally reaps the honor she's due.

Betty Crocker continued on the radio through the 1950s, but by the end of the '40s, radio no longer had the nation in thrall. Certainly to advertisers, radio was starting to seem a little dowdy compared with the up-and-coming medium of television. According to a study of one hundred "TV families" conducted by A.C. Nielsen in 1950, people listened to the radio nearly five hours a day until they bought TV sets. Nine months into TV ownership, they were devoting that same amount of time to television. They were still tuned in to radio every day for about two and a quarter hours, but the trend was clearly in the direction of pictures. General Mills started running TV ads on "The Lone Ranger" in 1949 and was planning to sponsor other shows. But for a company eager to reach consumers through TV, there were opportunities much bigger than mere commercials. As with radio, it was permissible in the early years of television for sponsors to write and produce an entire show, thus making sure it was a good showcase for the product. What's more, the audience for television was shaping up to resemble the radio audience, especially during the day: women at home doing their housework or taking a break. To General Mills, daytime TV looked like a perfect vehicle for Betty Crocker.

Culinary expertise was nowhere in the job description when General Mills went looking for a television-age Betty Crocker. What the company needed wasn't a home economist but a woman who could give human form to a treasured image. Adelaide Hawley, a Manhattan divorcée who was raising a daughter alone and hated to cook, had all the right credentials. Her morning radio show, the "Adelaide Hawley Program," ran from 1937 to

1950 and featured news and interviews aimed at housewives; she also had TV experience, covering fashion shows and women's issues. In 1948 she had even been a guest on "The Betty Crocker Magazine of the Air," discussing her travels in Europe (and little dreaming she was soon to be Betty Crocker herself). Despite a total lack of interest in domesticity, she did have a background in fictional housework. For a time she portrayed Procter & Gamble's "Ann Bradley," who promoted Spic and Span. Most important, she had the height, the cheekbones, and the calm, professional bearing that would bring to life Neysa McMein's now-famous portrait.

The Betty Crocker Show had its premiere in the fall of 1950 on CBS. A long, loving shot of the General Mills flag rippling in the breeze opened the show, and then the scene shifted to an inspirational *tableau vivant*. A young woman was posed outdoors on a promontory against the sky, two small children clinging to her hands. Her chin was lifted, her gaze was unflinching, and her purpose was grave. As she paused with her little brood on their arduous journey, the announcer made it clear just what she symbolized. "Homemaking," he intoned. "A woman's most rewarding way of life."

Not until this essential background had been established did Betty Crocker greet the nation in person for the first time. There was no mistaking her: Here was the nation's best-known domestic expert, seated behind an office desk. Her features were firm and pleasant, her hair was designed in well-controlled waves around her face; she wore a white collar, and she carried herself with natural dignity. "Hello, everybody," said Betty Crocker, exactly as she did on the radio. Adelaide Hawley's name was never spoken.

Much of the program took place right at General Mills headquarters, with Betty Crocker moving back and forth between her office and her kitchen. In her office she talked about freedom, family life, religion, and America. In the kitchen she introduced an assistant named Ruth and gave detailed lessons in the use of Stir 'n Roll pastry, which was made of flour, milk, and oil rather than flour and solid shortening, and so was easier to handle. Back in the office, Betty Crocker explained to viewers what had inspired the invention of Stir 'n Roll pastry. She had received a letter from a homemaker who needed a "surefire" recipe for mince pie, because she was having very special guests for Thanksgiving. This led to a dramatization of the letter, showing how the homemaker and her husband had made friends with new neighbors, recent and very blond immigrants called the Voltags. The two families shared Thanksgiving dinner, and Mr. Voltag expressed all their feelings when he haltingly said, "We come, we eat, we talk—we aren't strangers anymore. We are one family." In the final moments of the program, Betty Crocker returned to her office and offered a few reflections on how important it was to take time during the holidays for "family living and loving." At the very end she read a hymn.

For all the mawkishness of the script, Betty Crocker came to life as a woman far more businesslike than motherly. The "first lady of food" made her debut in an office, without so much as a pot holder anywhere in sight. Walking into the kitchen, she tied an apron around her waist, but it was Ruth who did the work as Betty Crocker conducted the lesson. Indeed, viewers never saw Betty Crocker cooking. She was knowledgeable, but she was management. She was self-possessed and authoritative, with a well-modulated speaking voice and enunciation so precise she couldn't say "Stir 'n Roll." It came out "Stern Roll." She was a career homemaker with no need for a home. Her sermonette on "family living and loving" was as out of place as a doily on a desk.

Perhaps because of the dazzling incongruity of the imagery, perhaps because of the stodgy writing and leaden patriotism,

The Betty Crocker Show was a flop. General Mills made another try with a different format, this one featuring Betty Crocker as the hostess of an entertainment show with guest stars. It flopped as well. Americans went right on listening to Betty Crocker on the radio, they wrote her thousands of letters a week, they bought her cookbooks in record numbers, but they were never at ease with a real, live Betty Crocker who sat down in their living rooms once a week for a visit. Apparently the cognitive dissonance was just too overwhelming. She remained on television, but only in the carefully circumscribed format of a short commercial. Here, promoting cake mix, she played the simple role of saleswoman, which viewers found much easier to take than the part-real, part-fictional persona of the TV show. One series of Betty Crocker's television ads featured George Burns and Gracie Allen, and the ads often began with Gracie bemoaning to George that she couldn't think of anything to make for her club meeting or for a holiday dinner. "Why don't you ask your friend Betty Crocker?" George would say. In a minute Betty Crocker had materialized, and the two women were admiring a marble or spice cake that had been produced with almost no visible effort. "It's so easy, even I can bake a Betty Crocker cake!" Gracie would exclaim with relief at the end. Perhaps because Gracie, like Betty Crocker, was a seamless blend of the real and the imaginary, the two women seemed thoroughly comfortable together.

Husted retired from General Mills in 1950, and although many of the traits she had developed for Betty Crocker continued to flourish for the next several years on radio, they disappeared completely on television. Unlike Betty Crocker's radio world, where a woman's voice took the lead and women's accomplishments earned full recognition, she and Gracie had practically nothing to do in the TV kitchen. It took no skill to come up with this particular marble or spice cake—indeed, that was the point of their delighted self-congratulation. Betty Crocker, who had started her career by sharing a vast store of culinary expertise, had dwindled in size and scope until she was little more than a cheerleader. By the mid-'50s her personality in print followed the tone set by TV. "In strawberry season—or anytime—you have it all over mother's generation," she told readers in a 1954 angel food cake mix ad. "Much of the guesswork is gone from cooking. Kitchen time is cut way down. By the ready-to-eat and ready-to-cook foods. By magical appliances that practically *think* for you. . . . These days, you can even *bake* without experience." Two decades earlier Betty Crocker had been explaining how easy it was to bake with Bisquick, but she never claimed that Bisquick would do the thinking. Now, as she became increasingly identified with packaged-food cuisine, she was promoting the notion that women's work need have nothing to do with women's minds.

It was during this time that Betty Crocker's commercials introduced a tagline that would become famous. "I guarantee a perfect cake, every time you bake—cake after cake after cake," she announced in 1953, conjuring an image of identical flawless cakes rolling off an assembly line. With this epigraph the woman in the kitchen effectively became redundant, and not long afterward, so did Betty Crocker. Although she continued to show up in print, by the mid-'60s she had disappeared from radio and television, as if a human presence was no longer relevant to cooking. In one of the TV cake-mix commercials that followed her departure, nobody cooked at all—a cartoon spoon merrily mixed batter in a cartoon bowl. This image of the cake that baked itself represented a culmination of sorts for postwar women's cuisine. Here was the most sentiment-laden dessert in America arriving on the table almost without human intervention, yet deserving the accolade "homemade." Betty Crocker was never perceived as a gastronome, but at the height of her powers she helped women believe that their presence in the kitchen made a difference. Now, as her human shape faded from public life, the message the food industry had been trumpeting for decades—that women couldn't wait to get out of the kitchen, that the culinary revolution had been successful and cooking had been vanquished—finally began to sound plausible. If Betty Crocker wasn't cooking anymore, maybe nobody was.

※

While Betty Crocker and her sisters were busy attending to the nation's housewives in the years right after World War II, the increasingly chic world of male cuisine was fielding experts of its own—figures who had a very different message to deliver. These authorities from the opposite end of the culinary spectrum were fewer in number than the women created by the food industry, and they rarely hovered over the home kitchen in the manner of their pen-and-ink counterparts. They cooked and ate in a far more splendid milieu, for these were creatures of American literature rather than creatures of advertising. Their influence on the nation's cooking habits was negligible, but that was no surprise; they didn't really try to teach cooking. They simply wished to affirm that there were better ways to eat than those represented by packaged-food cuisine, and to mourn the fact that so many Americans were missing out on one of life's great pleasures. Most important, they treasured the conviction that glorious cuisine was by its very nature beyond the ken of ordinary housewives. At the heart of an exquisite dish lurked a mystery, not just a recipe. Merely to venture into the presence of such culinary grandeur required instincts and sensibilities that belonged to men, and probably Frenchmen at that. True, some of the best-known authorities in the domain of food and literature were female—but not irreparably. Like their invented colleagues in home economics, they inhabited a realm with a remarkably porous border between real life and the imagination.

Mary Frances Kennedy Fisher was the acknowledged lodestar in this genre, although she had no very lofty ambitions when she began writing essays on food in the 1930s. She liked cooking and eating, she loved reading, and she had always wanted to write, so during the Depression she spent hours in the Los Angeles Public Library, paging through its extensive culinary collection. Then, with care, she started putting her own words on paper. One of her early stories was about César, the butcher in the French village where she and her husband, Al, had lived for a few weeks. "César was all that every man wants secretly to be: strong, brave; foul, cruel, reckless. . . . César was man. Man noble and monstrous again after so many centuries." The village women feared and despised him, and he had nothing but contempt for them; nonetheless, before Fisher and her husband left the village, they invited César for dinner. He brought the meat—"a massive filet of beef"—and Fisher went off to cook it. Then the meal began, uncomfortably at first. But the meat was superb, and as Fisher was enjoying it, César suddenly spoke up. " 'She likes it, she likes good food!' he said, wonderingly, to Al. 'She cannot be a real woman!' After that things were very pleasant."

Fisher went on to write hundreds of stories and essays, many of them memoirs of meals past, and her work appeared in print regularly for the next six decades. W. H. Auden called her the best prose writer in America, and magazines known for their elegant writing snapped up her work and felt honored to publish it. Nobody handled the subject of food the way she did, with an intoxicating appreciation for the sensual, emotional, and intellectual experiences inherent in touch and taste. Especially arresting was her narrator, the woman who moved through Fisher's nonfiction in love or despair, hinting at much in the way of emotional entanglements but conveying their substance only by suggestion, with food as the metaphor. The meals she described could be as simple as a few sections of tangerine or as elaborate as a multicourse dinner in a great restaurant. What made this elusive narrator compelling wasn't what she ate but how—hungrily, passionately, reveling in the bitter as well as the pleasurable, unwilling to miss a single dimension of taste whatever the morsel she put in her mouth. Or as César put it, "She cannot be a real woman!"

To be typecast as a real woman, Fisher decided early on, would be fatal for her work. Women weren't supposed to be able to eat with gusto or wisdom, and their thoughts on cuisine would never merit the attention of literary-minded readers. The people who commanded respect on this subject were men. So she altered her sex just a bit. Her work was published under the byline "M.F.K. Fisher"—"an adequately equivocal name for someone who did not write about the pleasures of the table in correctly female and 'home economics' fashion," as she explained later. M.F.K. Fisher became the person who traveled and lived and dined and loved in Fisher's work, and who ate like a man, because Fisher herself was not.

Fisher's accounts of her many sojourns in Europe, especially France, were at the heart of her literary and culinary reputation. After her early stay in Dijon as a newlywed, she settled with her husband in California; but their marriage failed when she fell in love with an artist and writer named Dillwyn Parrish. With his encouragement she published her first collection of food essays, *Serve It Forth,* in 1937. She and Parrish spent only a few years together, living in Switzerland and California, before a debilitating and painful condition known as Buerger's disease drove him to suicide in 1941. Their relationship—a handful of years marked by towering devotion and devastating sorrow while Europe toppled into war—became the defining motif in Fisher's writing about

food and love, notably in her 1943 memoir, *The Gastronomical Me.*
After a third marriage ended in divorce, Fisher had two daughters
to raise on her own. She and the children lived with her father in
Whittier, California, where she cared for him until his death in
1953, and then they moved to the Napa Valley. There she made
her home for the rest of her life, cooking and keeping house and
writing, though she traveled to Europe as often as her finances
permitted. By the time she died in 1992, she had published some
two dozen books and reams of journalism, and was widely acclaimed as the finest food writer the nation had ever produced.

Fisher spent many years of her life enmeshed in domesticity,
and for the most part she enjoyed it. In fact she relished nearly
everything about being female: She loved men, and raising children, and cooking for the people who flocked to her house. But it
was never easy for her to identify with other women. Too much
feminine timidity trailed them everywhere, too much coyness and
fraility. Fisher preferred to stand apart, even at the cost of splitting
herself in two. Time and again in her correspondence she referred
to her writing persona in the third person. "Do I marry M.F.K.
Fisher and retire with her-him-it to an ivory tower and turn out
yearly masterpieces of unimportant prose?" she wondered deject-
edly in a letter to her psychiatrist. On another occasion, during a
period when she was overwhelmed with family demands and un-
able to write, she became convinced that her career was over and
told her sister it was time to "hold a private funeral" for M.F.K.
Fisher. "The old girl is weak and gasping already, a genteel has-
been," she wrote despairingly. "If I killed off Fisher, professionally at least, how would it affect me emotionally? Could I create
enough other ways to satisfy my basically fertile nature . . . ?" In
this dark mood, contemplating a future without writing, she characterized M.F.K. Fisher as "genteel" to the point of dessication, a
female force drained of its fertility and left "weak and gasping."

When she feared her writing self was about to fade and die, that is, she associated that persona with femininity—the deadliest sort of ladylike femininity, the sort of femininity she had always been determined to avoid. Fisher's voice and vision, and her entrancing prose style, won accolades throughout her long career; but she was never certain it was she who deserved the praise. After all, M.F.K. Fisher was the one everybody thought was a genius.

Perhaps for this reason one of the recurring themes in the essays was M.F.K. Fisher's image as strangers perceived it—the image she conveyed when, for instance, she was traveling by herself. She liked to describe almost tenderly what an unusual and compelling figure she made, sitting alone in a restaurant or on board a plane, attracting curious stares from the people around her. They were curious because Fisher wasn't behaving like the other women or eating the way women usually ate. At a hotel in Mexico the other Americans felt "hurt and snubbed, and in a blind way angry at me" because she didn't want to spend an evening with them. She took a table by herself in the dining room, where guests were silently ingesting the horrible food prepared for tourists: "a tasteless *sopa de pasta,* a salad of lukewarm fish and bottled dressing, some pale meat. . . . I simply could not eat it." Meanwhile, strange and wonderful smells reached her, as if delicious food was being cooked somewhere in the kitchen but never carried into the dining room. Finally, a waiter took notice of her and whispered in her ear that there was one kitchen for Americans and another for the staff; he would bring her what the waiters were eating. Soon she was downing quantities of hearty, aromatic beans and dipping big tortillas into the bowl—"enough for three or four probably"—while the tourists obediently ate their pablum.

On another such occasion she stopped at a famous restaurant in Burgundy in the course of a long walk. The waitress automatically offered the foreigners' menu—"shoulder of lamb in the English style, with baked potatoes, green beans, and a sweet." M.F.K. Fisher looked appalled, and the waitress instantly recognized that a true eater had arrived. For Madame, the chef would send out his famous pâté, his little baked onions, pickled herring, *truite au bleu,* tiny potatoes . . . each dish sublime. There was another moment of truth when the waitress asked about wine, and Fisher promptly replied, "I think I shall drink a bottle of Chablis 1929—*not* Chablis Village 1929." The waitress was amazed. "For a second her whole face blazed with joy, and then subsided into a trained mask," wrote Fisher. "I knew that I had chosen well."

She always chose well. "I know what I want, and I usually get it because I am adaptable to locales," she explained once. "I order meals that are more typically masculine than feminine, if feminine means whipped-cream-and-cherries. I like good wines, or good drinkin'-likka, and beers and ales." This seriously pleasurable attitude toward food made people uneasy, she noted. "Women are puzzled . . . and jealous of the way I am served, with such agreeable courtesy, and of what I am eating and drinking, which is almost never the sort of thing they order for themselves." As for men, "I make it plain that I know my way around without them, and that upsets them." Like Betty Crocker, M.F.K. Fisher appeared before her public as a woman free and clear of crippling femininity, forever sporting that enviable sense of self-possession most often the birthright of men.

Fisher's reputation was based to a great extent on her writing about Europe, where food and sensuality had every reason to be tumbled together. In her most highly regarded essays, her narrator was swathed in romance or tragedy while encountering the luscious dishes of France or Switzerland. This was the M.F.K. Fisher who made American food-lovers swoon. Yet Fisher also wrote as a cook, publishing quantities of magazine journalism with recipes—

work she undertook largely for the income it provided. These pieces tended to be less heady than the European ones; often she wrote about growing up and making a home in California. The recipes, intended for ordinary cooks and written in standard format, reflected the honest, flavorful food she liked best. Oxtail stew, a good steak on the grill, spinach tart starting with two boxes of frozen spinach—no mysteries lurked about these dishes. They were practical, they were lucid, and they attracted relatively little attention from an otherwise devoted public. Her readers gladly worshiped M.F.K. Fisher as a culinary authority as long as she kept that sensuous prose swirling around a fragrant stew in Vevey or a cauliflower sprinkled with Gruyère in Dijon. But her aura dissipated the moment it touched the can of beets that went into Fisher's summer borscht. Even Fisher didn't have the literary clout to make plain American recipes into an object of desire.

There was simply no such thing as high-art American cooking, and there never had been. It could be delicious, it could be expensive, it could call for extraordinary skill, but American cooking just didn't breathe status and classical grandeur the way French cooking did. Traditional epicures permitted no other food to share the glory of French cuisine, while fledglings in gastronomy knew that with French food they were on safe as well as holy ground. James Beard was passionate and knowledgeable about the regional foods of his own country, yet even he couldn't work up much enthusiasm about some of the good-hearted home cooking he encountered outside his circle. Once he dined with old friends in the suburbs who served a Sunday-best meal in the American style—"a crown of lamb filled with mashed potatoes, green peas, a salad of avocado, tomato and lettuce with a sweet 'French' dressing, homemade strawberry ice cream and homemade coconut layer cake," he wrote to Helen Evans Brown. "Also homemade cinnamon bread with the dinner. No wine." He admired the cinnamon bread—in fact, he said it should have been the main course—but rued everything else. "Contrast that with luncheon yesterday at Baroque—just goujonettes of sole, with fried parsley, a little Chablis and a macaroon—delicious," he added. Compared with the simple, delicate French lunch, the all-American dinner was going to seem impossibly stodgy even if the dishes themselves were prepared perfectly. It was hardly surprising, moreover, that Beard found himself comparing home cooking with restaurant food. For all intents and purposes, American cooking was home cooking—an identity that amounted to a shortcoming almost by definition. No matter how excellent the steamed clams and the lemon meringue pie, a codified three-star restaurant cuisine for such foods did not exist. And if American cooking was home cooking, that meant it was women's cooking—a fatal association when the popular stereotype for women's cuisine was Harriet Hepplewhite, the Happy Housewife.

The French were troubled by no such inanity when it came to female culinary stereotypes. Happy Housewives were strictly an American problem. As far as the French were concerned, women might not be capable of true greatness in the kitchen, but in their own private realm these endearingly simple creatures could work culinary miracles from the humblest ingredients. How lovingly the gourmets evoked her, the farmwife whose greatest joy was to carry fragrant platters out to a long table under the vines at harvest time. Round and rosy-cheeked, her apron full of fresh leeks, this creature of untutored wisdom held the highest position available to women in French cuisine. So when sophisticated Americans went looking at midcentury for the finest in home cooking—home cooking, that is, with the best pedigree—they took their cues from the French. Sure enough, in the pages of *Gourmet* magazine they found a wise, rosy-cheeked French home cook named Clémentine Bouchard.

Clémentine worked for an American family called the Becks who spent a dozen years before World War II living in France. The family had grown devoted to the local food and wine, as well as to a French way of life centered on the delights of the table, so when the war forced them to return to the United States, they brought Clémentine with them. In their new home outside Boston, Clémentine continued cooking the wonderful food she knew so well, while Phineas Beck described her adventures and wrote up her recipes in a long-running serial published in *Gourmet*.

Readers quickly discovered that nothing Clémentine turned out could possibly be mistaken for American cooking even when the recipes had the same name. Her Blanquette de Veau, for instance, began with the making of a broth from pieces of veal simmered with onions and carrots. Then she mixed flour and butter, and added the broth to make a sauce, which simmered until it was reduced. She added the sauce slowly to a mixture of egg yolks, butter, and lemon juice, and heated it all gently until it thickened. Finally, she stirred in the pieces of veal, along with a few mushrooms. Right around that time Betty Crocker, too, was making what she called Blanquette of Veal: She browned veal steaks in hot fat, added a little vinegar, cooked them until they were tender, and served them with a white sauce to which sliced mushrooms had been added. "A French chef gave me this recipe. . . . It's wonderful," she confided to her readers. But if the food diverged wildly, the two women themselves had a great deal in common. Like Betty Crocker, Clémentine made a career in professional home cooking. Like Betty Crocker, she had amassed a tremendous amount of experience and information over the years. And like Betty Crocker, Clémentine was imaginary—a trait that assured her success, just as it did her colleague's.

Eternal French female that she was, Clémentine was a man. She was the creation of Samuel Chamberlain, a Boston artist and writer who really did live with his family in France and fall under the spell of that charmed way of life. When the war forced their return to America in 1939, Chamberlain's friend Earle MacAusland asked him to contribute to a new food magazine that MacAusland was planning, to be called *Gourmet*. Chamberlain became one of the mainstays of the magazine early on, appearing in the very first issue with an article about the food of Burgundy. His enormously popular running feature, "Clémentine in the Kitchen," began in the second issue. In 1943 the Clémentine stories and their recipes were published in book form, with an appendix of 106 additional recipes, and remained in print for the next four decades. Although the tale was a swirl of fact and fiction, nothing in the introduction or on the book jacket so much as hinted that this warm, engaging narrative was anything but a memoir. The book was illustrated with Chamberlain's own etchings of shops and neighborhoods in France and New England, and the new recipe appendix was called "Extracts from Clémentine's Notebook." The only obvious touch of fantasy was the author's pen name: Phineas Beck was a play on the French term *bec fin,* used to describe someone very discriminating about food.

Clémentine was everything Americans recognized as good and true in a French home cook: bright-eyed, pink-cheeked, "a demure and smiling little person" raised in a legendary wine-making family and brought up on her *grand-mère*'s superb *boeuf en daube.* At one level the serial recounted what happened when she, the very essence of France and its food, arrived in the land of cellophane and hot dogs. Her forays into the shops, her frustrated search for coffee with chicory, the dinner party so spectacular it propelled the family to the highest ranks of local society—all this Chamberlain described with affection in graceful, witty prose.

But the story he really wanted to tell was about France, which fell to the Germans shortly before he started writing. "Clémentine in the Kitchen" allowed him to wander back into the remembered past, which played just as prominent a role in the serial as did the American present. When he evoked the little town his family sadly left, with its pâtisserie and charcuterie, the strawberries and truffles and snails, the branches of tarragon perfuming the young roasted chickens, *Gourmet* readers with their own blissful memories of France could see and taste it all again. That was the place, he wrote, where the Beck family discovered "civilized living." France was where they learned to drink wine with their meals and to shudder at the combination of cranberry sauce with turkey. France was where their teenage daughter came to love snails, sheep's brains, and calf's head. His readers knew just what he meant. They were as homesick as he was even if they had never been to France. They longed for exactly the life the Becks had so treasured, the life this lucky family seemed to be re-creating in New England. They wanted mousse and caneton, they wanted charm and wine and children who liked pâté, and they wanted Clémentine.

It was all out of reach. Of course, American readers could try the recipes; and if they found carrots and strawberries as sweet as the ones in France, and sausages as rich and tangy, and if they could differentiate between "a good lump of butter," "a heaping teaspoon of butter," and "generous quantities of fresh butter," then Clémentine's wonderful cooking might be theirs. (More than forty years later, Chamberlain's wife, Narcisse, revised and expanded the recipe section for a new edition of the book, putting the instructions in the clear, precise format of American cookbooks. "Mr. Beck removed himself from this process of modernization; it was not at all close to his heart," she wrote. "He preferred a recipe written with resonance and uninterrupted by statistics.") But in most homes *Clémentine in the Kitchen* was less a cookbook than a wish book. Chamberlain poured into it his love for a time and place that could never be recovered, and readers brought precious, unrealizable fantasies of their own. If Betty Crocker's mission was to make her products and recipes accessible to every family with a newspaper or a radio, Clémentine's was to be caretaker for a dream. Betty Crocker was a source of practical information; Clémentine, the very embodiment of kitchen mysteries that only the French understood—and a highly select handful of American acolytes. Betty Crocker shared, sold, explained, offered, and persuaded. Clémentine kept her wisdom locked behind glass, like the jewel-encrusted crowns in a museum.

The success of *Clémentine in the Kitchen* inspired MacAusland to send Chamberlain back to France in 1949 for a gastronomic tour of the provinces. Chamberlain and his wife drove all around the country in a Peugeot, gathering the material for a series of knowledgeable and evocative travel articles. These appeared in *Gourmet* with recipes the Chamberlains had collected from French cookbooks or gathered from chefs they encountered on their trip. Three years later the travel stories and recipes were published as a book. Despite its heft—*Bouquet de France* was a 619-page hardcover—it accompanied numerous Americans on their long-awaited pilgrimages to the cradle of haute cuisine.

One of the Americans who hurried to buy a copy of *Bouquet de France* was a woman who had been living in France for years and was intensely curious about everything concerning French cooking. In fact, she was at work on a cookbook herself, a book meant to teach American housewives how to employ French culinary techniques in their own kitchens and prepare dinners as delicious as those in any French household. Her name was Julia Child, and she thought perhaps the Chamberlains' method of recipe writing could give her some tips as she tried to make this wonderful cuisine accessible. She opened *Bouquet de France*, studied the recipes, and grimaced. As far as she could tell, these instructions were going to make novice cooks hurl their sauté pans across the room in anguish and frustration.

Suppose, for example, that some eager new wife tried to make Escalope de Veau according to the directions given to the Chamberlains by a chef in Auvergne. The hapless cook would pound the veal slices and then try to do what the book instructed: "Cook them slowly in butter until the slices are tender and a fine golden-brown color on both sides." It was a recipe for nothing but failure, Child wrote in distress to a friend back home. "They won't brown if cooked slowly, butter has got to be just turning blond before meat is added, then browned quickly, the heat lowered. Etc." She was amazed to learn that *Gourmet* hadn't reviewed the recipes before publishing them. "The tragedy is, young brides will try out the recipes and conclude that only a genius can cook," she fumed.

Gourmet did not, in fact, test recipes as rigorously as the women's magazines did. Any reader who couldn't interpret a French chef's recipe didn't belong on *Gourmet*'s subscription list, as far as MacAusland was concerned. To him, great cuisine was all the greater for remaining the property of a fortunate few. He didn't even want *Bouquet de France,* which was published under the magazine's own imprint, to be sold indiscriminately in bookstores. His plan was to make the book available only from *Gourmet* itself, by mail order, and perhaps allow a few copies to be seen in the better bookshops.

Here was an approach to France and its food that Child knew all too well. She had met plenty of French gastronomes who felt just the way MacAusland did about their precious national resource, and she was fed up. The French had developed a splendid cuisine based on principles and techniques that made very good sense. Why not share it? Why not help everyone learn to eat well? Child had no patience with the notion that good cooking began with exclusivity. Later that year she went to a party, listened to a circle of Frenchmen discussing food, and came home in a rage. "At the party was a dogmatic meatball who considers himself a gourmet but is just a big bag of wind," she wrote to her friend. "They were talking about Beurre Blanc, and how it was a mystery, and only a few people could do it, and how it could only be made with white shallots from Lorraine and over a *wood fire*. Phoo." As Americans were just about to discover, Child had Betty Crocker's zeal for teaching, M.F.K. Fisher's love for food, and Clémentine's happy command of the kitchen. But unlike her colleagues who were most at home in the imagination, living on a carefully constructed borderline between genders, Julia Child was real—and every inch of her six-foot frame was exuberantly female.

Chapter 6

Now and Forever

Julia Child and Betty Friedan sprang up simultaneously as national icons. The French Chef *began its long run on public television in February 1963; eight days later,* The Feminine Mystique *was published. There was no lag time; an audience was waiting for both. The message they conveyed went straight to women's hearts and into women's history.* (Photo of Betty Friedan used by permission of the Schlesinger Library, Radcliffe Institute, Harvard University. Photo of Julia Child by Paul Child, 1965. Used by permission of the Schlesinger Library, Radcliffe Institute, Harvard University.)

THE NAME OF the show had to have immediate appeal. It had to have at least one French word. And it had to be short—preferably no more than three words—so that it would fit into a column of television listings. Eventually the three shows that made up the pilot were aired under a tentative title; but it didn't satisfy the whole team, and ideas continued to fly about the station.

Cuisine Magic?
Cooking Chez Vous?
Kitchen Francaise?
Savoir Faire?
French Cuisine at Home?
Cuisinavision?

Finally, six weeks before the series was scheduled to make its official debut, station manager Bob Larson sent a memo to everyone involved. "After having racked our collective brains for weeks to find a good alternative title for the French Chef we have decided that a good alternative title does not seem to be available. And since both Julia and Paul Child are extremely fond of the original title I have capitulated. Let us call it: THE FRENCH CHEF now and forever!"

His joyful baptism was prophetic. The moment Julia Child looked into a television camera and started to talk, Americans were smitten for good. Child had a charisma that blossomed with remarkable grandeur on screen, turning her into an authority figure who defied all the imagery the food industry had been promoting for decades. She was wholeheartedly in favor of taking the time and trouble that good cooking demanded, yet she wasn't a dowdy, old-fashioned grandmother and she positively gloried in the chance to plunge her hands into fresh, raw ingredients. What's more, she believed anybody could cook with distinction from scratch, and that's what she was out to prove. Among the women who tuned in to *The French Chef* that first season were many who had surrendered at least in part to the rust of indifference and industrialization that was creeping across American kitchens. Others were enthusiastic cooks, and some were the best in town. But they all needed a focal point for the ambitions and dissatisfactions that swirled confusingly around life at home. The old compass wasn't working; it was never clear anymore whether making dinner was an honor or an obligation or even a necessity. And if dinner went, what was left? You didn't have to cook Child's recipes to bask in the comfortable moral certainty she embodied. On television, at least, there was high pleasure and welcome clarity at the kitchen counter.

Child wasn't the first cooking teacher to take her skills to the screen, but she was the first who was able to exploit every inch of its potential. Cooking had been a staple on television since its early years, starting with a show called *I Love to Eat!* on NBC's fledgling network in 1946. *I Love to Eat!* starred James Beard, who greeted the public at 8:15 P.M., right after the Friday night boxing match at Madison Square Garden. Borden was the sponsor, and the announcer was Elsie the Cow. Beard was not very telegenic, and this particular experiment lasted less than a year; but it spawned many more cooking programs. By the early '50s local TV stations in all forty-eight states and Hawaii had developed cooking shows, mostly on daytime television. Often the cooks on camera were home economists from the area, and the women who sat down to watch between chores encountered a wide range of culinary styles true to the era. On WSPD-TV in Toledo, for instance, Dorothy Coon made gelatin eggs in emptied-out eggshells and displayed them on nests of shredded coconut, with salad dressing. Cordelia Kelly at WFMY-TV in Greensboro,

North Carolina, showed housewives how to brown squabs slowly in butter, then finish them with a poaching in wine. Breta Griem on WTMJ-TV in Milwaukee demonstrated a traditional hasenpfeffer calling for fourteen ingredients, including "wild cottontails"; Trudy McNall at WHAM-TV in Rochester made a layered salad with lemon gelatin, cream cheese, and apples; and in Omaha, Connie Cook of WOW-TV turned out a fresh peach pie topped with sour cream.

One of the most popular TV cooks of the '50s was Josie McCarthy, who had her own long-running show on NBC and also appeared on a daily program called *Hi Mom!* hosted by Shari Lewis and her puppet, Lamb Chop. McCarthy conveyed a relaxed, matronly presence; she enjoyed working with food and sharing her expertise, and she was comfortably at home on camera. "When your tutti-frutti is cool, you can if you like add a drop or two of pure vanilla," she remarked once, capably putting together a tutti-frutti sundae. "Vanilla always steps up the flavor of fruits. I didn't—I thought it was just fine the way I did it." McCarthy received thousands of letters and phone calls every year from viewers who had questions about recipes or needed help with a cooking problem; sometimes the calls started coming into the station even before the show was over. When she made Upside-Down Peach Cake, women picked up the phone on the spot to find out if they could use plums or apricots instead. The day McCarthy showed how to coat a ham with tinted mayonnaise and then apply decals to it, with pictures of birds and flowers, the calls didn't let up for hours.

Like the decorated ham, her recipes tended to be hearty and on the festive side—Roast Loin of Pork Floridian, Fish Teriyaki, Cottage Cheese Blintzes, Banana Split Salad—but she made a point of explaining any tricky steps in the cooking with special care. Describing a gravy she had thickened with a beurre manié, she recapitulated the procedure in the friendliest possible fashion. "Then we just dropped it into the gravy off of the tip of a spoon and stirred it through with a fork and let it boil up for about ten minutes, and the gravy thickened like that. Had you thought of that way of thickening the gravy?" When she made a custard pie on the air, she informed her viewers outright that they would never be able to keep the bottom crust crisp. The only solution to the problem of a soggy bottom crust was to bake the crust and the custard separately, in two pie plates the same size, then transfer the custard into the baked pie shell. "Yes! It can be done, and easily, too, with a little practice," she wrote in her 1958 cookbook, *Josie McCarthy's Favorite TV Recipes.* "I've done it on television several times with all eyes on me and under tension, with the Director's distracting speed-up cues. Just take a firm grip on your pans and yourself and let-er-fly!"

Familiar, all-American cooking was the rule in most TV studios. Poppy Cannon lost her job on NBC's *Home* show soon after her debut, apparently because the recipes—including quick vichyssoise and pots de crème—were too sophisticated for the audience NBC had in mind. "Maybe you can improve tastes, but gosh would somebody please tell me how to cook corned beef and cabbage without any smell?" complained an NBC executive in a memo a month after the show had its premiere. The only television cook to make a career as a public epicure was Dione Lucas, who had a series of programs on French cooking that started in 1946 and ran for a decade. She also wrote several cookbooks, along with running her restaurants and cooking school, and was a great favorite on the charity circuit. All over the country, women raised funds for schools, hospitals, and art organizations by presenting a Dione Lucas cooking demonstration or a series of classes. At the restaurant she was a widely recognized figure making omelettes in a pan she famously used for nothing else.

When she died in 1971, her omelette pan had not been washed in forty years.

The recipes she offered on television and in her public lectures were classics and often showstoppers—sole Joinville, eggs Benedict, chocolate roll, baked Alaska. Local newspapers reported on her visits, the recipes were widely reprinted, and in the mid-'50s she was the best-known spokeswoman in the country for fine French cooking. Yet her influence never ran very deep, perhaps because she wasn't a teacher at heart. Although her recipes were elaborate, she put little effort into making sure they were reliable and even less into conveying them in accessible fashion. Her skills were well polished, but her sensibility stopped there, as if the taste and texture of the ingredients and their interactions didn't interest her as much as the finale. "This one belongs to the Department of Utter Confusion," wrote a caustic reviewer in the New York Wine and Food Society's *Newsletter* when her *Cordon Bleu* cookbook came out. James Beard described her as "a great, great technician who doesn't know food." By the time her career disintegrated under the pressures of illness and business chaos, her name was known in many homes, but she had made little lasting difference in American kitchens.

Julia Child didn't resemble any of the TV cooks who came before her; indeed, she didn't resemble any of her culinary predecessors. They had all become food experts for the usual good reasons: either they loved food or they needed a job and found they were talented at this one. Child's impetus was different. She knew nothing about food, but she was in love with a man who relished great cooking, so she went barreling straight for it. Paul Child was helping to run the War Room for the Office of Strategic Services in Ceylon when he met Julia McWilliams, who headed the OSS Registry office there, in 1944. An artist and photographer who was nearly ten years older than she and far more worldly, he took his time falling in love with her. The rangy California girl was friendly and high-spirited, he thought, but not his type; the loves of his life tended to be intellectual, chic, and sophisticated. For Julia the differences between them were tonic. Paul lived with all his senses blazing, and he woke her up in dozens of ways, body and soul. She was ready for a future with him, and she was determined to have it. Chic was beyond her—she was too tall and too forthright—but she could certainly go to work on intellectual and sophisticated. And on food. After the war, their mutual plans still uncertain, Paul went back to Washington, D.C., and the State Department while Julia returned home to Pasadena, California. She started reading politics and Henry Miller, she wrote to Paul and said she loved him, and she threw herself into learning to cook.

Many years later Cecily Brownstone, food editor at the Associated Press, asked Child if she was a born cook. Child said no. She wasn't being modest; anybody who witnessed—or tasted—her first efforts in the kitchen would have rapidly agreed. At first she tried to teach herself at home, but it was frustrating to bushwhack her way through one dish after another. She never knew whether she would find success or failure when she opened the oven door, and worst of all, she didn't know why this recipe worked and that one didn't. She wanted lessons. Two Englishwomen, Mary Hill and Irene Radcliffe, ran a cooking school in Beverly Hills, and for several months Child took classes there three times a week. Her progress was erratic—a duck exploded in the oven when she neglected to prick the skin; a very French dish of brains in red wine came out an appalling mush—but as she often remarked in the years following, Paul married her anyway. After the wedding they moved into a house in Washington, and her experiments in the kitchen racketed on. Sometimes dinner was burned, sometimes they sat down at 10:00 P.M.—none of it came easily to Child, especially because she was tackling the most elaborate recipes she could find in *Gourmet* and other magazines. The whole process was frustrating and bewildering. She could read, she could follow a recipe, so why wasn't she more successful in the kitchen? Why so many disasters?

Not until they moved to Paris, where Paul had been posted to the United States Information Service, did she start to figure it out. If Paul had been her first great awakening, France was the second. She signed up for French lessons at Berlitz right away and surrendered herself to the city, wandering and discovering and exclaiming and tasting in a constant rapture. Everything sparked a response in her, from the streets and cafés to the last scraps of conversation at night with a crowd of French and American friends. And every day at meals and in the markets she was swept with new revelations about food. The hundreds of cheeses, the piles of fresh produce, the sausages and fish and wines were a school that never closed, and she the ravenous student. Clearly, she had no instinct for cooking. But just as clearly, she was blessed with a powerful instinct for food—an appetite, a palate, and a passion. In the fall of 1949, shortly after she turned thirty-seven, she took up a rigorous course of lessons in the elements of French culinary technique at the Cordon Bleu. This time she learned to cook.

Learning to cook at the Cordon Bleu meant breaking down every dish into its smallest individual steps and doing each laborious and exhausting procedure by hand. In time Child could bone a duck while leaving the skin intact, extract the guts of a chicken through a hole she made in the neck, make a ham mousse by pounding the ham to a pulp with a mortar and pestle, and turn out a swath of elaborate dishes from choucroute garnie to vol-au-vent financière. None of this came effortlessly, but she could do it. She had the brains, the considerable physical strength it demanded, and her vast determination. Most important, she could understand for the first time the principles governing how and why a recipe worked as it did. To be able to approach the kitchen with this kind of intellectual clarity made all the difference to a cook like Child, who lived right up front in her consciousness, not way back in any misty recesses of dream or instinct. Paul was the poet; she—as they discovered later—was the performer.

By the time she made her way to the Cordon Bleu, Child had decided that cooking would be her career. Women were barred by custom from the kitchens of the haute cuisine restaurants of France, and as a foreign service wife she had no thought of such a future anyway. Her goal was to teach, to be the very teacher she herself had been looking for without knowing it. She spent two days in the Cordon Bleu's amateur-level class, then insisted on transferring to a professional course, where she was the only woman. After six months of lessons she worked on her own for a year, studying with a chef and attending demonstration classes as well as practicing endlessly at home. The Childs' kitchen filled up with knives, whisks, pots and pans, and all the other tools necessary for classic French cuisine, including a huge mortar and pestle they lugged home from the Marché aux Puces. Meanwhile, she joined the Cercle des Gourmettes, a gastronomic club for women, and became good friends with two of the other gourmettes: Simone Beck and Louisette Bertholle. Among the three of them they had abundant energy and ambition, and soon started to talk about opening a school together. In January 1952 they did just that, right in the Childs' kitchen. L'École des Trois Gourmandes was tiny—only a handful of pupils could fit into the kitchen—but rigorously organized around technique as the most important body of information that could be transmitted to an aspiring home cook. Child was adamant that the recipes used in class be absolutely reliable, and she tested every one of them for what she called "scientific workability." Teaching was exhilarating, and she was deeply sorry to leave the school and Paris when Paul was transferred to Marseilles a year later.

But she had a new kind of teaching project at hand, and she took it with her when she moved. Her two friends had been working for some time on a book of French recipes aimed at an American readership, and they had produced six hundred pages. Child agreed to help by straightening out the English and started with the sauce recipes—which she couldn't resist testing. Nothing worked. By her standards the recipes needed a complete overhaul, especially since they were intended for American kitchens. At length the three women decided to work together on a fresh approach to the whole project. They wouldn't just amass recipes; instead, they would produce a technique-based manual for American home cooks. As Child said later, they wanted to write a book that would "break down French cooking into some kind of logical sequence—to make cooking make sense, in other words." Their own skills and experience would underlie everything that went into the book, but their goal wasn't to codify traditional procedures for their own sake, it was to help ordinary women prepare good food. The idea was to bring classical techniques up to date and introduce such appliances as the blender whenever possible—in short, to make demands on the tradition that had never been made before. Then they would lay out the information so precisely and comprehensively that a woman opening the volume could actually learn to cook. For Child it would be a hardcover version of her own culinary enlightenment, the approach to cooking that had redeemed and inspired her as she labored in the name of love.

For the next seven years, while she and Paul were transferred from city to city, the women tested and tasted and experimented and argued, working together whenever Child could get back to Paris, and by mail the rest of the time. In 1960 the manuscript was accepted by Knopf, and Child embarked on a year of revising and editing. Their editor at Knopf was Judith Jones, an accomplished cook herself who knew French food very well and shared with Child a determination to make this book usable. There was no mention in the soufflé chapter of tying a paper collar around the dish to help the soufflé rise high, she wrote to Child. Why not? "This is a lot of balderdash, the paper collar stuff, I think, and a damned nuisance, and it is not done in France," Child explained briskly. "Dione Lucas & those people use the paper collar, and to hell with them—why complicate things." Her point of view was always that of the woman in the kitchen, desperate to cook and dependent on having good information at hand. Child became furious when she opened a book or magazine and found a recipe written so carelessly that the cook was bound to fail. An article in *Gourmet* purporting to describe cooking methods for suprêmes de volaille—boned and skinned chicken breasts—left her exasperated. "In a variation, 'Add more butter and 2 TB meat glaze to the sauté juice', they say," she fumed in a letter to Jones. "That shows the breast is overcooked, as there should be no juices. . . . In another variation the cook is directed to 'reduce the sauce by ½ and stir in 1 cup heavy cream mixed with 2 egg yolks and simmer without boiling.' And when the egg yolks scramble the cook thinks she's the dumb one. *Ye gods!*"

Mastering the Art of French Cooking was published with all the honor due a major book from Knopf in the fall of 1961. The reviews were excellent, there was a gratifying burst of publicity all across the country, and the professional food world acknowledged a new star in Julia Child. What nobody knew for sure was whether everyday homemakers in the nation that invented the TV dinner would buy the book. The food industry had been proclaiming the death of traditional cooking for so long that most people, even traditional cooks, were sure they had been to the funeral. Everyone who cared about food had a grim story to relate about the hostess who passed canapés of curried peanut butter topped with shrimp or the neighbor who made Snow Ball Sandwiches for a bridge party (two-layer circular sandwiches, one layer of tuna fish and the other of crushed pineapple mixed with whipped cream, the whole frosted with cream cheese and garnished with a cherry). Food editors at the women's magazines were receiving complaints from subscribers who found the recipes overly long and complicated, and at *McCall's,* the widely respected Helen McCully had just been fired for being "too gourmet." Yet there did seem to be women out there who hadn't heard the news that they weren't cooking anymore. Suburban dinner parties in the Midwest featured veal parmigiana, stuffed cornish hens, apricot mousse, and cheesecake, all made from scratch. *The James Beard Cookbook,* which came out in 1959, was on its way to selling half a million copies, and *The New York Times Cook Book,* published in 1961, would become a classic as well. Both of these substantive manuals were aimed unapologetically at home cooks who liked spending time in the kitchen. Child, who regularly sent trial recipes to friends as she was working on her book, had come to believe that it would appeal to anyone who took food seriously. "Men like our recipes as well as women, young marrieds go for them, and maturer types who have a bit of leisure," she told the Knopf publicity department. "Den mothers, the TV-dinner crowd, and meat-and-potato families do not go for it at all."

Six months after publication about 12,500 copies of Child's book had been sold, and it was moving out of bookstores steadily at the rate of 40 to 100 copies a week. This was a respectable showing, though hardly a dazzling one. Beard's book, which had the advantage of simpler recipes and more familiar food, had sold 150,000 copies the first nine months it was out. But in August

1962, the Book-of-the-Month Club decided to make *Mastering the Art of French Cooking* a dividend selection. Orders for 6,000 copies came in right away, a response considered quite impressive by the BOMC, which predicted overall sales of about 12,000 copies. By the following January, to the amazement of BOMC officials, more than 35,000 orders were in, and by the end of the year the club had printed 84,000 copies. Child's book was the most popular dividend the BOMC had ever offered. Clearly, there was more of a market for Navarin Printanier and Pâté à Choux than the publishing experts had suspected, though how many of these curious home cooks were actually tackling the recipes could not be known. At any rate, the startling success of Child's book at the BOMC was the first hint that at least some mainstream home-makers were less narrowly fixated on canned soup casseroles than the food world had long assumed.

But nobody was prepared for the overwhelming response to *The French Chef*. When Paul left the foreign service in 1961, the Childs had settled into a big old clapboard house in Cambridge, Massachusetts, right outside Harvard Square. They liked Cambridge for its congenial people, its academic atmosphere, and its liberal politics; and they were still unpacking when *Mastering the Art of French Cooking* was published that fall. A few months later Boston's local public television station invited her to talk about the book on a show called *I've Been Reading*. Merely talking about food sounded a little bleak to Child, especially on TV—why not cook? She brought a dozen eggs, a copper bowl, a whisk, and a hot plate, and made an omelette. Viewers loved it, and twenty-seven of them wrote to WGBH to say so. Such a flock of enthusiastic letters was rare for a new station, especially one laboring in the sober realm of what was still called "educational television." Right away, station officials asked Child to work up a plan for a whole series of cooking shows.

"I think we could make an interesting, adult series of half-hour TV programs on French cooking addressed to an intelligent, reasonably sophisticated audience which likes good food and cooking," she wrote in a memo to WGBH. "'How to make cooking make sense' is an approach which has always interested me, and I would like to expound on it publicly." Over the summer of 1962 they taped three pilot programs and aired them, reaping another impressive round of fan mail, though Child herself could see how much she had to learn. "I find that the TV technique is far different from public demonstrations in that everything for TV must be done deliberately, under-waterly," she wrote to James Beard that summer. "Naturally, as our educational TV is short of cash, we had practically no rehearsals, and no playbacks. Had I at least seen a playback, I could have improved. The first to be shown was 30 minutes on omelettes, with Mrs. C. swooping about the work surface and panting heavily; I had put much too much into the program. The next, on Coq au Vin, was much better. The third . . . is on soufflés; I expect it to fall between the 2. Perhaps if I did 20 more, I'd get on to the technique a bit better."

With the help of Paul and an astute team at WGBH, she did get on to TV technique, or, more accurately, they managed to shape the technique around her particular skills, including an instinct for comedy and an ability to deal adroitly with the unexpected. The team also made sure that Child's mission—to make cooking make sense—was built into the structure of every program. "We have licked the timing quite well, by having the show broken up into sections, such as *Browning Chicken,* 5 minutes. Then, when the floor manager flashes me up the section and the timing, and then follows with cards saying '3' (3 minutes), etc., it works out pretty well," she wrote to William Koshland at Knopf, after taping the first eleven shows of the series. "All the material within each section, however, has to be pretty ad-lib, as one never quite knows what's going to happen on the stove. The least one can say is that the shows will have a definite informality and spontaneity! We'll soon know whether they are going over, I guess."

The first show was aired the next day—not during the morning or afternoon, when most cooking shows were scheduled in order to reach housewives, but at 8:00 P.M., a time slot dignified by the presence of men at home. Ten days later the station had received two hundred letters; by the time the fourth show was aired, another four hundred had arrived. Nothing in the short history of WGBH-TV had ever gone straight to the heart of an audience the way *The French Chef* did, and the other public TV stations promptly took notice. By the fall of 1963, half a dozen stations had picked it up; a year later two dozen more signed on; and by 1965 nearly all eighty-five stations in the network were carrying *The French Chef*. Sales of *Mastering the Art of French Cooking* shot up right alongside the TV audience numbers. In the summer of 1963, bookstore sales were about six hundred copies a month; a year later they had increased to about a thousand a month, and by October and November 1964, they were up to some four thousand copies a month. Whether or not the book was reaching den mothers and TV-dinner families, it was certainly making its way to a wider sphere of home cooks than Child had ever anticipated. "I find the book has been bought here by many non-chic types, such as the fishman's mother, the supermarket's checker-outer, etc., which is a good sign," she wrote to Koshland, adding that "none of these people I have known at all, which is good."

The chic as well as the "non-chic," anxious cooks and experienced cooks, working wives and full-time homemakers—they all watched *The French Chef*. Mail poured in to every station carrying the show as soon as it went on the air.

"I have tried a number of your recipes and we all (my husband, six children and myself) want them again. I like all the 'why' and 'wherefores' that you include."

"You make it look so easy. I used package piecrust but now I make my own and what a difference—flakier and better."

"Please continue the French Cooking Series with Julia Child on evening time. Thousands of new working housewives can enjoy this fine half hour at night and learn the fine points of cooking."

"Thank you for presenting a program interesting to the working woman who can be domestic only evenings and weekends."

"I go to business and of course do not have the time to spend on such luxurious cookings, but hope someday to have the time *and patience* to try some of your cookeries."

"We love to watch you cook—myself especially—with your mouth-watering recipes—positively *'smell' them cooking!* . . . And best of all you are not afraid to taste as you cook—to me that's cooking!"

They could smell the cooking, they could taste her passion for the kitchen. What Child had mastered was the art of American television. Nobody who had ever cooked on camera—nobody who had ever appeared on television in any starring capacity—conveyed such a striking image of unaffected good nature. The great performers on early TV, such as Lucille Ball and Sid Caesar, stood out for the way they brilliantly packaged their talents for the medium. Child's gift was different: She created no roles, not even the role of Julia Child. That's not to say that she didn't play to the camera—she was a tremendous ham, as she herself often remarked—but the persona she beamed around the country was in fact her own personality, biggest and brightest when it leaned toward the camera, like a rose toward the sun. Cooks and their families alike were enthralled by her buoyant enthusiasm and the glamorous food she pulled from the oven and displayed with a flourish. Standing behind the counter with a knife in hand, about to tackle a shallot or a whole pig, she exuded pleasure, confidence, and class—traits that Americans associated with the dining room, perhaps, but rarely with life in the kitchen.

Only Irma Rombauer, whose wit came through jauntily in the early editions of the *Joy of Cooking,* had made an impression on home cooks that was akin to Child's; but without television as a magnifier, Rombauer had to win an audience one housewife at a time. As for Beard, though his books sold well, they never conveyed his personality because he didn't write them himself. He did make many public appearances with great success, but throughout his career he was far more influential as a friend, colleague, and teacher than he was as a mass-market personality. Among the culinary authorities who preceded Child, only Betty Crocker reached more people, more powerfully, but by the 1960s her once-commanding presence was diminishing as she reverted to trademark status. And her message as well as her food diverged sharply from Child's. Both of these figures aimed to evoke the social and emotional rewards of good home cooking, but Betty Crocker promised she could make cooking easy, while Child promised she could make the cook strong. When the volume of mail became so enormous that Child had to answer many queries with form letters, she composed one especially for beginning cooks. "Do not lose heart, and do not think you are inept," she told them feelingly. "Cooks are made, geniuses are born, and you can learn to cook with the right instruction—especially if you are lucky enough to be married to someone who loves good food as that will always inspire you."

Despite her concern for nervous beginners, Child never explicitly directed her teaching to women. She always referred to her audience as "home cooks" and loved hearing from men who watched the program. Her own coming-of-age as a cook had necessarily taken place on the female side of the French food world, with the other gourmettes, but during those years in Paris she was affected far more profoundly by the food than by the misogyny. "It wasn't until I began thinking about it that I realized my field is closed to women," she remarked nearly a decade after leaving Europe. From the start of her TV career she aimed to attract a male audience, hence the evening time slot; and whenever an interviewer asked what she thought about men who cooked, she lavished praise on them. Nothing would help to resuscitate the art of cookery in America faster than bringing men into the kitchen, she believed, just as male participation assured that cooking would always enjoy high status in France. "It's good to know there are some enthusiastic men at the stove these days; men always have more daring and imagination than women—even if I do say so," she wrote in response to an early fan letter from a male viewer. Child herself identified most contentedly not as a woman but as the female half of a couple. Paul had been the first gastronome she knew, and falling in love with him had sparked her career. Once he left the foreign service the two of them became, in effect, Julia Child. He was manager, photographer, food stylist, lackey, and guru; he went everywhere with Child and shaped her thinking as well as her life's work. Her happiness and success flowed from their partnership, and it was as Paul's partner that she viewed the world.

To the audience, however, Paul was invisible, and the laughing giant in the kitchen was a woman. These viewers—and most of them were women since it was, after all, a cooking show—had never seen a female culinary authority approach her work the way Child did. They had been watching television and reading magazines for years; they expected to be addressed as if they were slow-witted, especially on domestic subjects, yet Child never talked down to them. On the contrary, she focused their gaze upward, as if the most exacting culinary standards were there for a reason and the whole, wonderful point of home cooking was to meet them. Her program dislodged truisms and preconceptions that had been welded into place for more than half a century, perhaps ever since the adjective *dainty* began showing up as the highest praise for a woman's cooking. There was nothing dainty about Julia Child and nothing stereotypically feminine about her kitchen, though it was firmly located in the realm of the senses. On this program the cook stood up tall and proud, and women's cuisine burst its boundaries at last.

Just eight days after the French Chef made her official debut on television, another woman stepped before the public with a new gospel for homemakers. Her name was Betty Friedan, and what she wanted to cook up was a radical redefinition of womanhood. As it happened, *The Feminine Mystique* was published on February 19, 1963, precisely when the very women Friedan wanted to reach were falling under the spell of a six-foot home cook who thought nothing of devoting two or three days to making cassoulet. Now, suddenly, an argumentative feminist was all over the news urging housewives to take themselves seriously, use their brains, and forget such pointless distractions as china painting and fancy cookery. In their different ways both Child and Friedan came across as larger than life, Child via the screen and Friedan via her electrifying words. Each one made an immediate impact and quickly amassed a following; each one proved to be so profoundly influential that she was credited with starting a revolution. Child put the kitchen at the center of home life, while Friedan put women at the center of their own lives, but there was more overlap than conflict in the huge welcome each received from the public. Homemakers read *The Feminine Mystique* for the same reason they watched *The French Chef*: They had been waiting for a long time, and they were hungry.

During the years leading up to Julia Child's appearance on television, American women made it increasingly clear that they were rejecting the idea of full-time domesticity as a life's work. The percentage of married women with jobs had been growing steadily since 1948; in 1960, nearly 40 percent of all households with school-age children had a mother in the workforce. Most employed women held clerical, factory, or service jobs, and many worked part-time, but only in the most affluent circles was it unusual for married women to bring home a paycheck. As the ranks of employed women expanded in the postwar era, they included more and more middle-class wives—women whose counterparts in past generations had rarely worked outside the home because they didn't need to and weren't expected to. Among married women with school-age children, more than 40 percent were working in 1957 even though their husbands earned $4,000 to $5,000 a year, the average wage. More than a quarter were working even though their husbands made $7,000 to $9,000. The trend was unmistakable: Women who could afford to choose between work and homemaking were beginning to choose work.

In the midst of this unsettled environment, as women's preference for paychecks was growing more and more visible, one of the most talked-about women in America was a generic creature who emerged in the press around 1960 and became known as the trapped housewife. "I don't feel like *me* anymore!" exclaimed the author of an article that ran in *Good Housekeeping,* a woman who described herself as "trapped at home" with nothing but a fussy baby and her housework to fill the tedious days. *Newsweek* examined the phenomenon in a cover story called "Young Wives with Brains"; *The New York Times* declared "Former Co-eds Find Family Routine Is Stifling Them"; and *Time* made "The Suburban

Wife" a cover subject and assigned an "expert" to report the story ("He is married to one"). *Redbook* commissioned a study on "Why Young Mothers Feel Trapped," and then invited readers to send in their own trapped-housewife narratives. Some twenty-six thousand responded, and the magazine published one every month for the next two years.

Like most of the women who came to life in magazines over the decades—the rapturous bride, the glowing mother, the brave patriot of the home front, and the happy homemaker—the trapped housewife was very much a media invention. Her vital statistics alone placed her in a tiny minority: college-educated, married to a rising young manager or professional, big house in the suburbs, several pretty children. But she spoke for many more women than those in her fantasy neighborhood when she talked about the intense boredom of housework, the pressure to be a flawless wife and perfect mother, how she resented her husband for his freedom and snapped at her children for their demands, and most of all how she was lost in a swamp of guilt and confusion. Magazines ran story after story about the trapped housewife because their readers responded avidly to the image, some with disapproval but most with recognition and relief. "I am so sick of being told I should want to be 'feminine' and enjoy the easy life my husband labors to give me," wrote a *Good Housekeeping* subscriber in 1960. "I don't want an easy life built on somebody's sweat. I want to be treated as *somebody* in my own right—because I am."

Two years after *Redbook* ran the story "Why Young Mothers Feel Trapped," the magazine reported on a new, bright side to the crisis. Among the letters and stories generated by the first article were many from women who said they had suffered the same problems but triumphed over them. "Most people solve their problems by arriving at a moment of truth," the editor noted, "a sort of perceptive 'click' that tells them that it is time to stop emoting and to start coping." A wide range of "click" solutions appeared in this second story, which the magazine called "I Don't Feel Trapped Any More." One woman threw out everything in the house that needed ironing except her husband's shirts and then signed up for ballet lessons. Others took up bowling, mountain climbing, gymnastics, or square dancing. Some persuaded their children to do more chores around the house, some took long walks or drives by themselves, and many made time for "creative activities" such as baking bread or painting. "These, then, are some of the many ways in which enterprising young mothers have freed themselves from 'that trapped feeling,'" the story concluded approvingly. Despite the number of women who were solving their problems by going out to work, *Redbook* and other magazines hesitated to promote such a step. They put a greater emphasis on purely domestic avenues of escape—gentle, spiritual solutions to women's distress that wouldn't offend readers who were proud of their mothering and homemaking. Often the stories quoted Anne Morrow Lindbergh, who remained the model for well-tempered protest.

And that might have been the end of trapped housewives, at least as a media fad, if a freelance journalist named Betty Friedan hadn't taken them up as her cause, applying furious energy and massive research to a study of women at midcentury. Her first published piece on the subject was a *Good Housekeeping* story that ran in 1960 called "I Say: Women Are *People* Too!" Under a picture of Friedan, the magazine described her as an author, suburban housewife, and mother of three. "It is not easy to put into words a feeling and a problem that women find harder to talk about than almost anything else—including sex," the article began. "Essentially, this feeling or problem is a strange stirring, a dissatisfied groping, a yearning, a search that is going on in the minds of women." Three years later "the problem that has no name" had become a phrase known nationwide. It was the title of the first chapter in *The Feminine Mystique,* and millions of women instantly recognized the dissatisfaction and the search that Friedan was describing.

Friedan was indeed an author, housewife, and mother, but she was also a hard-driving public intellectual with a mission that burned brighter than any home fire. Raised in Peoria, she went to Smith and graduated in 1942 as a psychology major with a flock of prizes and academic awards. Her politics were already firmly in hand: In the course of her four years at Smith she had become a prominent, outspoken campus radical with a strong interest in the rights of workers and women's equality. She spent a year at Berkeley in graduate school, studying psychology, and quickly won a fellowship so prestigious that Berkeley had never before found a student worthy of it. In a moment of personal crisis, aware that her success would alienate her then-boyfriend, she turned down the fellowship and dropped her pursuit of a graduate degree entirely. Years later this incident would become a cautionary tale at the crux of her life story, but in recounting it she tended to leave out what happened next—namely, that she discovered her true calling. Friedan was a fine scholar, but it's doubtful that life in the ivory tower would have satisfied her for very long. After Berkeley, she followed her politics to New York and a career in the labor movement, where she was an astute and committed journalist for the next nine years.

Arriving in New York in 1943, she began writing for Federated Press, a left-wing news agency that supplied articles to progressive and union newspapers, and later took a job at *UE News,* published by the United Electrical, Radio and Machine Workers of America. Her stories were sharp and colorful, tackling all the issues she found most pressing: the dangers of corporate greed, the importance of progressive tax laws, and the fight on numerous fronts for blacks, Latinas, migrant workers, and women workers. In a thirty-nine-page pamphlet called "UE Fights for Women Workers" she pointed out how the same corporations that pictured women so becomingly in advertisements for electrical appliances were busy exploiting women workers on the factory floor. She went on to discuss equal pay, sex discrimination, and the extra burden borne by black women. During these years Friedan and other women writers of the left were deeply involved in causes that would still be viewed as radical decades later.

With the rise of McCarthyism, however, the left wing of the labor movement was crippled, and many of the progressive initiatives that Friedan had supported so ardently disintegrated. Male union officials were backing away from feminist issues, sometimes because they feared women's concerns such as equal pay and child care made the labor movement vulnerable to red-baiting, and sometimes because the male leadership never took women's needs seriously in the first place. In 1952, UE was forced to cut back on staff and decided to fire two women, including Friedan. Married and pregnant with her second child, she appealed to her union, the Newspaper Guild, but it refused to help her. Her colleagues on the left had no interest in Friedan any longer—a rejection she never forgot. Meanwhile, voices like hers were growing quieter and quieter as McCarthyism spread its tentacles.

The next ten years were the ones that became the basis of her life story as she often recounted it later: I, too, was a trapped housewife in the '50s. Friedan was indeed at home with two and then three children, her husband was building up a career in advertising, and they lived in the suburbs. But staying home for Friedan was hardly synonymous with homemaking or even child care. She was a rabble-rouser by nature, with a zeal for social justice and community organizing. Wherever they lived she became the loudest, most demanding, and often the most effective local activist around. And she continued working, albeit at home as a writer. They needed the money, and she would have worked under any circumstances, because work was fundamental not only to her sense of self but to her sense of human dignity. She threw herself into her freelance career with all the determination she brought to her work in the labor movement, eager to master the formulas and make a name for herself.

For women writers the money was in mainstream women's magazines, which wanted bright, confident voices and optimistic messages that readers could take to heart. In some ways the requirements weren't too different from those of the labor press. Friedan transferred her skills quite handily and broke into a number of major magazines including *Charm, Redbook, Cosmopolitan, Mademoiselle, Parents,* and *Good Housekeeping*. She was full of ideas and turned out profiles of successful women in various professions, stories about women who worked together to improve their neighborhoods and towns, articles about marriage and social issues, and even a major science story that ran on the cover of *Harper's,* "The Coming Ice Age." Her pieces tended to lose much of their personality and most of their politics in the editing process, but she learned a great deal about how to package her thinking for a wide audience.

In 1957, Friedan's college class had its fifteenth reunion, and she put a considerable amount of time into planning and writing a lengthy questionnaire for her Smith classmates. Her own career was going well enough, but she certainly hadn't lived up to the promise of her brilliant academic achievements—what about other women's lives? Were they using their minds? Were they disappointed with their choices? Was domesticity enough for them? The answers indicated that her classmates were definitely experiencing frustration with the limits imposed on them by family responsibilities, and many found homemaking an irritant rather than any sort of creative or intellectual challenge. But they derived a great deal of satisfaction from volunteer and political activities, and those who wished to work outside the home were either doing so or planned to start when their children were older. Overall, they felt positive about their lives, and if significant numbers of them were clawing at the walls of their domestic prisons, they didn't say so in the questionnaire.

According to Friedan, it was the responses to this questionnaire that inspired her to undertake the research culminating in *The Feminine Mystique*. As she explained in the preface to the book, the guilt she experienced as a wife and mother trying to sustain a career provided her first hint that "something is very wrong with the way American women are trying to live their lives today." Then, she wrote, when she studied what her classmates had written in the questionnaire, she realized that these women bore no more resemblance than she did to the modern American female defined by the media, the educational establishment, medical and psychiatric authorities, and the social sciences. "There was a strange discrepancy between the reality of our lives as women and the image to which we were trying to conform, the image that I came to call the feminine mystique," she wrote. "I wondered if other women faced this schizophrenic split, and what it meant." Plainly, this analysis of the questionnaire was skewed by the conclusions she wanted to reach. But if her Smith classmates did not in fact play precisely the role she assigned them, her depiction of the feminine mystique and its influence rang true to millions of women—very likely including many in the class of '42.

Friedan spent five years at work on *The Feminine Mystique,* reading widely and conducting hundreds of interviews. What emerged in the book was a clear and gripping narrative of how American women, climbing steadily toward equality since the 1920s, stopped short in the postwar era and traded their independence for a fairy tale. In Friedan's telling, the war, the atom bomb, and the Mc-Carthy era all encouraged Americans to retreat to the safety of home. Women led the way, relieved to give up the anxieties of war-time in favor of simple, traditional pleasures. At the same time a growing body of wisdom derived from psychology, sociology, and anthropology seemed to indicate that home was exactly where women belonged. In harmony with such social theories was the postwar economy, which for its success relied on women who be-lieved new products would solve their problems. Soon millions of bright, inquisitive women found themselves deep in suburbia, changing diapers and hemming curtains and trying desperately to believe they were happy. Their college diplomas were tucked away in the attic, along with their long-ago dreams of being a doctor or a poet. Now they were wondering if they should have majored in home economics instead of political theory. The Freudians must be right: Education was a dangerous distraction for a woman, threatening to lead her away from the only road to genuine fulfill-ment, namely marriage and motherhood. Besides, what else was out there for her to do? The women's magazines littering the cof-fee table never printed a word about women who found satisfac-tion in anything but homemaking. Maybe she needed to go on a diet, invent a glamorous canapé, change her shampoo, buy new fur-niture for the patio. Maybe that would get her closer to the rapture that the women in the ads were always experiencing.

Every source of wisdom, every expert, every image, and every idea that women encountered in the '50s commanded them to re-joice in domesticity, according to Friedan. The only alternative that was ever put forth was the cold and lonely misery of the working woman. And if women did work, sex discrimination made it impossible for them to advance in their careers. What's more, women who confined their lives and minds to the home were vital to the nation's prosperity. If they ever started asking themselves whether they actually cared about cleaner laundry, quicker casseroles, or redder lipsticks, the cash registers might stop ringing. "Somehow, somewhere, someone must have figured out that women will buy more things if they are kept in the under-used, nameless-yearning, energy-to-get-rid-of state of being housewives," she wrote.

At the heart of *The Feminine Mystique* was Friedan's analysis of the great female symptom of the era: "the problem that has no name." Women who thought they had done all the right things—marrying young, having babies, decorating cakes, and making Halloween costumes—were wondering why each day seemed so empty and pointless. They went to doctors and psychiatrists, and they took tranquilizers. But they didn't dare ask anyone, especially themselves, the terrifying question: "Is this all?" Instead, they had more babies, decorated more dens, and struggled to be as blond, thin, and sexy as the magazines advised them to be for maximum happiness. "If I am right, the problem that has no name stirring in the minds of so many American women today . . . is far more im-portant than anyone recognizes," wrote Friedan. "We can no longer ignore that voice within women that says: 'I want some-thing more than my husband and my children and my home.'" The whole point, as far as Friedan was concerned, was the word *more*. Yes, increasing numbers of women were working, but they were content or simply stuck in low-level jobs that made few de-mands on their intelligence. Friedan wasn't impressed by the fact that one-third of American women were employed, for that left two-thirds who were not; and there were "increasing millions of young women who are not skilled or educated for work in any profession," she emphasized. If a woman did have career ambi-tions, she was likely to be derailed by her husband, her psychia-trist, her boss, or the unyielding disapproval of her family and community. And work alone wasn't the answer: Friedan was determined to expand women's lives, not shore up the historic division between home and career and thus imply that women had to choose. Getting married and raising children were just as basic to Friedan's own sense of fulfillment as they were to most women's, and she made a point of quoting mothers who took far greater pleasure in their family responsibilities once Cub Scout meetings were not the entire focus of the day.

Nobody but Friedan expected the book to sell, and she was so certain she had a triumph on her hands that she went out and bought a wardrobe of photogenic new clothes. The publisher printed only three thousand copies, however, and did very little promotion until Friedan persuaded the company to hire an outside publicist and send her on the road to talk up her findings in person. She was right. By summer the book was in its seventh printing, and full-page ads were trumpeting "America's controversial best-seller!" Just how controversial the book was, however, is unclear. Perhaps people were arguing about it at home or around the watercooler, but in public the book seems to have encountered remarkably little opposition, apart from the occasional on-air fracas between Friedan and an interviewer.

Far more striking was the warmth of the welcome. Even some of the women's magazines threw open their pages to her, despite the fact that the book excoriated the whole genre. Portions of her manuscript had appeared earlier in *Good Housekeeping* and *Mademoiselle*; when the book was published, there were excerpts in *McCall's* and *Ladies' Home Journal,* both of which continued their coverage in later issues. Most major newspapers and magazines ran positive reviews, and so did a flock of smaller, local publications across the country. "The key phrase is 'human being' and it is through this wonderfully wide and deep lens that Mrs. Friedan looks," ran a typical comment in a Charlotte, North Carolina, paper. Reviewers who disliked the book most often took issue with Friedan's emphasis on paid work as fundamental to women's self-fulfillment. "Many women do not want careers, are not qualified, are genuinely happy in their domestic roles, or can still remember the grimness of the 9 to 5 routine they worked before marriage and want no part of it," commented a critic in *Mark*, "The Magazine of Southwestern Fairfield County." "The ones who really hanker usually make solutions for themselves by part-time work or satisfying volunteer work. . . . I think the problem of the thirty-plus woman and where she is going is just not that important." But Friedan was receiving sacks of letters from readers who told her they experienced a powerful moment of revelation reading the book, that it gave them the clarity and courage to change their lives. "I have squeezed my usual four-hours-a-day housecleaning into a slashing one-hour after breakfast—with identical results—so I could get back to The Book," wrote one of her fans. "I have felt the explosive Click of Something Beginning that has been dead for eight years." Pitching it as "controversial" certainly helped make *The Feminine Mystique* famous, but what sold the book was its message.

As several reviewers pointed out at the time, very little in Friedan's thinking was new. She herself noted that the nagging stresses she had summed up as "the problem that has no name" had first been identified in the trapped-housewife stories running in all the magazines a few years earlier. But she scolded the magazines for trivializing the subject, ignoring the fact that occasionally their analyses anticipated her own. In a *Good Housekeeping* article published four months before hers in 1960, for instance, a housewife reported that she had talked over her troubles and dissatisfactions with her minister and found he was familiar with such problems, for he knew many women in her situation. "When a woman with a trained, active mind is shut away in a house with children and housekeeping chores . . . she comes to feel that she has nothing to offer as an individual, and she begins to have nagging feelings of worthlessness," he explained—words of wisdom that Friedan herself might have offered.

Nor were the more sophisticated aspects of her analysis particularly new. Ever since the 1940s, women writers had been airing pointed, feminist critiques of a society bent on keeping its females docile and domestic. "We will never grow up as long as we must devote the major part of our time or a great amount of our individual energy being servants for our husbands and children," wrote the left-wing journalist and reformer Elizabeth Hawes in her 1943 book, *Why Women Cry*. At the end of *Why Women Cry* she published a kind of declaration of domestic independence, calling for an end to "a seventeenth-century division of labor" and a new social and economic pact based on equality. Five years later, in *Anything but Love,* she analyzed the immense cultural pressures on the American woman to be beautiful, to marry, and to make a life for herself as a consumer of new products. That same year Ruth Herschberger's *Adam's Rib* appeared, a witty, original, and tough-minded assault on the stereotypes that shore up conventional thinking about sex and sex differences. "Cleanliness is to be distinguished from non-cleanliness, but it is time to call a halt to the hygiene anxiety tormenting America," she wrote in a chapter discussing sexual puritanism. "We have nightmares of drowning in a sea of Listerine and Lysol with nothing but bars of Lifebuoy to which to cling. The motivation behind this is a preposterous sexual fastidiousness which has selected women as its lucrative scapegoat. Women are expected to carry the purity tradition for the entire race of mankind, leaving men free to enjoy themselves in the dirty work of war, politics, business, and animal satisfaction." Then in 1953 came the first American edition of Simone de Beauvoir's *The Second Sex*. This sweeping, erudite examination of the sexual hierarchy would become the intellectual foundation for generations of feminist thinkers and activists. Drawing on copious literary and scholarly sources, de Beauvoir described a cross-cultural worldview in which man defined himself as the absolute, the measure of all things, and woman as "the other"—inferior, diminished, alien, and existing only by virtue of her relation to man.

But none of these predecessors had the impact of *The Feminine Mystique.* In part it was an issue of timing: By 1963, ideas like Friedan's had been swirling through American culture for years, readying the ground for action. Even the political climate was starting to change as the civil rights movement made harrowing headlines and the nation's complacent view of itself was thrown into turmoil. Women active in the Democratic Party, including Eleanor Roosevelt, were so angry at President John F. Kennedy for appointing only a handful of women to government posts— and for the patronizing attitude he brought to the issue—that they pressured him to appoint a Commission on the Status of Women in 1961. Its first report was published two years later, and although the language was exceedingly mild, it did call for increased child care and an end to sex discrimination in employment. That was also the year Congress finally passed the Equal Pay Act, after rejecting it for two decades. But Friedan's success wasn't simply a matter of the ground being prepared. Unlike Hawes, Herschberger, and de Beauvoir, she knew how to write to reach a mainstream audience. She had put years into learning the formula for women's magazine articles, massaging her politics until they fit smoothly into the tone and format of *McCall's, Good Housekeeping,* and all the others. When she set out to write *The Feminine Mystique,* she was already good at telling a story. Most important, she knew just the right story to tell.

Friedan placed her own experience at the moral core of *The Feminine Mystique,* because as a smart journalist she wanted to give readers somebody with whom they could identify. But in order to be that person, she had to tell a version of her life that wrenched it far beyond recognition. She pointedly omitted her work as a vigorous and committed labor movement journalist and erased every sign of the powerful political convictions that had inspired her since college. Instead, she offered herself up as Exhibit A in suburban housewifery, the conscience-plagued mother trying desperately to write in the odd moments when she wasn't driving the children to swimming lessons or rushing to get dinner ready. Not that Friedan didn't love and enjoy her children, but there was nothing of the dabbler about her writing career, which she pursued zealously straight through her young-mother years.

By the same token, her portrait of American life at midcentury was far more compelling than it was accurate. She described the "disuse of, the resistance to higher education" among women, citing statistics that showed the proportion of women attending college dropping since the 1920s. "If the present situation continues, American women may soon rank among the most 'backward' women in the world," she wrote. But at least part of the reason for the dwindling percentages was the G.I. Bill, which greatly boosted the number of men in higher education. By the late '50s the proportion of women enrolling in college was on the rise. She also stressed the fact that college women in the '50s "showed no signs of wanting to be anything more than suburban housewives and mothers." It's true that a wedding-ring culture was widespread on campus during the decade, but that was far from the whole picture. When the Women's Bureau of the Department of Labor surveyed a sample of the eighty-seven thousand women graduating from college in 1956, it found that three-quarters of those surveyed were working full-time six months after graduation. Even among those who married, more than two-thirds were working. They were not particularly career-minded—more than half of those working expected to quit when they married or had children—but it was already clear from trends beginning in 1950 that women were going back to work once their children were older.

Similarly, Friedan dwelt at length on the happy-homemaker imagery she found throughout the culture, but ignored the constant and copious references to working women in magazines, newspapers, and advertising. She emphasized the pernicious influence of a 1947 book called *Modern Woman: The Lost Sex,* which advised women to forget their ambitions lest they turn into Lady Macbeth, unsexed and raving. Yet she never pointed out that ten years after this book was published, a significant body of sociological research began to emerge with very different findings about working women. In study after study examining women's well-being and that of their families, there were virtually no differences that could be traced to the mother's employment status. She did acknowledge that increasing numbers of women had been entering the workforce ever since the war years, but she made no mention of the labor union feminism she herself had witnessed in action. And despite the fact that she knew very well the impact of racism on black working women, she rarely looked away from the population she was scrutinizing most closely—white, educated suburban housewives. Friedan's assessment of American women in this period had a great deal of truth to it, and she backed it up with wider and more varied research than anyone except de Beauvoir had ever done. But she narrowed her perspective so sharply that the complexities and contradictions of the time fell away. Like all successful writers for popular magazines, she had studied and practiced the art of simplification, and the book was a masterpiece of the genre.

The Feminine Mystique became conventional wisdom almost as soon as it was published. Friedan's version of the '50s settled promptly into place as history itself. Her schema made sense: It gave the postwar years a plot that people could recognize. For the first time middle-class women were able to locate a usable past, a narrative that offered a coherent framework for their messiest ambitions and most damning imperfections. Women in the process of reimagining their place in the household and their relation to domesticity seized hold of *The Feminine Mystique* and treasured it for the clear hierarchy of values it spelled out. Marriage, children, home life—these were important, yes, but they weren't enough. What's more, there was no good reason why they should be enough. "The only way for a woman, as for a man, to find herself . . . is by creative work of her own," Friedan wrote. "There is no other way." Not everyone fell on this message with relief. Some women preferred the challenges of home life to those of the workplace and resented hearing that they were making the wrong choice. "I'm mad, I'm sick, I'm *tired* of being told by every article in every magazine that because I'm 'just a housewife' my husband finds me a dull companion, my children are not self-reliant, and my time and talents are being wasted on 'trivial unimportant matters,'" a subscriber wrote to the *Ladies' Home Journal* after it published a feminine mystique article by Friedan. "As for stretching my imagination and capabilities to the limit, my home and family demand far more than my former jobs." She signed it "One of those 'mindless drudges.'" But even women who rejected Friedan's analysis were moving, with everyone else, toward the world she was trying to invent.

Friedan believed ardently in work outside the home, but she also believed in the emotional sustenance uniquely associated with domestic life. She had a dream house: Everyone in the family contributed to its vitality, but nobody was expected to be one of the fixtures. Julia Child's dream house operated on much the same principle. They both nurtured the image of a world in which men and women sailed freely about the kitchen without bumping into sex roles. As their followers would learn in the course of the next several decades, domestic life was never going to shift from its ancient moorings in femininity until the workplace became as basic to women's lives as it was to men's. Even then, change would be slow; but of all the gender barriers in the house, the most fragile would prove to be the kitchen door. Child and Friedan maintained their stature over the years in part because they embodied for the public the very possibilities they so boldly envisioned: a future thrown open on all fronts to both sexes.

The revolutions that Child and Friedan would be credited with starting were well under way by the time the two women became famous: The ambitions and uncertainties that always fuel social and culinary progress had been churning out important changes for years. But a cause needs a conjurer to make it visible. Child's image in the kitchen, fearless and jovial at once, was precisely suited to its moment. Here was an activist who took full charge of the food, demonstrating over and over that the most important ingredient in her kitchen was conviction and the most useful shortcut was skill. Friedan, for her part, supplied the foundation for a feminist structure already inching skyward. She told the story that women were ready to hear, the story they could take to heart and trust with their lives. In Friedan's book and Child's cooking, women discerned a femininity far indeed from Anne Morrow Lindbergh's wise, reflective poet roaming the beach. The future as Friedan and Child offered it took place on a wide-open frontier that invited lifelong exploration, and their appetites for it were as big and eager as a man's.

Women responded instantly to *The French Chef,* instantly to *The Feminine Mystique.* The inspiration they drew from these two women was as crucial as the how-to, and it altered the domestic legacy for all the generations that came after. Not every woman who watched Child intently on TV, scribbling the recipe as fast as she could, was a fan of Friedan's; and not every woman who tore excitedly through Friedan's book and found her own life on each page was a dedicated cook. But they were all hearing the same words: You can do this yourself, with your brains and your own two hands. You don't need to get it from a package. You can take charge. You can stand at the center of your own world and create something very good, from scratch.

Epilogue

IN THE END, it took both a cook and a feminist to liberate the American kitchen. By liberation I don't mean freedom from cooking, though the women's movement is often construed in those terms. I mean that cooking itself has been freed, or at least notably loosened, from the grip of the food industry and the constraints of gender. There was nothing inevitable about these developments; on the contrary, centuries of moral authority and the vast reach of the modern food industry were invested in quite another outcome. But in the decades following that eventful week in February 1963, fundamental changes that had been stirring since the end of the war began to register across the country.

For Julia Child, as we've seen, the holy grail of cooking was technique—the traditional skills and procedures enshrined in French cuisine. Like all good cooks, she honored high-quality ingredients, but the glorious produce and meats she had loved in France simply weren't available in American supermarkets. Even James Beard, a lifelong champion of American regional foods who had no trouble finding greatness in a plain, ripe strawberry, made his career on complex dishes that displayed the artistry of the cook, not the flavor of the raw ingredients. He could hardly have done otherwise even if the culinary fashions of the time had been different. By the 1960s, fruits, vegetables, meats, and poultry had been so rigorously standardized through factory farming that a bland, mealy apple was becoming indistinguishable from a bland, mealy tomato. If Americans were going to develop a taste for good cooking that would see them through the assaults of the food industry and beyond, technique alone was not going to suffice.

The reeducation of the American palate started in California, far from the media nerve center of packaged-food cuisine, and farther still from the imposing standards of French classical cooking. Alice Waters was living in Berkeley, California, during the '60s, active in the counterculture and never happier than when she was cooking and eating with friends. Despite or more likely because of her talents at the stove, she didn't seek formal training. Unlike Child, she had instincts galore, and they served her splendidly. Waters, too, went to France and was forever changed by the food she tasted there, but her epiphany was different from Child's. She fell in love with the simple, seasonal food of the countryside and came home fired with the conviction that the heart, the soul, and the substance of great cooking are the ingredients; the rest is commentary. The only way for Americans to re-create French food, she decided, would be to choose ingredients the way French women choose theirs—by the time of year and the possibilities closest at hand. If asparagus is in season, that's when you cook asparagus, and at no other time. You get it right from the farm or from a source as close as possible to the farm, and it's a farm where produce is grown without any chemicals in the soil or pesticides on the crops. The cook's job is to give the finishing touches to work largely done in the field. In 1971, Waters and a few friends opened a restaurant they called Chez Panisse and put these principles into action.

From the start, Waters made a point of establishing relationships with local farmers, cheese makers, and other artisans who supplied her with extraordinary fruits and vegetables, meats and dairy products. Her talented and imaginative chefs—whom she hired for their ability to taste, not just for their knife skills—dedicated themselves to showcasing the abundant flavors that arrived at the kitchen door each morning. Chez Panisse became a success and then a landmark; for food lovers it has been the Plymouth Rock of contemporary American cuisine. More and more restaurants began opening in California and elsewhere under the banner of a new culinary mantra, "fresh and local," although the farther they were from California, the more loosely the chefs tended to interpret the phrase. Nevertheless, the demand for high-quality farm products soared among chefs and home cooks alike, and helped spawn a network of farmers' markets across the country. Food shoppers hungry to taste and touch fresh produce with nature still clinging to it pour into these markets wherever they open, and their popularity has given a huge boost to the movement for organic agriculture. Even the food industry has awakened to the trend, although the industry's contributions—for example, overpriced salad ingredients shipped across country and sold in plastic containers engineered to fend off wilting—aren't precisely in the spirit of either "fresh" or "local." Nonetheless, it is possible today in many cities and towns for home cooks to ferret out fresh ingredients, sometimes even in supermarkets, of a quality all but unknown to most grocery shoppers in the 1950s.

With or without Waters, indeed with or without Child, home cooking was going to change in the 1970s and 1980s as the number of working mothers skyrocketed. Traditionally, as noted earlier in this book, working women made no greater use of convenience foods than full-time homemakers. Today it seems irrelevant even to make the comparison. Work is the standard for women now; whatever the statistics of the moment on how many mothers are staying home with their children, the reality is fluid. Children get older, and mothers go looking for jobs. But, remarkably, even in the domestic flurry that descends on many households after 5:00 P.M., dinner does not plummet irrevocably to frozen burritos. Thanks to the influence of Child, Waters, and the popularizers who followed in their wake, recipes for quickly made meals using fresh ingredients pour constantly through the media, from *Gourmet* to the food pages of the local paper to the Internet. Of course, there's no telling how many harried cooks turn to them of an evening, but this emphasis on simple cooking from scratch is not confined to the upper reaches of cuisine. Betty Crocker herself, who remains one of the most practical and widely consulted culinary authorities in the country, makes relatively little use now of packaged foods in many of her cookbooks. Convenience products are entrenched in most kitchens and show up on many a dinner table, but they haven't redefined what we know as cooking or flattened the culinary terrain.

What characterizes middle-class American home cooking, and has for more than a century, is the way it careens from appalling to exquisite and back again—sometimes in a single neighborhood, sometimes in a single family. Green bean casserole doesn't adequately sum us up; neither does a hot dog or a dozen glistening oysters or a slab of pizza with pineapple on top or an omelette with freshly snipped herbs. This enormous country is continually infused with immigrants and committed at least in principle to social mobility; ambition and curiosity keep us restless, and many people have the means to travel abroad. The food will never be monolithic. We're a nation of niche markets, and any two of them are likely to contradict each other. Nonetheless, food writers still get press releases every day announcing the death of traditional home cooking. Nothing except perhaps the women's movement has died so repeatedly and with such devoted publicity.

There's no question, however, that the food industry has exerted profound and far-reaching influence on every aspect of American eating habits, from our palates to our family lives. By now the steady accumulation of packaged grease, salt, and artificial flavors in the American diet constitutes a genuine threat to health and culture. Back at the turn of the twentieth century, we began the long process of turning over to the food industry many of the decisions about what we eat, in the name of habit or convenience or taste. Today our staggering rates of obesity and diabetes are testimony to the faith we put in corporations to feed us well. But the food industry is a business, not a parent; it doesn't care what we eat as long as we're willing to pay for it. Although some people think of cooking as a choice now, no more necessary to learn than sewing or shoemaking, that perspective holds up poorly when we gaze around a mall or an airport at Americans en masse. Home cooking these days has far more than sentimental value; it's a survival skill.

Do women like to cook? Some do and some don't; what's clear now is that women and cooking are no longer a single entity. Although women still prepare most of the family meals, cooking has become the first domestic chore to float free of sex roles. Most important, men are making dinner even when they don't particularly want to. They're cooking, that is, in the fine, thoroughly pedestrian spirit of home cooking: because someone has to feed the family. An obvious next step would be for domestic life as a whole to become a natural venue for both sexes, just as the workplace has become over the years. But nothing in the long history of women doing what used to be man's work has ever seemed to Americans as unnervingly radical as the notion of men wholeheartedly engaged in woman's work. To help out is noble; to place domestic responsibilities on a par with one's job remains suspect.

Near the park in my New York City neighborhood there's a short stretch of roadway that has been blocked off for as long as I can remember. Sometimes trucks and machinery are in evidence, and sometimes a worker is drilling amid the torn-up asphalt; but often it's quiet, and nothing much seems to change from year to year. As far as I can tell, the place is a permanent construction site.

In many ways I think the relationship between women and their domestic lives has been a permanent construction site ever since the end of World War II. Participating in the labor force has had its difficulties, but the most stubborn problems associated with work have been the ones churned up at home: children, housework, cooking, love, and guilt. The old, smooth surface of the road has been definitively ripped apart, and while various experts have come up with plans for how to restore it, from cake mix to consciousness raising, the mess defies simple solutions. The problem, of course, is that domestic life as a purely female preoccupation is an anachronism, as ill-suited to most families today as coal-burning stoves and live chickens underfoot. Yet we chip away at the rubble, millions of women with millions of little shovels, until the next generation picks up the task. Perhaps we accomplish more than we know, for the daughters do seem to start out well ahead of the place where their mothers began, way back in the olden days.

Notes

INTRODUCTION: DO WOMEN LIKE TO COOK?

Page

xxiii "You don't cook it": *Better Homes & Gardens*, February 1950, 88.

xxiv Cookbook author Sylvia Schur: Sylvia Schur, ed., *New Ways to Gracious Living*, 4.

xxiv "time, work and the task": *Life*, May 17, 1954, 7.

xxiv "Won't someone": *Boston Globe*, January 16, 1948, 20.

xxv Chatters— : Ibid., September 20, 1963, 23.

CHAPTER 1: THE HOUSEWIFE'S DREAM

Page

3 One night he: Beard to Brown, February 21, 1954, in *Love and Kisses and a Halo of Truffles*, ed. John Ferrone, 49.

3 a few days later: Beard to Brown, February 24, 1954, ibid., 50.

3 "Smells divine": Ibid.

3 "Dean of American Cookery": Robert Clark, *James Beard*, 158.

3 For every dinner: Beard to Brown, August 13, 1954, in Ferrone, 60.

3 "the Home Ec side": Clark, 155.

3 "I have been": Beard to Brown, June 26, 1960, in Ferrone, 268.

4 "Where, oh where": Clark, 148.

4 Not in Portland: Ibid., 151.

4 "missionary work": Beard to Brown, May 18, 1953, in Ferrone, 12.

4 "Try to get": Ibid., 51.

4–5 "It's easy to cook": Poppy Cannon, *The Can-Opener Cookbook*, 3.

5 Like Beard, she made: Cannon, *The Bride's Cookbook*, 137.

5 Her "French" and "*so romantic*": *Mademoiselle*, April 1950, 54.

6 "How long is it": *Boston Globe*, January 1, 1954, 28.

6 "We've had repercussions": Ibid., January 6, 1954, 23.

7 "It was a sweltering August day": E. W. Williams, "Frozen Foods 2000 A.D.: A Fantasy of the Future," *Quick Frozen Foods*, February 1954, 101.

8 "My predictions": Ibid.

8 "Foods formerly manufactured": *American Cookery*, February 1946, 8.

8–9 **Along with the indestructible luncheon meats:** Pauline Arnold and
     Percival White, *Food: America's Biggest Business,* 157; **canned-ham-and-**
     sweet-potato: *American Cookery,* February 1946, 8.

   9 **The magazine also welcomed:** *American Cookery,* April 1946, 6; June
     1946, 6; May 1946, 6.

   9 **An ingenious New York engineer:** Ibid., June 1946, 8.

   9 **"Froz-n Coff-e":** Ibid.

  10 **"From its reception":** *Better Food,* June 1946, 22.

  10 **At General Mills the first shortcut:** General Mills, "Cutting the
     Homemaker's Time Budget," *Progress Thru Research* 1, no. 3 (1947).

  11 **"Fresh produce":** Williams, *Quick Frozen Foods,* February 1954, 108.

  11 **"No pots or pans":** Arnold and White, 110.

  12 **As early as 1944:** Williams, *Frozen Foods, Biography of an Industry,* 36.

  12 **"dinner plates":** *Quick Frozen Foods,* February 1948, 84.

  12 **During the war, the National Research Corporation:** See Robert
     Buzzell, *Product Innovation in Food Processing, 1954–1964,* 49. See also
     Williams, *Biography of an Industry,* 47, 82, 85.

  13 **By 1950 a quarter of Florida's:** Williams, *Biography,* 82, 47; *Quick
     Frozen Foods,* June 1951, 50.

  13 **A jubilant Minute Maid:** *Quick Frozen Foods,* June 1951, 50.

  13 **According to a study:** "Frozen Orange Juice Leads in Urban Home
     Servings," ibid., December 1953, 47.

  13 **These were trumphant statistics:** "Battle of Fresh vs. Frozen to Be
     Fought on Nutritional Value," ibid., December 1952, 41.

  13 **In yet another skirmish:** Ibid., October 1952, 92.

  14 **In terms of sales:** "What Has Happened to Concentrated Milk?" ibid.,
     December 1951, 47. See also "Frozen Concentrate Held Answer to
     Milk Surplus Problem," ibid., November 1954, 54.

  14 **E. W. Williams:** *Quick Frozen Foods,* December 1952, 37. Williams con-
     tinued to seek new frontiers in freezing. "Can the body be quick-
     frozen and kept in that state long enough to add years to life?" he
     wondered once in an editorial (July 1954, 31).

  14 **Processors started:** Ibid., September 1951, 55; March 1952, 88.

  14 **The apple industry:** G. E. Hilbert, "What's New in Concentrates,"
     ibid., September 1951, 55.

  15 **The next orange juice:** "Fish Sticks Score with All-'Round Conve-
     nience," ibid., September 1953, 81. See also "Birdseye Sends Fish Sticks
     into N.Y. Market," October 1953, 57.

  15 **More than 7 million pounds:** *Quick Frozen Foods,* April 1954, 87.

  15 **"This is the way":** *McCall's,* January 1956, 79.

  15 **These alternatives:** Ibid., October 1954, 71; November 1954, 173;
     March 1956, 105; January 1957, 15.

15 **By the same token:** Ibid., December 1953, 87; August 1956, 122.

15 **Why wouldn't people:** Ibid., February 1954, 186.

15 **What prejudice kept:** Ibid., March 1953, 25.

16 **When would the market:** Ibid., February 1953, 77.

16 **"If the truth":** Marvin R. Polkow, "Frozen Bakery Products Are Here to Stay," ibid., October 1949, 63.

16 **One reason frozen food:** Ibid., February 1952, 4; March 1952, 85; June 1952, 190; January 1953, 37.

16 **In a small study of homemakers:** Elizabeth Wiegand, *Comparative Use of Time of Farm and City Full-Time Homemakers and Homemakers in the Labor Force in Relation to Home Management,* 42.

17 **International Harvester:** *Quick Frozen Foods,* February 1953, 135.

17 **Then *Quick Frozen Foods:*** "Getting the Home Freezer into the Living Room," ibid., March 1953, 120.

17 **That year the first frozen dinners:** "Frozen Dinners Debut with Premium," ibid., December 1952, 66.

18 **Swanson came late:** "Frozen Meals a Hit After Many False Starts," ibid., July 1954, 63.

18 **Television was still:** Lynn Spigel, *Make Room for TV,* 1.

18 **Previous frozen dinners:** *Quick Frozen Foods,* January 1955, 107.

18 **"The day of the complete meal":** Ibid., January 1954, 35.

19 **While the company hurried:** Ibid., September 1954, 143; January 1955, 107.

19 **"When I'm having":** McCall's, *Congress on Better Living,* 1958, 46, 47.

20 **Two years later, marketing researchers:** "Consumer Attitudes Toward Frozen Foods," *Quick Frozen Foods,* October 1960, 86.

20 **Despite statistics:** "Nargus Convention Is Told Frozen Foods Revolutionized American Way of Life," ibid., July 1964, 51.

20 **Only 3 percent:** Ibid.

20 **A year later about half:** "FF Buyer Spends 80% More Than Non-User, Can Help Independents Boost Sales," ibid., March 1956, 59.

20 **Even frozen vegetables:** "Breaded Vegetables—New Concept in Frozen Food Products," ibid., June 1956, 48.

21 **"New convenience foods":** "Convenience Foods Have Scant Impact on Housewife, Agriculture Dept. Study Says," *Advertising Age,* February 4, 1957.

21 **From the spring of 1959:** Harry H. Harp and Denis F. Dunham, *Comparative Costs to Consumers of Convenience Foods and Home-Prepared Foods.*

21 ***Parents Magazine:*** Parents Magazine, *Consumption and Use Study of Foods and Home Products,* 1960, 38–41.

21 **"To date the average homemaker":** Janet Wolff, *What Makes Women Buy,* 212.

22 **Wolff thought it was:** Ibid., 143.

23 **"Most of the 16":** *Consumer Reports,* June 1947, 200.

23 **Yet even then:** Wolff, 212.

23 **A team of food technologists:** W. F. Cruess and Florence Pen Ho, "Studies of Frozen Food Samples Bought in the Open Market," *Quick Frozen Foods,* April 1949, 70.

23 **A decade later:** Nancy Hale, "Lack of Uniform Quality Is Found Hurting Repeat Business," ibid., February 1956, 131.

24 **In 1962:** Kermit Bird, *Freeze-dried Foods: Palatability Tests,* July 1963.

24 **In January 1952:** "Battle of Fresh vs. Frozen to Be Fought on Nutritional Value," *Quick Frozen Foods,* December 1952, 41.

26 **In the '50s and early '60s:** Cannon, "Swift and Elegant Meals," *House Beautiful,* April 1956, 160; Beard to Brown, December 2, 1962, in Ferrone, 316. See also Stringfellow Barr and Stella Standard, *The Kitchen Garden Book* (New York: Viking, 1956), 9. Barr attacked "agricultural science" for concentrating on size and shipping qualities at the expense of flavor. Among most food lovers, to be sure, the concept of organic farming meant little in the '50s. When Julia Child heard that her editor, Judith Jones, had "an organic Thanksgiving" in 1962, she expressed her sympathy. "Surprisingly enough our 'organic' Thanksgiving dinner was delicious!" Jones wrote back. "The truth is that things like chickens which have not been stuffed with estrogen pellets to make them put on those extra ounces of fat before killing have a lovely fresh flavor that takes one back to one's childhood or to the happy days of European markets. You must try one if you have a health store in your neighborhood." (Jones to Child, December 18, 1962. Julia Child papers, Schlesinger Library.)

27 **Many of these:** According to the *Oxford English Dictionary* (1992), the term *gracious living* was appearing in print by the 1930s.

27 **Incomes had been rising:** Susan M. Hartmann, *The Home Front and Beyond,* 8.

27 **From 1950 to 1960:** Robert H. Bremner, "Families, Children, and the State," in *Reshaping America: Society and Institutions, 1945–60,* ed. Robert H. Bremner and Gary W. Reichard, 116–17.

28 **Stories in every issue:** "Mr. and Mrs. in the Kitchen," *Living,* April–May 1949 (the magazine was also called *Living for Young Home-makers*); September 1950, 78; Janet W. Misch, "Thanksgiving Without Turkey," ibid., November 1950, 107.

28 **In 1954 the magazine:** *Life,* May 24, 1954, 94.

28 **"Here is my favorite":** *Forecast,* February 1950, 26.

28 **Cookbooks of every sort:** *The New York Times,* June 12, 1952, 42.

29 **When the renowned:** Mary Margaret McBride, *Mary Margaret McBride's Harvest of American Cooking* (New York: Putnam, 1957), xviii.

29 **At the *Ladies' Home Journal*:** I am indebted to Jean Anderson and Geraldine Rhoads for information about the *Ladies' Home Journal.*

29 *Life* **ran a series:** See *Picture Cook Book*, 1958, which contains many of the magazine's food features published from 1951 to 1958.

30 **Nearly all the major:** See, for example, Poppy Cannon, "The Noble Wines of Burgundy," *House Beautiful,* March 1958, 132. But the wine industry didn't confine its efforts to writers at the glossy magazines. When the American Home Economics Association met in California in 1949, members went on a tour of Almaden, where they learned the art of making champagne. See Mary Meade's column in the *Chicago Tribune,* August 7, 1949, part 7, 7.

30 **"The best of the experts":** "Wine Buying," *Picture Cook Book,* 109.

30 **In 1948 she brought:** *Ebony,* June 1948, 44.

31 **Her teacher was:** Ibid., March 1950, 58.

31 **Ruth Ellen Church:** *Chicago Tribune,* January 14, 1950, part 1, 12.

31 **Her culinary convictions:** *Ebony,* March 1947, 36.

32 **"What is the secret":** Ibid., March 1950, 58.

32 **"If one has been compelled":** Roberta Lee, "Modern Etiquette," *Amsterdam News,* January 31, 1948, 12.

32 **The paper offered:** Betty Granger, "Do the Unusual for Dramatic Summer Entertaining: Serve Chilled Soups," ibid., August 14, 1954, 11.

32–33 **"Integration took place":** Granger, "Bit of Sweden Invades Brooklyn via Smorgasbord," ibid., February 9, 1957, 10.

33 **In Kansas City:** "Skill in Fine Cooking," *Kansas City Star,* May 11, 1955, n.p.

33 **Helen Worth:** I am indebted to Helen Worth for information about the school and her teaching.

33 **In Minneapolis:** See *Verna Meyer's "Way with Food,"* 1964. I am indebted to Suzanne Weil for information about Verna Meyer.

33 **In Princeton:** "The Schools That Make Good Cooks Better," *Good Housekeeping,* May 1960, 176.

34 **"You are *dated*":** Mary Elizabeth Wiley and Alexandra Field Meyer, "What America Needs Is a New Domestic Philosophy," *House Beautiful,* April 1951, 105.

34 **Reviewing a flock:** A.I.M.S. Street, "The Gastronomical Year," *Saturday Review,* February 13, 1954, 35.

34 **"I particularly enjoy":** Mrs. H. Ranzenhofer, Clifton, N.J., letter to the editor, *Living,* November 1952, 16.

35 **But Pillsbury decided:** "A $50,000 Piece of Baked Goods," *Life,* December 26, 1949, 16.

35 **"The goodwill":** "A New Era at Pillsbury," *Tide,* December 15, 1950, 40.

35 **The event was:** Pillsbury, "Pillsbury Bake-Off Contest Backgrounder," 1987. I am indebted to Pillsbury for company information sheets and publicity materials pertaining to the Bake-Off and its history. See also Ann Burckhardt, "Bake-Off," *Minneapolis Star,* March 18, 1981, 3T.

36 **Pillsbury officials:** "A $50,000 Piece of Baked Goods," *Life.*

36 **"I was real":** Ibid.

36 **But the judges:** The recipe is in Pillsbury, *100 Prize-Winning Recipes,* 1950. The recipe booklets published after the contest each year contain details of all the winning recipes as well as contest rules.

37 **Mrs. Richard W. Sprague:** Ibid., 6.

37 **"Submit a recipe":** Gladdie B., "Warm-Up for the Bake-Off," *Contest Magazine,* June 1961, 37.

38 **"Look, Mom":** Ibid., 33.

38 **Bertha Jorgensen:** Ibid.

38 **"When your recipes":** Ibid., 37.

38 **Amaizo was marketing:** Buzzell, 61; *Ladies' Home Journal,* March 1949, 181.

39 **"What do you think":** Marjorie Husted, "Women, Our Most Important Customers," a speech delivered to the Copywriters' Meeting, Minneapolis, Minn., June 21, 1948, 9. Marjorie Child Husted papers, Schlesinger Library.

40 **"My first plane ride":** Pillsbury, publicity booklet, 1962.

CHAPTER 2: SOMETHING FROM THE OVEN

Page

43 **"Women who gave up":** "Home-Finished Foods," *Look,* May 9, 1950, 122.

43 **"When the food manufacturers":** "It's a Revolution in Eating Habits," *BusinessWeek,* September 6, 1952, 40.

43 **"The loathing with which":** "The Fabulous Market for Food," *Fortune,* October 1953, 135.

44 **"When the American housewife":** Helen McCully, "Short-Cut Foods Revolutionize American Cooking," *McCall's,* January 1955, 42. McCully, a friend of James Beard's and a lover of good food, turned out sentiments like these strictly at the command of her editor.

44 **As late as 1960:** *Parents Magazine,* "Consumption and Use Study of Foods and Home Products," 1960, 24.

44 **Between 1938 and 1961:** Francille Maloch, "Characteristics of Most and Least Liked Household Tasks," Cornell, 1962, 4. Maloch analyzed nine previous studies and conducted her own.

45 **In his thousands:** Ernest Dichter, *Handbook of Consumer Motivations,* 1964, 33. Referring to a study of two thousand women he conducted for *Woman's Home Companion,* Dichter divided women into three categories: the "pure housewife," the "career woman," and the "balanced woman." According to his analysis, the first and the third were actively interested in cooking; the second was primarily interested in competing with men. But he also emphasized that "the modern woman," whatever her category, had a "basic readiness to enjoy homemaking" (28).

45 **Pierre Martineau:** Pierre Martineau, *Motivation in Advertising,* 1957, 87.

45 **Although Dichter once claimed:** Dichter, "Electrical Home Appliances in the Postwar World," typescript, n.d., 18. This was a study undertaken for Crowell Collier, which published it in 1945. I am indebted to Daniel Horowitz for this document and many other Dichter materials.

45 **Other studies, including a 1949 poll:** "Would You Rather Cook? Clean House?" *Woman's Home Companion,* April 1949, 7. The magazine polled more than two thousand readers; 56 percent said cooking was the task they liked most, and 7 percent said they liked it least. The second most popular task was cleaning house, preferred by 12 percent; **a 1951 Gallup poll:** George H. Gallup, *The Gallup Poll,* 1972, vol. 2, 964. Cooking was the most-liked household job for 43 percent of women; housecleaning was second, preferred by 17 percent. Cooking was the most disliked for 7 percent.

45 **True, housework:** Joann Vanek, "Time Spent in Housework," *Scientific American,* November 1974, 116.

46 **Women spent:** Ibid., 119.

46 **When a Los Angeles company:** Ed Green, "A Low-Cost Consumer Survey for the Specialty Packer," *Quick Frozen Foods,* November 1952, 47.

46 **As one Ph.D. student:** Maloch, "Characteristics," 18.

46 **When a doctoral student:** Jane Rees, "The Use and Meaning of Food in Families with Different Socio-Economic Backgrounds," Pennsylvania State University, 1959, 53–56.

47 **In a study conducted:** Howard Trier, Henry Clay Smith, and James Shaffer, "Differences in Food Buying Attitudes of Housewives," *Journal of Marketing,* July 1960, 66.

47 **Mirra Komarovsky:** Mirra Komarovsky, *Blue-Collar Marriage,* 1962, 58.

48 **In 1955:** "Frozen Meats Are More Economical, Taste Better, Consumers Report," *Quick Frozen Foods,* August 1956, 142.

48 **Another study:** Elizabeth Sweeney Herbert, "When the Homemaker Goes to Work," *Journal of Home Economics,* April 1952, 257.

48 **The study was based:** Gary A. Marple and Harry B. Wissman, "Who Buys Convenience Food," in Marple and Wissman, eds., *Grocery Manufacturing in the U.S.* (New York: Praeger, 1968), 368, cited in Mary Anne Anselmino, "Factors Influencing the Emergence and Acceptance of Food Innovations in Twentieth-Century America," Teachers College, 1986, 44. After analyzing the available research on this subject, Anselmino concludes that the studies indicate no significant differences between working and at-home wives in their purchases of convenience products (54).

49 **"Frankly, we were surprised":** "A Very Special McCall's Recipe," *McCall's,* November 1954, 72.

49 **Two pages later:** Helen McCully, "Canned Meat Meals," ibid., 74.

49 **Tuna croquettes:** *Denver Post,* March 24, 1954, 26; **bread-and-butter pickles:** ibid., July 26, 1954, 15; **rhubarb crisp:** ibid., April 26, 1955, 19; **meat loaf . . . pineapple:** ibid., August 3, 1953, 15; **rarebit:** ibid., May 11, 1956, 32.

50 **"Could a double-crust":** *Boston Globe,* January 16, 1948, 20.

50 **Some Chatters:** Ibid., February 19, 1959, 28.

50 **If Chatters prepared:** Ibid., April 5, 1959, 44A; ibid., April 24, 1952, 26.

51 **"Is Home Cooking":** Ibid., January 1, 1954, 28.

52 **Women were avoiding:** Ben Duffy, "Why We Buy What We Buy," *Look,* June 12, 1956, 94.

52 **They resisted products:** Wolff, 109.

52 **"How often have we heard":** Mason Haire, "Projective Techniques in Marketing Research," *Journal of Marketing,* April 1950, 649.

53 **"I was a little slow":** *Chicago Tribune,* June 7, 1948, part 2, 8.

54 **"Apparently, she likes":** Haire, 653.

57 **There wasn't much:** Ruth Wakefield, *Ruth Wakefield's Toll House Tried and True Recipes* (New York: Barrows, 1938), 112.

57 **Hence, canned fruit:** *Denver Post,* April 18, 1955, 31; **peanut butter:** *Boston Globe,* March 4, 1954, 18; **frozen lemonade:** *Woman's Home Companion,* August 1953, 76.

58 **A cook who:** H. J. Heinz Co., *57 Prize-Winning Recipes,* 1957, 29.

58 **In a story:** Helen Churchill, "Bananas Are Back," *Household,* February 1948, 36.

58 **English muffins:** "Tricks and Treats with Bread and Cake," *Woman's Day,* April 1954, 65.

58 **Nabisco promised:** *Woman's Day,* June 1948, 69.

58   Betty Crocker decided: *Better Homes & Gardens,* July 1953, 96.

59   Campbell's thought: *Forecast,* October 1956, 57.

59   "Gone are the days": *Household,* February 1954, 24.

59   "Honestly, it's good!": *Woman's Home Companion,* August 1956, 54.

59   Hovering restlessly: *Chicago Tribune,* March 16, 1953, part 3, 3.

59   Perhaps it seemed: The Seven-Up Company, *"Fresh Up" Familiar Foods and Party Treats . . . with That Famous Lively 7-UP Flavor!* (St. Louis, Mo. 1953).

60   When Kraft introduced: *San Francisco Chronicle,* August 18, 1955, 19.

61   "Cooking is *not*": Virginia Stanton, "Cooking Is *Not* Work," *House Beautiful,* July 1949, 62.

62   "One opens a box": "100 Years of Living," *Living,* January 1956, 53.

62   "If you're a typical": Mary Odegard, "The Food Scout," *Household,* September 1954, 12.

62   According to Kellogg: *Forecast,* February 1951, 32.

62   "In this fast-moving era": Ibid., November 1951, 10.

63   "Baby fussing?": *Life,* March 24, 1952, n.p.

63   Soon no excuse: *Household,* July 1956, 46.

63   "Quick fix desserts!": Ibid., August 1956, 56.

63   "Suppers": Ibid., December 1956, 62.

63   "It's just 1-2-3": "Meals in Minutes," *Better Homes & Gardens,* September 1953, 93.

63   He and his staff: Dichter, "Today's Woman as a Consumer," *Motivations,* September 1956.

64   Instead, she developed: Dichter, *The Strategy of Desire,* 183. ("She 'doctors up' the ready-made food, she adds to it original ingredients, on occasion she tries to surprise her husband and her children with new combinations, new taste experiences.")

64   "The question is often asked": Edalene Stohr, "Harvest Abundance for Holidays," *Forecast,* November 1956, 18.

65   "The show in Cleveland": Beard to Brown, April 1955, in Ferrone, 99.

66   An economical cake: *Boston Globe,* June 19, 1952, 17.

66   According to *House Beautiful*: "You Have 1001 Servants in Your Kitchen," *House Beautiful,* March 1951, 74.

66   "For instance, a really good": "Is Your Grandmother Standing Between You and Today's Freedom?" ibid., 150.

67   Canned mushrooms: *Forecast,* March 1952, 55; September 1954, 109; *Household,* June 1958, 54.

67   Even instant coffee: *Living,* May 1957, 144.

67   Sure enough: Wellesley-in-Westchester, comp., *Favorite Recipes of Wellesley Alumnae,* n.d., 59.

67   **A housewife in Topsfield:** *Landmarks in Cooking,* 1960, 39.

67   **In Milwaukee a member:** *Be Milwaukee's Guest,* 1959, 8.

68   **"Can you think":** Husted, "A Critical Evaluation of Modern Home Service," a speech to the Mid-West Regional Gas Sales Conference, April 23, 1952. Husted papers, Schlesinger Library.

68   **They couldn't, and neither:** *Advertising Age,* October 2, 1950, 66. *McCall's* considered this such a risky departure that it went to press with two different covers, sending half its subscribers a "girl cover" and the other half a food cover. The editors urged readers to locate a friend or relative who had received the other cover and compare them, then write to the magazine to say which they preferred (*McCall's,* March 1950, 4).

68   **"Cakes from every land":** Betty Crocker, *Betty Crocker Cook Book of All-Purpose Baking,* 1942, n.p.

69   **Even when she evoked:** Ibid., n.p.

69   **"The crowning indignity":** To combat this perception when it arose in the 1930s, Marjorie Husted of General Mills sought out Hollywood movie stars and invited them to be interviewed on Betty Crocker's radio program, which reached millions of listeners, talking about how eating bread did no harm to their figures.

69   **"The era of the hundred-pound":** Paul Gerot, "Convenience, Ease and Success from the Oven," 193. Gerot's article, not otherwise identified, was included in materials made available to me by the publicity staff at Pillsbury.

70   ***"Betty Crocker says":*** *Household,* December 1951, n.p.

70   ***"Remember":*** *Household,* ibid., 55. ("When you want to bake a mandazzling beauty, you've *got* to make your cake with Swans Down Cake Flour!")

70   **"Love and Kisses":** Ibid., February 1951, 77.

70   **"He'll think he married":** *Ladies' Home Journal,* May 1949, 68.

70   **"Nothing says lovin'":** Cake mix ad, 1960, General Mills/Pillsbury archives.

70   **"When my beloved":** *Boston Globe,* January 5, 1956, 28.

70   **In 1959:** Ibid., April 5 and 12, 1959.

70   **"What recipes":** *Chicago Tribune,* November 8, 1948, 3.

70   **"My staff and I":** Ibid., September 5, 1949, part 6, 5.

71   **Two hundred women:** Ibid., September 15, 1949, part 4, 12.

71   **When a 1953 Gallup poll:** Gallup, *The Gallup Poll,* vol. 2, 1136.

71   **"Before my sponge cake":** *Household,* April 1951, 57.

71   **"Why does the brown coating":** Ibid., October 1951, 75.

71   **"Here is my recipe":** Ibid., March 1953, 65.

71   **A Connecticut woman:** Letter to Irma Rombauer, March 16, 1953, Rombauer-Becker papers, Schlesinger Library.

71   A San Francisco woman: Ibid., August 5, 1953.

71   A Cincinnati woman: Ibid., September 23, 1953.

72   Rombauer scribbled: Ibid., February 25, 1955.

72   Duff cake mixes: Gerot, 192. See also Buzzell, 39.

72   General Mills was first: "General Mills Research Brings a 'Delicacy of the Ages' Up to Date," *Progress Thru Research* 3, no. 1, 1948.

72   Pillsbury was right on: Gerot, 196.

72   That same year: "Eat Your Cake and Have It, Too," *Progress Thru Research* 4, no. 1, 1949, 9.

72   Pillsbury launched: Gerot, 198; General Mills, "Cake Mixes" (company information sheet); "Three Rival Cake Mixes Race for the National Market," *Tide,* August 15, 1952, 22.

72   Meanwhile, Nebraska Consolidated: "Duncan Hines—New Name in Mix Market," *Tide,* January 30, 1953, 21.

73   Throughout the '50s: See "Deep Breath for Mix Makers," *Business Week,* August 6, 1955, 58; "Have Cake-Mix Sales Hit a Plateau?" *Printers Ink,* December 9, 1960, 9.

73   "These were the days": "Have Cake-Mix Sales Hit a Plateau?" *Printers Ink*, December 9, 1960, 9. "Betty Crocker Primps for Cake-Mix Campaign," ibid., July 8, 1960, 12.

73   In 1953, General Mills: "Old Treat with a New Taste," *Progress Thru Research* 7, no. 2, 1953.

73   two years later: "The History of Betty Crocker's Cake Mixes," 1955 (company information sheet); "Deep Breath for Mix Makers," *Business Week,* August 6, 1955, 58.

73   More plausible numbers: Rees, "The Use and Meaning of Food," 43. ("In spite of the introduction of partially-prepared foods, homemakers continued to make products from the basic ingredients because their families like them even though it requires more time.")

74   In fact, they had been puzzling: Buzzell, 39.

74   The homemakers who were buying: "General Mills Horizons," a report published for stockholders, February 1952.

75   When home economics students: Bernice J. Gross and Kay Young Mackley, "Should the Homemaker Use Ready-Made Mixes?" *Journal of Home Economics,* June 1950, 451.

75   In 1954 a study: Pauline Paul, Olive M. Batcher, and Lilian Fulde, "Dry Mix and Frozen Baked Products," ibid., April 1954, 249.

75   Other studies: Mary Morr, "Food Mixes and Frozen Foods," ibid., January 1951, 14; Mary Helen Bradley Morrison, "Ready Mixes for Chocolate Cakes," ibid., April 1957, 283.

75   "Yes, I'm using a cake mix'": Dichter, *Strategy of Desire,* 157.

76   this story came to be a favorite: See, for example, "Inside the Con-

sumer," *Newsweek,* October 10, 1955, 89; and Vance Packard, *The Hidden Persuaders* (New York: David McKay, 1957), 77–78.

76 **"You and Ann Pillsbury":** *Life,* December 5, 1949, n.p.

76 **Paul Gerot, the CEO:** Gerot, 189.

76 **For the industry:** "Eat Your Cake and Have It, Too," 10.

77 **"Unlike most cake mixes":** *Life,* June 2, 1952, n.p. According to the ad, "Hundreds of homemakers in Philadelphia, Cincinnati, St. Paul recently compared 3 leading cake mix brands. . . . On the average, the preferences for the cakes made from the Betty Crocker Cake mixes, calling for fresh eggs, were more than two to one over the cakes made from the 'dried egg' cake mixes tested."

77 **This Arctic home cook:** "Time for Betty Crocker," typescript, January 21, 1955. Adelaide Hawley Cumming papers, Schlesinger Library.

77 **Pillsbury conducted:** Gerot, 196.

77 **His research spurred:** *Living,* April 1948, 98.

77 **"Now, success in cakemaking":** Myrna Johnston, "Glamour Tricks with Cake Mix," *Better Homes & Gardens,* September 1953, 90.

78 **Cover a quick angel food cake:** "Angel Food Cake Without Tears," *Living,* February 1953, 102.

78 **Or split the cake:** Ibid.

78 **Fill and frost:** *Household,* March 1957, 79.

78 **Cover an oblong cake:** Betty Crocker, *Betty Crocker's Beautiful Cakes,* 7.

78 **Cut a hole in the center:** "Glamour Tricks," 91.

78 ***McCall's* gave directions:** "Our Humpty-Dumpty Cake," *McCall's,* February 1962, 125.

79 **"I really don't know":** McCall's, *Congress on Better Living,* 43.

80 **"These mixes eliminate":** Eloise Davison, "Correct Techniques Produce Correct Results from Mixes," *Forecast,* November 1955, 12.

80 **Such an attitude:** Beard to Brown, January 12, 1957, in Ferrone, 177.

81 **"I know damned well":** Ibid., July 1955, 122.

81 **"There are some good mixes":** Ibid., January 1, 1960, 255.

81 **"How simply horrid":** Angelica Gibbs, "With Palette Knife and Skillet," *The New Yorker,* May 28, 1949, 53.

81 **A year later she had come:** *Mademoiselle,* February 1950, 60.

82 **The homemaker who baked:** Mrs. John Cabbell Roy, "Crusty French Bread," Pillsbury, *100 Prize-Winning Recipes,* 86.

82 **And, of course, many:** Pillsbury, *100 Grand National Recipes,* 1954, 68.

82 **"In these busy days":** Pillsbury, *Pillsbury's Best 10th Grand National Bake-Off Cookbook,* supplement, 1.

83 **"Ease and simplicity":** Pillsbury, "Easy Rules," *The Pillsbury Busy Lady Bake-Off Recipes,* 95.

83 **Pillsbury went so far:** Ibid., 93.

83 **A year later the prize:** "Easy Livin' Caramel Cake," Pillsbury, *Bake-Off Cook Book*, 19.

83–84 **They made Gourmet Pâté de Foie Gras:** June Fete Committee, *The June Fete Cook Book,* 7.

84 **"gracious living":** Ibid., 1.

CHAPTER 3: DON'T CHECK YOUR BRAINS AT THE KITCHEN DOOR

Page

87 **Murrow wasn't really there:** Murrow's interview on *Person to Person* with Poppy Cannon and Walter White was broadcast on October 1, 1954.

90 **The truth, which she never:** I am indebted to Poppy Cannon's daughters, Cynthia White and Claudia Philippe, for much of the information in this chapter. Any conclusions about Cannon's skills and foibles are my own.

92 **In 1928 when she was:** See Poppy Cannon, *A Gentle Knight*, 20. Cannon gives 1929 as the date for this meeting, but later correspondence suggests that the year was 1928. See, for example, Walter White to Poppy Cannon, January 29, 1949: "Well, Angel, I guess that's all the news to now. Except the perennially new and exciting, although now old enough to vote, news that I love you." Walter Francis White and Poppy Cannon White Correspondence, Yale Collection of American Literature, Beinecke Rare Book and Manuscript Library. (All citations of letters to or from Cannon or White refer to the Beinecke collection.)

93 **White's great-grandfather:** Kenneth Robert Janken, *White: The Biography of Walter White, Mr. NAACP* (New York: The New Press, 2003), 3.

94 **Years later, in a letter:** White to Cannon, February 20, 1949.

94 **"We would collect":** Cannon, *Knight,* 23.

94 **They received an advance:** Ten years later William Koshland of Knopf wrote to White to cancel the contract "for a book on Negro cooking" and offered to forgive the advance (Koshland to White, October 27, 1947). White wrote back that he and Cannon still hoped to write the book but would prefer to return the money (White to Koshland, October 31, 1947).

94 **"It was a subtle thing":** Cannon, *Knight,* 24.

95 **"White got an advance":** E. J. Kahn, Jr., "The Frontal Attack—II," *The New Yorker*, September 11, 1948, 48.

96 **"After taking his hat":** Marie Blizard, "Cocktails for Two," *Mademoiselle,* January 1940, 71.

96 **"Fair reader":** "Eat and Run," ibid., February 1940, 116. (This

column is signed "Snack," evidently Cannon's first idea for a pseudonym.)

97　"This is a true story": "Eat and Run," ibid., September 1940, 70.

97　When she wanted, "a splotch of wine": "Food for Fun and Fitness," ibid., February 1947, 38; "a drift of caraway seeds": ibid., October 1948, 76; "a flurry of fresh coconut": ibid., May 1947, 54; "a great swish": ibid., June 1947, 34; "a generous flutter": "Eat and Run," ibid., January 1941, 30; "a fleck of allspice": "Food for Fun and Fitness," ibid., October 1944, 42.

98　"snorkier dinner-parties": "Eat and Run," ibid., March 1942, 40; "mix furiously": ibid., January 1941, 30; "stir like crazy": ibid., March 1942, 40; "fling": "Eat and Run," ibid., December 1941, 14: "salad-flinging": ibid., February 1941, 24.

98　"When up a tree": Ibid., October 1944, 42.

98　"Those as yearn": "Food for Fun and Fitness," ibid., February 1947, 38.

98　To "work on it": Ibid., December 1946, 76.

98　"Any haughty Creole cook": Ibid., October 1946, 26.

98　"Hungarian salami goulash": Ibid., October 1948, 76.

98　Once she published: Ibid., September 1940, 70.

99　"Honest to God": Ibid., December 1940, 209.

99　Trained in Europe: See George Lang, *Nobody Knows the Truffles I've Seen,* for a description of Philippe at work.

100　Three years later: *Denver Post,* October 14, 1952, 28.

100　In a 1946 feature story: "The White House," *Ebony,* April 1946, 3.

101　"Darling, were ever two people": White to Cannon, February 3, 1949.

101　"Our marriage": White to Cannon, March 1, 1949.

101　Cannon wrote back: Cannon to White, February 24, 1949.

101　The next day she was: Cannon, *Knight,* 35.

101–2　"No interracial marriage": "Famous Negroes Who Married Whites," *Ebony,* December 1949, 20.

102　As for Philippe: Philippe to Cannon, July 28, 1949.

102　As a reader: "Letters to the Editor," *Ebony,* August 1952, 6.

103　It is unlikely: Cannon to President Dumarsais Estime, Republic of Haiti, October 20, 1949.

103　One day she accompanied him: Cannon, "How We Erased Two Color Lines," 47.

103　For years White was deeply involved: White to Governor William Hastie, the Virgin Islands, December 19, 1947.

103　Perhaps only a husband: Cannon, *Can-Opener Cookbook,* 7.

104　On another occasion: Cannon, *Knight,* 174.

104　Her original idea: Cannon to White, February 21, 1950.

104 **"Domestic Villanella"**: Cannon, *The Bride's Cookbook,* 376.

105 **"Yolks must be whipped"**: "Rule for a Cake," ibid., 64.

105 **Or, from "To Make a Salad"**: Ibid., 272.

106 **"Time is a savor"**: "Time Is the X-Thing," ibid., 372.

106 **"But in this day and age"**: Ibid., 371.

106 **Its dashing editor**: *House Beautiful,* November 1956; May 1957. Gordon devoted the entire issue of November 1955 to Wright.

107 **"Have you discovered"**: Gordon, "Have You Discovered the New Freedom in Homemaking?" *House Beautiful,* March 1951, 73.

107 **"If you want to dine well"**: Cannon, "The Modern Epicure," ibid., May 1953, 161.

108 **"If they are perfect"**: Ibid., 165.

108 **Again and again she wrote**: Cannon, "How to Be a Pace Setting Gourmet," ibid., November 1953, 264.

108 **"Not the quickest-maturing"**: Ibid., 267.

109 **"Canned chicken fricassee"**: "The Modern Epicure," ibid., May 1953, 239.

109 **"Why, oh why"**: Cannon, "Memo to a Modern Epicure," ibid., June 1956, 184.

109 **She wrote a detailed**: Cannon, "Pancakes Are Your Yardstick," ibid., April 1956, 155; "Swift and Elegant Meals," 199.

109 **Then she offered**: Cannon, "Delights for Your Table," ibid., June 1955, 174.

109 **"Franco-American beef gravy"**: Cannon, "The Modern Epicure," ibid., May 1953, 205.

109 **"Assembling a list"**: Cannon, "How, Where, and Why to Read a Cookbook," ibid., February 1957, 147.

110 **"Every single one"**: M.F.K. Fisher, "How to Catch a Sea Monster," ibid., April 1957, 246.

111 **After all, she was**: *Park East,* November 1951, 5. Cannon was the magazine's food editor from November 1951 through March 1953, and the expression appeared in a biographical note published about her when she began the job. The note continued: "Hers is a brand-new philosophy in the field of edibles and notables, a conviction that ease, speed, and simplicity can be compatible with gracious living, epicurean eating, memorable entertaining—and a full life."

112 **"I am nothing"**: Alice B. Toklas to Carl Van Vechten, May 21, 1958, Burns, *Staying on Alone,* 358.

112 **She poached the fish**: Toklas, "Food, Artists, and the Baroness," *Vogue,* March 1950, 165.

112 **She called the job**: Toklas to Van Vechten, April 24, 1953, Burns, 276.

112 **had to beg her friends:** Toklas to Louise Taylor, March 14, 1953, Burns, 274. ("About the cook book. You wont think too badly if I throw myself upon you with a thud will you . . . You will see the grind this is. So one chapter . . . will be devoted to recipes of friends—undoubtedly the only thing of merit in the deadly dull offering.")

113 **She sent all the recipes:** See Linda Simon, *The Biography of Alice B. Toklas,* 217–19.

113 **"What do you think":** Toklas to Van Vechten, March 23, 1954, Burns, 301.

113 **"Do you suppose":** Ibid.

114 **"Alice Toklas by the way":** Cannon to White, n.d.

114 **When Cannon published:** Toklas to Cannon, December 2, 1956.

115 **"I have a new trick":** Toklas to Isabel Wilder, April 8, 1956, Burns, 336.

115 **"Gertrude had said":** Samuel Steward, ed., *Dear Sammy,* 81.

115 **"The Mix master came":** Gertrude Stein to Samuel Steward, March 25, 1940, ibid., 147.

115 **"Day and night":** Stein to Steward, April 4, 1940, ibid., 148.

116 **". . . you see you can use":** Stein to Steward, November 18, 1940, ibid., 151.

116 **He also sent:** Stein to Steward, October 27, 1945, ibid., 155.

116 **Although it had been:** Cannon, "Introduction," Toklas, with Cannon, *Aromas and Flavors of Past and Present,* xiii.

116 **A month later:** Ibid., xiv.

116 **"Delicious!":** Ibid.

116 **"It has revolutionized":** Toklas to Cannon, October 13, 1954.

117 **"The blended tomatoes":** Toklas to Cannon, April 23, 1955. Toklas's article, "A Blessed Blender in the Home," appeared in July 1955.

117 **Harper & Bros. had an option:** See Simon, *Biography,* 235–36. See also the letters from Toklas to John Schaffner, her literary agent, in the John Schaffner Collection, Rare Book and Manuscript Library, Columbia University.

117 **The manuscript she submitted:** "I spend my days trying to achieve fifty thousand words from the box of recipes—to be delivered to Harper's at the end of November! Not likely. Half that has become my goal." (Toklas to Steward, September 21, 1956, Steward, 216.) Two years later, after she had begun revising the manuscript with Cannon's help, she wrote: "I have nine recipes to send to Poppy Cannon tomorrow morning—no wonder [Michael] Bessie of Harper's was enraged with my carelessness—but I wrote to him sharply before he had a chance to do so." (Toklas to Steward, January 15, 1958, Steward, 224.)

118 **Cannon had edited:** The note is in Toklas, "A Blessed Blender," 85.

118   **Even so, they battled:** Cannon, "Introduction," *Aromas and Flavors,* xxi.

118   **"How should I know":** Ibid.

118   **She refused to let:** Ibid., xxii.

118   **The questions she was:** Ibid.

118   **In the end, Toklas hated:** "It is not my fault if you have gotten now a cookbook of which I can not be proud." (Toklas to Steward, November 29, 1958, Steward, 229.) See also Steward's note on this letter, describing how Toklas "deplored" the book. Edward Burns makes a similar point in an editorial note on this subject (*Staying,* 359).

119   **She told her literary agent:** Toklas to Schaffner, July 12, 1959. Schaffner Collection, Columbia; Toklas to Schaffner, May 29, 1958. Schaffner Collection.

119   **"There is about as much Alice":** Beard to Brown, September 14, 1958, in Ferrone, 230.

119   **"What makes this book fun":** Charlotte Turgeon, "Favorite Dishes of Gertrude Stein and Others," *The New York Times Book Review,* December 7, 1958, 60.

119   **She lavished admiration:** Cannon, "Introduction," *Aromas and Flavors,* xxi.

119   **She told a friend:** Toklas to Steward, April 3, 1958, Steward, 226.

120   **"This book is for":** Cannon, *The Electric Epicure's Cookbook,* n.p.

121   **One minute she was making:** Cannon, *Poppy Cannon's Eating European Abroad and at Home,* 175; Cannon, *Unforbidden Sweets,* 44.

121   **A classic salmon soufflé:** Toklas, with Cannon, *Aromas and Flavors,* 31; **blender Hollandaise:** Cannon, *Electric,* 196.

121   **And there was a love poem:** Cannon, *Knight,* 190.

122   **"Even though you have visited:** Cannon, *Eating European,* xiv.

124   **Even if her Coupe Royale:** Cannon, *The Frozen Foods Cookbook,* 208.

124   **"Perhaps it is retribution":** Cannon, *The Fast Gourmet Cookbook,* 13.

125   **"Much of the difference":** Cannon, *The Can-Opener Cookbook,* 4.

125   **"Drama incarnate":** Cannon, *Electric,* 124.

125   **For salmon mousse:** Ibid., 107.

125   **Or she might sit:** Ibid., 109

125   **Or she could broil:** Cannon, "Avoid the Food Clichés-of-the-Season," *House Beautiful,* December 1952, 188.

125   **Perhaps the most dazzling:** Cannon, *Electric,* 270.

126   **As she saw it:** Cannon, *Can-Opener,* 98.

126   **Canned mushrooms:** Ibid., 163.

126   **"Consider the drama":** Cannon, "Avoid the Food Clichés," *House Beautiful,* December 1952, 132.

126   **She liked the idea:** Cannon, *Electric,* 144.

126 **And she loved:** Cannon, "The Cocktail Party Comes of Age," *Park East,* November 1951, 52.

126 **Most elaborate of all:** Cannon, *Can-Opener,* 256.

127 **"Pour on warmed rum":** Cannon, "Avoid the Food Clichés," *House Beautiful,* December 1952, 187.

127 **" 'I' stands for Intelligence":** Cannon, *The Bride's Cookbook,* n.p.

127 **One of the very last recipes:** Cannon, *Poppy Cannon's All-Time No-Time Any-Time Cookbook,* 21.

CHAPTER 4: I HATE TO COOK

Page

131 **"I've never made *anything*":** Dorothy Thompson, "Occupation Housewife," *Ladies' Home Journal,* March 1949, in Nancy Walker, ed., *Women's Magazines 1940–1960,* 161.

131 **"The businessman":** Lillian Gilbreth, Orpha Mae Thomas, and Eleanor Clymer, *Management in the Home,* 5.

132 **Half a century earlier:** Laura Shapiro, *Perfection Salad,* 37.

132 **"Vice President":** "Vice President in Charge of Home," *Living,* June 1956, 70.

132 **"The homemaker":** Thompson, 164.

132 **When home economists:** Shapiro, 164.

133 **" 'Be a prince' ":** Margaret Halsey, *With Malice Toward Some,* 7.

133 **But as it turned out:** Lynn Weiner, *From Working Girl to Working Mother,* 95.

134 **The number of working women:** Susan Hartmann, *The Home Front and Beyond,* 21.

134 **Two years earlier:** "The Fortune Survey," *Fortune,* August 1943, 10, cited in Hortense Glenn, *Attitudes of Women Regarding Gainful Employment of Married Women,* 9.

134 **In 1945:** Leila Rupp, "The Survival of American Feminism," in Bremner and Reichard, eds., *Reshaping America,* 36.

134 **A survey conducted:** Weiner, 111.

134 **A year later:** Ibid.

134 **Although many did return:** Ibid., 95.

134 **At that point women:** Esther Lloyd-Jones, "Progress Report of Pertinent Research," in Irma Gross, ed., *Potentialities of Women in the Middle Years,* 23.

134 **In the mid-'50s:** Weiner, 5–6.

135 **A study published:** Raymond Payne, "Adolescents' Attitudes Toward the Working Wife," *Journal of Marriage and Family Living,* November 1956, 345, cited in Glenn, 8.

135   **That same year a study:** Harold Christensen and Marilyn M. Swihart, "Post-Graduation Role Preference of Senior Women in College," *Journal of Marriage and Family Living,* February 1956, 52, cited in Glenn, 7.

135   **Because women were marrying:** Paul C. Glick, *Some Recent Changes in American Families* (Washington, D.C.: Bureau of the Census, 1975), 1–2, cited in Bremner, 28.

135   **In 1955:** Eli Ginzberg, "Shortage Occupations: New Opportunities for Women," in Women's Bureau, *The Effective Use of Womanpower,* 63.

135   **In 1957, Ph.D. student:** Glenn, 32–36.

136   **If these changes:** Weiner, 88–89.

136   **In 1940 a third:** Paula Giddings, *When and Where I Enter,* 238, 241.

136   **Segregation and discrimination:** Jacqueline Jones, *Labor of Love, Labor of Sorrow,* 261.

136   **By 1960 nearly half:** Giddings, 232.

136   **Psychiatrists attributed:** See, for example, William G. Niederland, "Some Psychological Disorders of Femininity and Masculinity," in J. E. Fairchild, ed., *Women, Society and Sex* (1956; reprint, New York: Fawcett, 1962), 91.

136   **No matter how:** Lois Wladis Hoffman, "Effects on Children: Summary and Discussion," in F. Ivan Nye and Lois Wlaldis Hoffman, eds., *The Employed Mother in America,* 190.

137   **By the early '50s:** Frances Lomas Feldman, "Supplementary Income Earned by Married Women," in National Manpower Council, *Work in the Lives of Married Women,* 93.

137   **"Working wives are one":** Quoted in John Harris, "Are Working Wives a Threat to Male Labor Markets?" *Boston Globe,* July 11, 1954, 66.

137   **The revolution had happened:** see National Manpower Council, *Work in the Lives,* passim.

137   **Even Congress could read:** Susan M. Hartmann, "Women's Employment and the Domestic Ideal in the Early Cold War Years," in Joanne Meyerowitz, ed., *Not June Cleaver,* 95.

138   **The anti-Communist witch hunt:** See, for example, Harriet Hyman Alonso, "Mayhem and Moderation: Women Peace Activists During the McCarthy Era," in Meyerowitz, 128.

139   **"When a woman":** Quoted in Hartmann, "Women's Employment," 86.

139   **This was a time:** Glenn Ramsey, Bert Kruger Smith, and Bernice Milburn Moore, *Women View Their Working World,* 5.

139   **"*House Beautiful* has watched":** "Reporting on a New Breed of Woman," *House Beautiful,* August 1956, 41.

139   **They emphasized how fast:** See, for example, *Life,* April 12, 1954, 118, where a Maytag ad shows mother and daughter in similar skirts as the daughter helps her mother with the laundry. In a variation on this

theme, *Living* ran a story about a woman who planned her "at-home" clothes so that she would always match the walls and furniture of her house. (Louise Richards, "It Was a Stable . . . Now It's Our Home!" *Living,* Autumn 1947, 175.)

140 **Story after story:** See, for example, *Quick Frozen Foods,* March 1953, 75; March 1954, 84; August 1954, 130; January 1957, 107.

140 **"How to Be a Volunteer Worker":** *Parade,* December 6, 1959, 9.

140 **Food stories featuring:** "Meal Suggestions for the Bread-Winner and Homemaker," *Boston Globe,* January 13, 1950, 27; Mary Meade, "Quickly Prepared Dishes Are Boon to Career Wives," *Chicago Tribune,* January 17, 1954, part 7, 7.

140 **An ad for Betty:** *Journal of Home Economics,* February 1956, 76.

141 **"Woman's hard-won right":** "The Married Woman Goes Back to Work," *Woman's Home Companion,* October 1956, in Walker, ed., *Women's Magazines,* 87.

141 **"Now is the time":** "How to Be a Girl," *Woman's Day,* February 1956, 18.

141 **"A woman, like a man":** Patricia Hunt, "I'll Stay Home and Like It," ibid., March 1954, 168.

141 **Singer Sue Bennett:** Joe Cullinane, "How a Mother Splits Time Between a Year-Old Son and TV," *Boston Sunday Globe Magazine,* July 11, 1954, 1.

141–42 **Pete's salary and the "driblets":** "Penny and Pete Find an Apartment and Furnish It," *Living,* Autumn 1947, 34.

142 **Dorothy Dandridge was:** Freda De Knight, "Coffee Breads for Sunday Morning," *Ebony,* March 1947, 38; De Knight, "Chocolate Potato Cake," ibid., May 1952, 74.

142 **A 1952 photo feature:** "Housework in Ballet," ibid., April 1952, 53.

143 **"I am twenty-four":** *Boston Globe,* October 23, 1952, 24.

143 **A few days later:** Ibid., October 29, 1952, 15.

143 **"I've so many questions":** Ibid., October 26, 1961, 34.

144 **"The problem is not":** Anne Morrow Lindbergh, *Gift from the Sea,* 29.

146 **"I won't write":** Quoted in Judy Oppenheimer, *Private Demons,* 145. Oppenheimer's biography of Jackson has been my chief source for information about her personal and home life.

146 **"Serve them coffee":** Shirley Jackson, *Life Among the Savages,* 32.

148 **"I went into the kitchen":** Ibid., 63.

150 **Then she departs:** Jackson, *Raising Demons,* 79.

150 **"Never, in this reviewer's":** Jane Cobb, "Chaos Can Be Beautiful," *The New York Times Book Review,* June 21, 1953, 6.

150 **The *Christian Science Monitor*:** M. W. Stoer, *Christian Science Monitor,* July 9, 1953, 7.

151   **"I have met the caterpillar's"**: Cynthia Lindsay, *Home Is Where You Hang Yourself,* 103.

152   **"I would like to know"**: *Boston Globe,* May 28, 1956, 19.

152   **"Please! Will everybody:"** Adeline Daley, "Some of My Best Friends Are Kids," *Coronet,* June 1961, 33.

152   **"Finally, last fall"**: Daley, in a note from "The Editors," ibid., 3.

153   **"I've always wanted"**: Lesley Conger, *Love and Peanut Butter,* 48.

154   **"I will read *anything*"**: Jean Kerr, *Please Don't Eat the Daisies,* 16.

155   **What she never mentioned**: According to her husband's obituary, they were divorced around 1957. ("Willard Espy, Who Delighted in Wordplay, Is Dead at 88," *The New York Times,* February 25, 1999, B12.)

156   **"For years I really believed"**: [Martha Gilbreth], "A Large Family Is Fun!" typescript, Ernestine Gilbreth Carey papers, Sophia Smith Collection, Smith College. All citations of Carey's manuscripts, letters, or diaries refer to the Smith collection. Biographical information has been drawn from the collection as well.

157   **"Mother and I"**: Carey, typescript, June 24, 1970.

157   **Her outline for the book**: Carey, typescript, 1943.

158   **It was a "really serious challenge"**: Fanny Butcher, "The Literary Spotlight," *Chicago Sunday Tribune,* March 25, 1956.

159   **Planning a chapter**: Carey, typescript.

159   **"Mother is a miracle"**: Carey, typescript of diary entry, January 8, 1963.

160   **Returning to work**: Carey, *Rings Around Us,* 77.

160   **"Mother, dad, son and daughter"**: Ibid., 108.

160   **"Like an old fire horse"**: Ibid., 117.

160   **Finally, she accepts**: Ibid., 201.

161   **"Thank goodness I've retired"**: Ibid., 216.

161   **"Thank goodness we're back"**: Ibid., 225.

162   **"This chapter contains"**: Peg Bracken, *The I Hate to Cook Book,* 3.

163   **During the 1940s and 1950s**: Susan L. Crowley, "Done to Perfection," *AARP Bulletin,* June 1999, 14.

163   **"My Husband Ought"**: Bracken, "My Husband Ought to Fire Me," *Saturday Evening Post,* January 11, 1958, 38; Crowley, "Done to Perfection," 14.

164   **"Never believe the people"**: Bracken, *I Hate to Cook,* 55.

164   **The terms**: Ibid., 81.

164   **"When you hate"**: Ibid., 113.

165   **Bracken writes**: Ibid., xi.

165   **In many instances**: Ibid., 43.

166   **James Beard summed up**: Clark, 240.

166   **"We live in"**: Bracken, *I Hate to Cook,* 27.

166   Yet she also assumes: Ibid., 76.

167   First, always remember: Ibid., 152.

CHAPTER 5: IS SHE REAL?

171   She was still working: Myra Waldo, *The Bride's Cookbook,* 15.

171   And if visionary home cooks: *Picture Cook Book,* 126, 133.

171   "Does anyone have": *Boston Globe,* June 12, 1959, 26.

171–72   Other Chatters . . . chicken cacciatore: Ibid., September 14, 1959, 19; sabayon: Ibid., January 26, 1961, 32; café au lait: Ibid., September 15, 1959, 14.

172   "those nice Italian cookies": Ibid., July 25, 1961, 31.

172   It was a visiting Frenchman: Waldo, 171.

172   "He was almost professional": Ibid., 141.

172   True, her source: Ibid., 110.

173   "I realize now": Ibid.

173   By 1952, makers: "Outdoor Cooking: The California Export Is Turning Fast into a New National Habit," *Tide,* September 12, 1952, 46.

173   "Possibly it is the closest": Ibid.

174   Thanks to a legacy: Shapiro, 94–97.

174–75   Hence, on the American side: Lang, *Nobody Knows the Truffles I've Seen,* 153.

175   Although the New York branch: See the *Wine and Food Society's Newsletter,* produced by the New York branch of the organization beginning in 1938 and written by Jeanne Owen, secretary of the branch. "We must say this, however, for the San Francisco branch: they are polite and quite friendly toward your secretary. Whereas the Los Angeles branch has such contempt for women and wine—in this particular sense—that when we are in Southern California and phone the members merely to wish them good morning, they don't even answer. Just how seriously can you take yourself!" (*Newsletter,* November–December 1949.)

175   "If the Chef": *Gourmet,* February 1941, 45.

175   Paul could pan-broil: "Mr. and Mrs. in the Kitchen," *Living,* April–May 1949, 98.

176   "Nothing, not even salads": Letter to Irma Rombauer, June 4, 1953, Rombauer-Becker papers, Schlesinger Library.

176   At [a wedding shower]: Betty MacDonald, *Onions in the Stew,* 178.

176   There was "Harriet Hepplewhite": Waldo, 175.

177   When Irma Rombauer published: Irma Rombauer, *Streamlined Cooking,* n.p.

178   Marie Gifford of Armour: "The Current State of Live Trademarks," *Tide,* March 22, 1957, 28.

178   **Kellogg dismissed:** Ibid.

178   **General Foods was grooming:** Ibid.

178   **Even so, she lasted:** *Woman's Home Companion,* May 1953, 100.

178   **Known in the business:** "The Current State of Live Trademarks," ibid.

178   **"Ideally, the corporate character":** Ibid.

179   **Mary Alden of Quaker Oats:** Mary Alden, "Breakfasting Well . . . *and Economically,*" *Forecast,* January 1952, 16; **a charming luncheon:** "Diary of an Editor," ibid., October 1948, 8.

179   **"I came home":** Ibid., April 1948, 71.

179   **That was Aunt Jemima:** See M. M. Manring, *Slave in a Box,* for a complete history and analysis of Aunt Jemima. Except for the point about Aunt Jemima in relation to the other corporate spokeswomen, the information here is drawn from Manring's book.

180   **During her glory years:** General Mills, "Betty Crocker . . . 1921–1954" (Minneapolis, privately printed, [1954?]), Appendix A, n.p.

180   **They knew her face:** Mary Hart, "$2,000,000 Cookbook Preview," *Minneapolis Sunday Tribune,* August 27, 1950.

180   **The Betty Crocker whose voice:** See Anna Rothe, ed., *Current Biography: Who's News and Why 1949* (New York: H.W. Wilson, 1950), 286. See also General Mills, "Outline of Career in Advertising of Marjorie Child Husted," typescript from the Department of Public Services, February 1950; and General Mills, "Marjorie Child Husted," in General Mills, *Siftings from the General Mills Test Kitchen* 2, no. 2, n.d.

180   **The company made a practice:** Carol Pine, "The Real Betty Crocker Is One Tough Cookie," *Twin Cities,* November 1978, 46; General Mills, "Outline of Career," 1.

181   **The school was a local:** General Mills, oral history of Marjorie Child Husted, conducted by Jean Toll, July 26, 1985.

181   **Betty Crocker had been created:** See James Gray, *Business Without Boundary,* 170; Pine, 46.

181   **"What makes my cake":** Pine, 46.

181   **"How do you make":** Gray, 170.

182   **"Comfortable chairs":** General Mills, *Siftings.*

182   **"I could see":** General Mills, oral history of Husted.

183   **Eventually, General Mills developed:** Gray, 178.

183   **"Have you tried Wheaties":** Ibid., 160.

183   **In 1924 the company:** Ibid., 176–77.

184   **"The radio made Betty":** "General Mills of Minneapolis," *Fortune,* April 1945, 117.

184   **"Thanks to the War Food":** General Mills, "Betty Crocker . . . 1921–1954," 8.

184 **Her free pamphlet:** *Fortune,* ibid., 118.

185 **During the early 1930s:** General Mills, "Outline of Career," 2.

185 **She conducted interviews:** General Mills, "Betty Crocker . . . 1921–1954," 9.

185 **After the war:** Ibid.

185 **"But as I came to know":** Husted, "The Women in Your Lives," a speech to 4A's Pacific Coast Council Convention, October 13, 1952. Husted papers, Schlesinger Library.

185 **Husted went home:** Pine, 50.

185 **"Women needed a champion":** Ibid., 49.

186 **Even though she was:** Ibid., 50.

186 **"Management is dominated":** Husted, "What Price Women in the Business World?," a speech to the American Association of University Women State Conference, Columbia, South Carolina, January 20, 1951. Husted papers, Schlesinger Library.

187 **"At first, I'd hedge":** Pine, 49.

187 **"The trend in American life":** Husted, "What Price Women."

188 **"Daily Betty Crocker and her staff":** General Mills, *Betty Crocker Cook Book of All-Purpose Baking,* n.p.

188 **"Our Mildred has a son":** "From Betty Crocker's Kitchen," *Chicago Tribune,* September 16, 1949, part 3, 2.

188 **"Our Vicky, who is":** Ibid., September 8, 1949, part 3, 10.

188 **By the time the artist:** General Mills, "Betty Crocker . . . 1921–1954," 5.

189 **"And here she is":** *Time for Betty Crocker,* typescript, January 21, 1955. Adelaide Hawley Cumming papers, Schlesinger Library.

189 **"You know we've found":** Script, *Time for Betty Crocker,* October 20, 1954, in "Betty Crocker on Net Radio: Ultimate in Integrated Sell," *Sponsor,* December 27, 1954, 34. At the General Mills archives I had the privilege of listening to tapes of Betty Crocker speaking on the radio.

191 **According to a study:** "Listening & Viewing Related to Length of TV Set Ownership," *Advertising Age,* December 11, 1950, 46.

191 **General Mills started:** "General Mills Moves," *Tide,* September 1, 1950, 16.

191 **Adelaide Hawley:** Obituary, *The New York Times,* December 25, 1998, B11. Other information was obtained from the Adelaide Hawley Cumming papers, Schlesinger Library. See especially Marcia Hayes, "Now It's Dr. Betty Crocker, the Speech Teacher," *Morning Call,* June 15, 1967, in Cumming papers. (Adelaide Hawley Cumming was Hayes's mother.)

192 **In 1948 she had even been:** *Betty Crocker. . . . 8/30/48,* typescript of the *Betty Crocker Magazine of the Air.* Cumming papers.

192 **For a time she portrayed:** Ibid.

192 ***The Betty Crocker Show:*** General Mills archives. I am grateful to Gen-

eral Mills for the opportunity to view a videotape of the first show, the only surviving record of Betty Crocker on her own television program. See also *Betty Crocker, Pioneer Advertising Woman,* typescript of a talk given by Adelaide Hawley to the Eastern Conference of Women's Advertising Clubs, February 5, 1956. ("Al Ward of BBDO, who was our producer, tells me that the Betty Crocker films we made in the winter of 1951 were the first half-hour films ever made for TV—cost $7,300 apiece.") Cumming papers.

194 **General Mills made another try:** See *Sponsor,* 82.

194 **"Why don't you ask":** General Mills archives. I am grateful to General Mills for the opportunity to watch a series of Betty Crocker ads preserved on videotape.

195 **"In strawberry season":** *Life,* May 17, 1954, 16.

195 **"I guarantee":** The slogan was used for six years, with a number of variations perhaps designed to tone down the implication that all those cakes came from a factory. "We guarantee a perfect cake—homemade perfect," Betty Crocker was saying in 1959. (General Mills archives.)

197 **She liked cooking:** M.F.K. Fisher, Guggenheim application, 1948. M.F.K. Fisher papers, Schlesinger Library. See also the entry on Fisher in Charles Moritz, ed., *Current Biography Yearbook 1983* (New York: H. W. Wilson, 1983), 133; and Joan Reardon, *Celebrating the Pleasures of the Table,* 25–110.

197 **"César was all":** Fisher, "César," *The Art of Eating,* 116.

197 **W. H. Auden called her:** Reardon, *Celebrating,* 57.

198 **Her work was published:** Fisher, Guggenheim application.

199 **"Do I marry M.F.K. Fisher":** Fisher to Dr. George Frumkes, June 6, 1950, in Norah K. Barr, Marsha Moran, and Patrick Moran, eds. *M.F.K. Fisher: A Life in Letters,* 86.

199 **"hold a private funeral":** Fisher to Norah Kennedy Barr, April 6, 1952, in Barr et al., 99.

200 **At a hotel in Mexico:** Fisher, "The Measure of My Powers," *The Art of Eating,* 544.

200–201 **The waitress automatically:** Fisher, "Define This Word," ibid., 474.

201 **"I know what I want":** Fisher, "The Lemming to the Sea," ibid., 518.

202 **Oxtail stew:** Fisher, "B Is for Bachelors," ibid., 588; **a good steak:** Fisher, "U Is for Universal," ibid., 699; **spinach tart:** Fisher, *With Bold Knife and Fork,* 192.

202 **But her aura dissipated:** Fisher, "K Is for Kosher," *The Art of Eating,* 638.

202 **"a crown of lamb":** Beard to Brown, May 14, 1955, in Ferrone, 106.

204 **Clémentine worked for:** See Phineas Beck [Samuel Chamberlain], *Clémentine in the Kitchen,* 1943.

204 **Her Blanquette de Veau:** Ibid., 195.

204   **Right around that time:** Betty Crocker, *Betty Crocker's Picture Cook Book,* 272.

205   **Clémentine was everything:** Beck, 6.

206   **That was the place:** Ibid., 55.

206   **Of course, American readers:** Ibid., 210, 186, 152.

206   **"Mr. Beck removed himself":** Beck, *Clémentine* (New York: Modern Library, 2001), 159. Narcisse Chamberlain's revisions first appeared in 1988 in an edition published by David R. Godine.

208   **"Cook them slowly":** Chamberlain, *Bouquet de France,* 259.

208   **"They won't brown":** Julia Child to Avis DeVoto, January 5, 1953. Avis DeVoto Collection, Schlesinger Library.

208   *Gourmet* **did not:** Child to DeVoto, March 6, 1953. DeVoto Collection.

209   **"At the party":** Child to DeVoto, February 12, 1953. Julia Child papers, Schlesinger Library.

CHAPTER 6: NOW AND FOREVER

Page

213   **The name of the show:** Note, Paul Child to Julia Child, May 24, 1962. Julia Child papers, Schlesinger Library.

213   **"After having racked":** Memo, Larson to staff, December 24, 1962. Child papers.

214   *I Love to Eat!* **starred James Beard:** Clark, *James Beard,* 121–22.

214   **By the early '50s:** William I. Kaufman, ed., *Cooking with the Experts,* vii.

214   **On WSPD-TV ... gelatin eggs:** Ibid., 127.

215   **squabs:** Ibid., 115; **"wild cottontails":** 76; **layered salad:** 129; **peach pie:** 207.

215   **"When your tutti-frutti is cool":** *Hi Mom!,* NBC-TV, December 11, 1957 (videotape, Museum of Television and Radio, New York).

215   **McCarthy received thousands:** Josephine McCarthy, *Josie McCarthy's Favorite TV Recipes,* 2.

215   **When she made Upside-Down Peach Cake:** Ibid., 199.

215   **The day McCarthy:** Ibid., 112.

216   **"Then we just dropped it":** *Hi Mom!*

216   **"Yes! It can be done":** McCarthy, 193.

216   **"Maybe you can improve":** Quoted in Lynn Spigel, *Make Room for TV,* 82. It's also possible that she lost the job because she seemed ill at ease on camera the first few times she appeared on the show. Jack Gould, the television critic at *The New York Times,* said she "lacked assurance" in his review of the show's first week. (Gould, "Television in Review," *The New York Times,* March 6, 1954, 26.)

216 **The only television cook:** Typescript biography prepared by Marion Gorman for use in Lucas's obituary. Dione Lucas papers, Schlesinger Library.

217 **The recipes she offered:** See, for example, "Mrs. Lucas Cooks Brioche," in *Greenwich Time*, May 21, 1954, 14. Lucas papers. This and other newspaper clippings describe her public appearances around the country.

217 **"This one belongs to":** "A Little Rough Shooting," [New York] *Wine and Food Society Newsletter,* April 1947.

217 **James Beard described her:** Beard to Brown, June 8, 1953, in Ferrone, 14.

217 **By the time her career:** See, for example, Child to Beard, September 18, 1963: "Craig [Claiborne, food editor of *The New York Times*] has told me that he dare not mention her school in the *Times* anymore because of the number of people who call in complaining who have suits against her. How tragic for one with her abilities!" Child papers.

217 **Paul Child was helping:** Much of the biographical information in this discussion of Child is drawn from Noel Riley Fitch's biography, *Appetite for Life*. The analysis and its attendant speculation are my own.

218 **Many years later:** Author's interview with Brownstone, April 18, 2002, New York.

220 **Child was adamant:** Fitch, 191.

221 **As Child said later:** *Cooking Biography of Julia Child,* typescript. Child papers.

222 **"This is a lot of balderdash":** Child to Jones, September 14, 1960. Child papers.

222 **"In a variation":** Child to Jones, January 13, 1961. Child papers.

223 **Everyone who cared:** I am indebted to Ann Phillips and Wendy Phillips Kahn for the Snow Ball Sandwiches recipe and other recipes from Helen D'Esopo's collection.

223 **Food editors:** William Koshland to Avis DeVoto, n.d. [1958]. DeVoto Collection ("Never before has this country been so gourmet-minded. . . . I have two cooking ladyfriends at *McCall's* and their problem is to keep that section corned up for the subscribers and the advertisers. Those housewives don't have the time to cook fancy things but the U.S. is filled with real cooks and hobby cooks."); Clark, 205.

223 **Suburban dinner parties:** I am indebted here to Carey Rosen for her extensive menu notes.

223 *The James Beard Cookbook*: Clark, 184, 201.

223 **"Men like our recipes":** Knopf, "Author's Questionnaire," filled out by Child on August 10, 1960. Child papers.

223 **Six months after publication:** Jones to Child, April 11, 1962. Child papers.

223 **Beard's book:** Clark, 184.

223–24   **But in August 1962:** See Koshland to Child, November 29, 1962; January 11, 1963; January 17, 1963; March 14, 1963; December 4, 1963. Child papers.

225   **"I think we could make":** Memo, Child to WGBH-TV, April 26, 1962. Child papers.

225   **"I find that the TV":** Child to Beard, August 20, 1962. Child papers.

225   **"We have licked":** Child to Koshland, February 11, 1963.

226   **Ten days later:** Child to Beard, February 21, 1963. Child papers; **another four hundred:** Child to Koshland, March 7, 1963. Child papers.

226   **By the fall of 1963:** Ruth Lockwood (assistant producer, *The French Chef*) to Paul and Julia Child, September 3, 1963; September 10, 1963; September 23, 1963. Child papers; **two dozen more:** Helen Peters (publicity director, WGBH) to Jean Muir (writer), July 24, 1964. Child papers.

226   **In the summer of 1963:** Koshland to Child, July 23, 1963. Child papers; **a thousand a month:** Koshland to Child, November 24, 1964. Child papers.

226   **"I find the book":** Child to Koshland, July 30, 1963. Child papers.

226   **Mail poured in...**"I have tried a number":** Jamaica Plain, Mass., April 29, 1964.

227   **"You make it look":** Kennebunk, Maine, April 9, 1964; **"Please continue":** Canton, Mass., n.d.; **"Thank you for presenting":** Fitchburg, Mass., n.d.; **"I go to business":** Long Island City, N.Y., January 6, 1964; **"We love to watch":** (no address), January 27, 1964. Child papers.

228   **As for Beard:** For example, Beard's friend and assistant Isabel Callvert was behind much of his work, including his best-known book, *The James Beard Cookbook*. See Clark, 144.

228   **"Cooks are made":** Child, typescript, n.d. Child papers.

228   **She always referred:** "I don't speak about women or housewives, it's 'the home cook.'" Author's interview with Child, September 23, 1989, Cambridge, Mass.

229   **"It wasn't until I began":** Edith Efron, "Dinner with Julia Child," *TV Guide*, December 5, 1970.

229   **"It's good to know":** Child, letter to a fan in Roslindale, Mass., July 31, 1963. Child papers.

230   **As it happened:** Memo, W. W. Norton sales department. Betty Friedan papers, Schlesinger Library.

231   **The percentage of married women:** F. Ivan Nye and Lois Wladis Hoffman, "The Socio-Cultural Setting," in Cynthia Fuchs Epstein and William J. Goode, eds., *The Other Half*, 88, 96.

231   **Among married women:** Ibid., 92.

231 **"I don't feel like *me*"**: Anne Jayson, "I Don't Feel Like *Me* Anymore," *Good Housekeeping*, May 1960, 47.

231 *Newsweek* **examined**: Edwin Diamond, "Young Wives with Brains," *Newsweek*, March 7, 1960, 57; Phyllis Lee Levin, "Road from Sophocles to Spock Is Often a Bumpy One," *The New York Times*, June 28, 1960; Jesse Birnbaum, "The Suburban Wife," *Time*, June 20, 1960, 14.

232 *Redbook* **commissioned**: Jhan and June Robbins, "Why Young Mothers Feel Trapped," *Redbook*, September 1960, 27.

232 **Some twenty-six thousand**: "Between the Lines," *Redbook*, September 1962, 4.

232 **"I am so sick"**: Letter, "Sincerely Yours," *Good Housekeeping*, November 1960, 19.

232 **"Most people solve"**: "Between the Lines," ibid.

233 **"These, then, are some"**: Jhan and June Robbins, " 'I Don't Feel Trapped Anymore,' " ibid., 45.

233 **"It is not easy"**: Betty Friedan, "I Say: Women are *People* Too!" *Good Housekeeping*, September 1960, 59.

234 **Her politics**: Much of my analysis of Betty Friedan relies on Daniel Horowitz's political biography *Betty Friedan and the Making of "The Feminine Mystique."* For some aspects of her life and work I also made use of Judith Hennessee's *Betty Friedan: Her Life*.

235 **"UE Fights"**: Horowitz, 138.

237 **Overall, they felt positive**: Ibid., 209.

237 **As she explained**: Friedan, *The Feminine Mystique,* 11.

239 **"Somehow, somewhere"**: Ibid., 207.

239 **"If I am right"**: Ibid., 32.

239 **Friedan wasn't impressed**: Ibid., 428.

240 **"Nobody but Friedan"**: Hennessee, 75.

240 **By summer the book**: Full-page ad, *The New York Times Book Review,* June 30, 1963.

240 **Portions of her manuscript**: Excerpts appeared in *Good Housekeeping*, March 1961; *Mademoiselle*, May 1962; *McCall's*, March 1963; and *Ladies' Home Journal*, January and February 1963. See Hennessee, 76.

240 **"The key phrase"**: Elizabeth Hinson, *News* (Charlotte, N.C.), March 23, 1963. Friedan papers.

241 **"Many women do not"**: Arlene Wood, "Distaff Dissent," *Mark,* April 6, 1963. Friedan papers.

241 **But Friedan was receiving**: Friedan, *It Changed My Life*, 18.

241 **"I have squeezed"**: Letter to Friedan, May 19, 1963. Friedan papers.

241 **As several reviewers**: See, for example, Diane Ravitch, "Mama in Search of Herself," *The New Leader,* April 15, 1963, 28. ("Like [Vance]

Packard, she is a journalist of the social sciences running down a story on a Big Idea. She too is more concerned with publicizing the subject than with the subject itself.")

241 **She herself noted:** Friedan, *Mystique,* 22.

241 **"When a woman":** Jayson, "I Don't Feel Like *Me,*" 198.

242 **"We will never grow up":** Elizabeth Hawes, *Why Women Cry,* 36, 219.

242 **Five years later:** Horowitz, 129.

242 **"Cleanliness is to be":** Ruth Herschberger, *Adam's Rib,* 45.

243 **Even the political climate:** See Miriam Schneir, ed., *Feminism in Our Time* (New York: Vintage, 1994), 38–41.

243 **That was also the year:** See the Equal Pay Act in Toni Carabillo, Judith Meuli, and June Bundy Csida, *Feminist Chronicles, 1953–1993* (Los Angeles: Women's Graphics, 1993), 45.

244 **By the same token:** See Horowitz, especially chapter 10, "The Development of *The Feminine Mystique,*" 197. See also Joanne Meyerowitz, ed., "Beyond the Feminine Mystique," in *Not June Cleaver,* 229.

244 **She described the "disuse of":** Friedan, *Mystique,* 425; **the proportion of women:** Women's Bureau, *Today's Woman in Tomorrow's World,* 121.

244 **She also stressed:** Friedan, *Mystique,* 150.

244 **a sample of the eighty-seven thousand:** Women's Bureau, *College Women Go to Work,* 1–2.

245 **Yet she never pointed out:** See F. Ivan Nye and Lois Hoffman, eds., *The Employed Mother in America,* 1963.

246 **"The only way for a woman":** Friedan, *Mystique,* 344.

246 **"I'm mad, I'm sick":** "Our Readers Report," *Ladies' Home Journal,* June 18, 1964. Friedan papers.

Bibliography

Anselmino, Mary Anne. "Factors Influencing the Emergence and Acceptance of Food Innovations in Twentieth-Century America," Ph.D. diss., Teachers College, Columbia University, 1986.

Arnold, Eleanor, ed. *Voices of American Homemakers*. Bloomington: Indiana University Press, 1985.

Arnold, Pauline, and Percival White. *Food: America's Biggest Business*. New York: Holiday House, 1959.

Barr, Norah K., Marsha Moran, and Patrick Moran, eds. *M.F.K. Fisher: A Life in Letters*. Washington, D.C.: Counterpoint, 1997.

Batchelder, Ann. *Ann Batchelder's Cook Book*. New York: M. Barrows, 1949.

———. *Start to Finish*. Woodstock, Vt.: Elm Tree Press, 1954.

Be Milwaukee's Guest. With an introduction by Edward Harris Heth. Milwaukee: Junior League of Milwaukee, 1959.

Beck, Phineas [Samuel Chamberlain]. *Clémentine in the Kitchen*. New York: Hastings House, 1943.

Benell, Julie. *Let's Eat at Home*. New York: Crowell, 1961.

Berheide, Catherine White, Sarah Fenstermaker Berk, and Richard A. Berk. "Household Work in the Suburbs," *Pacific Sociological Review* 19, no. 4 (1976): 491–518.

Bernays, Doris Fleischman. *A Wife Is Many Women*. New York: Crown, 1955.

Bird, Kermit. *Freeze-dried Foods: Palatability Tests*. Marketing Research Report no. 617. Marketing Economics Division, U.S. Department of Agriculture. Washington, D.C., July 1963.

Bitting, H. W. *Purchases of Frozen and Canned Foods by Urban Families as Related to Home Refrigeration Facilities*. Marketing Research Report no. 60. Agricultural Marketing Service, U.S. Department of Agriculture. Washington, D.C., February 1954.

Blood, Robert O., Jr., and Donald M. Wolfe. *Husbands & Wives: The Dynamics of Married Living*. Glencoe, Ill.: The Free Press, 1960.

Boddy, William. *Fifties Television*. Urbana and Chicago: University of Illinois Press, 1993.

Bose, Christine, Philip Bereano, and Mary Malloy. "Household Technology and the Social Construction of Housework." *Technology and Culture* 25, no. 1 (1984): 53–82.

Bracken, Peg. "My Husband Ought to Fire Me!" *Saturday Evening Post,* January 11, 1958.

———. *The I Hate to Cook Book.* New York: Harcourt, Brace & World, 1960.

Bremner, Robert H., and Gary W. Reichard, eds. *Reshaping America: Society and Institutions 1945–1960.* Columbus: Ohio State University Press, 1982.

Brobeck, Florence. *Cook It in a Casserole.* New York: M. Barrows, 1943.

———. *The Good Salad Book.* New York: M. Barrows, 1952.

Burk, Marguerite C. *Consumption of Processed Farm Foods in the United States.* Marketing Research Report no. 409. Agricultural Marketing Service, U.S. Department of Agriculture. Washington, D.C., June 1960.

Burns, Edward, ed. *Staying on Alone: Letters of Alice B. Toklas.* New York: Liveright, 1973.

Buzzell, Robert D., and Robert E. M. Nourse. *Product Innovation in Food Processing, 1954–1964.* Boston: Graduate School of Business Administration, Harvard University, 1967.

Cannon, Poppy. *The Can-Opener Cookbook.* New York: Crowell, 1952.

———. *The Bride's Cookbook.* New York: Henry Holt, 1954.

———. *A Gentle Knight.* New York: Popular Library, 1956.

———. *Unforbidden Sweets.* New York: Crowell, 1958.

———. *The Electric Epicure's Cookbook.* New York: Crowell, 1961.

———. *Poppy Cannon's Eating European Abroad and at Home.* New York: Doubleday, 1961.

———. *The Fast Gourmet Cookbook.* New York: Fleet Publishing House, 1964.

———. *The Frozen Foods Cookbook.* New York: Crowell, 1964.

———. *Poppy Cannon's All-Time No-Time Any-Time Cookbook.* New York: Crowell, 1974.

Carey, Ernestine Gilbreth. *Jumping Jupiter.* New York: Crowell, 1952.

———. *Rings Around Us.* Boston: Little, Brown, 1956.

———. *Giddy Moment.* Boston: Little, Brown, 1958.

Chafe, William H. *The American Woman: Her Changing Social, Economic, and Political Roles, 1920–1970.* New York: Oxford University Press, 1972.

Chamberlain, Samuel. *Bouquet de France.* New York: Gourmet, 1952.

Child, Julia. *The French Chef Cookbook.* New York: Knopf, 1978.

Child, Julia, Simone Beck, and Louisette Bertholle. *Mastering the Art of French Cooking.* New York: Knopf, 1961.

Claiborne, Craig. *A Feast Made for Laughter.* New York: Doubleday, 1982.

Clark, Robert. *James Beard.* New York: HarperCollins, 1993.

Clawson, Augusta H. *Shipyard Diary of a Woman Welder.* New York: Penguin, 1944.

Conger, Lesley. *Love and Peanut Butter.* New York: Norton, 1961.

———. *Adventures of an Ordinary Mind.* New York: Norton, 1963.

Coontz, Stephanie. *The Way We Never Were*. New York: Basic Books, 1992.

Cowan, Ruth Schwartz. *More Work for Mother*. New York: Basic Books, 1983.

Crocker, Betty. *Betty Crocker's Beautiful Cakes*. Student Booklet. Minneapolis: General Mills, n.d.

———. *Betty Crocker's 101 Delicious Bisquick Creations*. Minneapolis, Minn.: General Mills, 1933.

———. *Betty Crocker Cook Book of All-Purpose Baking*. Minneapolis, Minn.: General Mills, 1942.

———. *Betty Crocker's Picture Cook Book*. New York: McGraw-Hill; Minneapolis, Minn.: General Mills, 1950.

———. *Betty Crocker's Cook Book for Boys and Girls*. New York: Simon and Schuster, 1957.

———. *Betty Crocker's Guide to Easy Entertaining*. New York: Golden Press, 1959.

———. *133 Quicker Ways to Homemade . . . with Bisquick*. Minneapolis, Minn.: General Mills, 1959.

de Beauvoir, Simone. *The Second Sex*. New York: Knopf, 1953.

Dichter, Ernest. *The Strategy of Desire*. New York: Doubleday, 1960.

———. *Handbook of Consumer Motivations*. New York: McGraw-Hill, 1964.

Dinnerstein, Myra. *Women Between Two Worlds*. Philadelphia: Temple University Press, 1992.

Dolson, Hildegarde. *Guess Whose Hair I'm Wearing*. New York: Random House, 1963.

Epstein, Cynthia Fuchs, and William J. Goode, eds. *The Other Half*. Englewood Cliffs, N.J.: Prentice-Hall, 1971.

Espy, Hilda Cole. *Quiet, Yelled Mrs. Rabbit*. Philadelphia and New York: Lippincott, 1958.

———. *Look Both Ways*. Philadelphia and New York: Lippincott, 1962.

Ferrone, John, ed. *Love and Kisses and a Halo of Truffles*. New York: Arcade, 1994.

Fisher, M.F.K. *The Art of Eating*. Cleveland, Ohio: World Publishing Co., 1954.

———. *With Bold Knife and Fork*. New York: Putnam, 1969.

Fitch, Noel Riley. *Appetite for Life*. New York: Doubleday, 1997.

Friedan, Betty. *The Feminine Mystique*. 1963. Reprint, with a new introduction by the author, New York: Norton, 1998.

———. *It Changed My Life*. New York: Random House, 1976.

———. *Life So Far*. New York: Simon and Schuster, 2000.

Gage, Marie Geraldine. *The Work Load and Its Value for 50 Homemakers, Tompkins County, New York*. Ph.D. diss., Cornell University, 1960.

Gallup, George H. *The Gallup Poll: Public Opinion 1935–1971*. New York: Random House, 1972.

Giddings, Paula. *When and Where I Enter*. New York: Morrow, 1984.

Gilbreth, Lillian, Orpha Mae Thomas, and Eleanor Clymer. *Management in the Home*. New York: Dodd, Mead, 1954.

Ginzberg, Eli. *Life Styles of Educated Women*. New York: Columbia University Press, 1966.

Glenn, Hortense. *Attitudes of Women Regarding Gainful Employment of Married Women*. Ph.D. diss., Florida State University, 1958.

Gray, James. *Business Without Boundary*. Minneapolis: University of Minnesota, 1954.

Gross, Irma H., ed. *Potentialities of Women in the Middle Years*. East Lansing: Michigan State University Press, 1956.

Grossack, Martin M., ed. *Understanding Consumer Behavior*. Boston: The Christopher Publishing House, 1964.

Halberstam, David. *The Fifties*. New York: Ballantine Books, 1993.

Hall, Joan Wylie. *Shirley Jackson*. New York: Twayne, 1993.

Halsey, Margaret. *With Malice Toward Some*. New York: Simon and Schuster, 1938.

———. *The Folks at Home*. New York: Simon and Schuster, 1952.

———. *This Demi-Paradise: A Westchester Diary*. New York: Simon and Schuster, 1960.

Hanepe, Edward C., Jr., and Merle Wittenberg. *The Lifeline of America*. New York: McGraw-Hill, 1964.

Harp, Harry H., and Denis F. Dunham. *Comparative Costs to Consumers of Convenience Foods and Home-Prepared Foods*. Marketing Research Report no. 609. Marketing Economics Division, U.S. Department of Agriculture. Washington, D.C., June 1963.

Harrison, Cynthia. *On Account of Sex*. Berkeley: University of California Press, 1988.

Hartmann, Susan M. *The Home Front and Beyond*. New York: Twayne, 1982.

Harvey, Brett. *The Fifties*. New York: HarperCollins, 1993.

Hawes, Elizabeth. *Why Women Cry, or Wenches with Wrenches*. Cornwall, N.Y.: Cornwall Press, 1943.

Heinz, H. J., Co. *57 Prize-Winning Recipes*. n.p., 1957.

Hennessee, Judith. *Betty Friedan: Her Life*. New York: Random House, 1999.

Herschberger, Ruth. *Adam's Rib*. New York: Pellegrini & Cudahy, 1948.

Heth, Edward Harris. *The Wonderful World of Cooking*. New York: Simon and Schuster, 1956.

Heywood, Anne. *There Is a Right Job for Every Woman*. New York: Doubleday, 1951.

Hibben, Sheila. *American Regional Cookery*. Boston: Little, Brown, 1946.

Hines, Duncan. *Duncan Hines' Food Odyssey*. New York: Crowell, 1955.

Honey, Maureen. *Creating Rosie the Riveter*. Amherst: University of Massachusetts Press, 1984.

Horowitz, Daniel. *Betty Friedan and the Making of "The Feminine Mystique."* Amherst: University of Massachusetts Press, 1998.

Hyman, Stanley Edgar, ed. *The Magic of Shirley Jackson*. Farrar, Straus and Giroux, 1966.

Jackson, Shirley. *Life Among the Savages*. New York: Farrar, Straus and Young, 1953.

———. *Raising Demons*. New York: Farrar, Straus and Cudahy, 1957.

———. *Come Along with Me*. Edited by Stanley Edgar Hyman. New York: Viking, 1968.

Johnston, Carolyn. *Sexual Power*. Tuscaloosa: University of Alabama Press, 1992.

Jones, Evan. *Epicurean Delight: The Life and Times of James Beard*. New York: Knopf, 1990.

Jones, Jacqueline. *Labor of Love, Labor of Sorrow*. New York: Vintage, 1995.

June Fete Committee of the Women's Board of the Abington Memorial Hospital, comp. *The June Fete Cook Book*. Abington, Pa.: 1955.

Kaledin, Eugenia. *Mothers and More*. Boston: Twayne, 1984.

Kampen, Irene. *We That Are Left*. New York: Doubleday, 1963.

Kaufman, William I., ed. *Cooking with the Experts*. New York: Random House, 1955.

Kerr, Jean. *Please Don't Eat the Daisies*. New York: Doubleday, 1957.

———. *The Snake Has All the Lines*. New York: Doubleday, 1960.

Komarovsky, Mirra. *Blue-Collar Marriage*. New York: Random House, 1962.

Landmarks in Cooking. Collected by the Women of Trinity Church. Topsfield, Mass.: The Church, 1960.

Landry, Bart. *The New Black Middle Class*. Berkeley: University of California Press, 1987.

Lang, George. *Nobody Knows the Truffles I've Seen*. New York: Knopf, 1998.

Langseth-Christensen, Lillian. *The Instant Epicure Cookbook*. New York: Coward-McCann, 1963.

———. *Voyage Gastronomique*. New York: Hawthorn Books, 1973.

LaPrade, Malcolm. *That Man in the Kitchen*. Boston: Houghton Mifflin, 1946.

Lazar, David, ed. *Conversations with M.F.K. Fisher*. Jackson and London: University Press of Mississippi, 1992.

Levenstein, Harvey. *Paradox of Plenty*. New York: Oxford University Press, 1993.

Liebling, A. J. *Between Meals*. New York: Simon and Schuster, 1962.

Lindbergh, Anne Morrow. *Gift from the Sea*. New York: Pantheon, 1955.

Lindsay, Cynthia. *Home Is Where You Hang Yourself or How to Be a Woman—and Who Needs It?* New York: Simon and Schuster, 1962.

Lopata, Helen Znaniecki. *Occupation: Housewife*. New York: Oxford University Press, 1971.

McCall's. *Congress on Better Living: Final Report 1958–60*. Privately printed.

McCarthy, Josephine. *Josie McCarthy's Favorite TV Recipes*. Englewood Cliffs, N.J.: Prentice-Hall, 1958.

McCue, Lillian Bueno, and Carol Truax. *The 60 Minute Chef*. New York: Macmillan, 1947.

MacDonald, Betty. *The Egg and I*. Philadelphia and New York: Lippincott, 1945.

———. *Anybody Can Do Anything*. Philadelphia and New York: Lippincott, 1950.

———. *Onions in the Stew*. Philadelphia and New York: Lippincott, 1954.

McGinley, Phyllis. *The Province of the Heart*. New York: Viking, 1959.

———. *Sixpence in Her Shoe*. New York: Macmillan, 1964.

Maloch, Francille. *Characteristics of Most and Least Liked Household Tasks*. Ph.D. diss., Cornell University, 1962.

Manring, M. M. *Slave in a Box*. Charlottesville: University Press of Virginia, 1998.

Marchand, Roland. *Advertising the American Dream*. Berkeley: University of California Press, 1985.

Marling, Karal Ann. *As Seen on TV*. Cambridge, Mass.: Harvard University Press, 1984.

Martineau, Pierre. *Motivation in Advertising*. New York: McGraw-Hill, 1957.

Matthews, Glenna. *Just a Housewife*. New York: Oxford University Press, 1987.

May, Elaine Tyler. *Homeward Bound*. New York: Basic Books, 1988.

Mellow, James R. *Charmed Circle: Gertrude Stein & Company*. New York: Praeger, 1974.

Mendelson, Anne. *Stand Facing the Stove*. New York: Henry Holt, 1996.

Merriam, Eve. *After Nora Slammed the Door*. Cleveland, Ohio: World Publishing Co., 1964.

Meyer, Verna. *Verna Meyer's "Way with Food."* (self-published) 1964.

Meyerowitz, Joanne, ed. *Not June Cleaver*. Philadelphia: Temple University Press, 1994.

Miller, Douglas, and Marion Nowak. *The Fifties*. New York: Doubleday, 1977.

Morehouse, Ward, III. *The Waldorf-Astoria: America's Gilded Dream*. New York: M. Evans, 1991.

Murphy, Patricia. *Glow of Candlelight*. Englewood Cliffs, N.J.: Prentice-Hall, 1961.

Muscatine, Doris. *A Cook's Tour of San Francisco*. New York: Scribner, 1963.

National Manpower Council. *Work in the Lives of Married Women*. New York: Columbia University Press, 1958.

New Party Cakes for All Occasions. With a foreword by Betty Crocker. Minneapolis, Minn.: General Mills, 1931.

Nye, F. Ivan, and Lois Hoffman, eds. *The Employed Mother in America*. Westport, Conn.: Greenwood Press, 1963.

Oppenheimer, Judy. *Private Demons*. New York: Putnam's, 1988.

Packard, Vance. *The Hidden Persuaders*. New York: David McKay, 1957.

Parents Magazine. Consumption and Use Study of Foods and Home Products. 1960.

Pepper, Beverly. *The Glamour Magazine After Five Cookbook*. New York: Doubleday, 1952.

Perl, Lila. *What Cooks in Suburbia*. New York: Dutton, 1961.

Peterson, Alice, ed. *500 Favorite Recipes*. New York: News Syndicate Co., 1955.

Picture Cook Book. New York: Time, Inc., 1958.

Pillsbury, Inc. *100 Prize-Winning Recipes: From Pillsbury's $100,000 Grand National Recipe and Baking Contest*. Minneapolis, Minn.: 1950.

———. *100 Prize-Winning Recipes: From Pillsbury's 2nd Grand National $100,000 Recipe and Baking Contest*. Minneapolis, Minn.: 1951.

———. *100 Prize-Winning Recipes: From Pillsbury's 3rd Grand National $100,000 Recipe and Baking Contest*. Minneapolis, Minn.: 1952.

———. *100 Prize-Winning Recipes: From Pillsbury's 4th Grand National $100,000 Recipe and Baking Contest*. Minneapolis, Minn.: 1953.

———. *100 Grand National Recipes: From Pillsbury's 5th $100,000 Recipe and Baking Contest*. Minneapolis, Minn.: 1954.

———. *100 Prize-Winning Grand National Recipes from Pillsbury's 6th Grand National $100,000 Recipe and Baking Contest*. Minneapolis, Minn.: 1955.

———. *Pillsbury's 7th Grand National Cookbook: 100 Easy-to-Follow Prize-Winning Recipes*. Minneapolis, Minn.: 1956.

———. *100 Grand National Recipes: Collected for You at Pillsbury's Best 8th Grand National*. Minneapolis, Minn.: n.d. [1957].

———. *9th Grand National Cook Book: 100 Prize-Winning Recipes from Pillsbury's Best 9th Grand National Bake-Off*. Minneapolis, Minn.: n.d. [1958].

———. *Pillsbury's Best 10th Grand National Bake-Off Cookbook: 100 Prize-Winning Recipes*. N.p., n.d. [Minneapolis, Minn.: 1959].

———. *Pillsbury's Best 11th Grand National Bake-Off Cookbook: 100 Prize-Winning Recipes*. N.p., n.d. [Minneapolis, Minn.: 1960].

———. *Pillsbury's Best 12th Grand National Bake-Off Cookbook: 100 Prize-Winning Recipes*. N.p., n.d. [Minneapolis, Minn.: 1961].

———. *Pillsbury's 13th Grand National Bake-Off Cookbook: 100 Prize-Winning Recipes with Pillsbury's Best Flour*. N.p., n.d. [Minneapolis, Minn.: 1962].

———. *Pillsbury's 14th Grand National Bake-Off Cookbook: 100 Prize-Winning Recipes with Pillsbury's Best Flour*. N.p., n.d. [Minneapolis, Minn.: 1963].

———. *100 New Bake-Off Recipes: From Pillsbury's 15th Grand National*. N.p., n.d. [Minneapolis, Minn.: 1964].

———. *100 New Bake-Off Recipes: From Pillsbury's 16th Grand National*. N.p. [Minneapolis, Minn.]: 1965.

————. *The Pillsbury Busy Lady Bake-Off Recipes: From the 17th Annual Bake-Off.* N.p. [Minneapolis, Minn.]: 1966.

————. *Bake-Off Cook Book.* N.p. [Minneapolis, Minn.]: 1967.

Powell, Kathryn Summers. *Maternal Employment in Relation to Family Life.* Ph.D. diss., Florida State University, 1960.

Rainwater, Lee, Richard Coleman, and Gerald Handel. *Workingman's Wife.* New York: Oceana Publications, 1959.

Ramsey, Glenn, Bert Kruger Smith, and Bernice Milburn Moore. *Women View Their Working World.* Based on a study in mental health for the Texas Federation of Business and Professional Women. Austin: Hogg Foundation for Mental Health, University of Texas, 1963.

Ray, Marie Beynon. *The Five-Minute Dessert.* New York: Doubleday, 1961.

Reardon, Joan. *Celebrating the Pleasures of the Table.* New York: Harmony Books, 1994.

Rees, Jane Louise. "The Use and Meaning of Food in Families with Different Socio-Economic Backgrounds," Ph.D. diss., Pennsylvania State University, 1959.

Robertson, Helen, Sarah MacLeod, and Frances Preston. *What Do We Eat Now?* Philadelphia and New York: Lippincott, 1942.

Rombauer, Irma S. *Joy of Cooking.* St. Louis, 1931; New York: Scribner, 1998.

————. *Streamlined Cooking.* Indianapolis, Ind.: Bobbs-Merrill, 1939.

Rosen, Ruth Chier. *The Big Spread.* New York: Richards Rosen, Inc., 1953.

————. *The Ancestral Recipes of Shen Mei Lan.* New York: Richards Rosen, Inc., 1954.

————. *Pardon My Foie Gras.* New York: Richards Rosen, Inc., 1956.

————. *Pop, Monsieur.* New York: Richards Rosen, Inc., 1956.

————. *Having a Ball.* New York: Richards Rosen, Inc., 1959.

————. *Spicemanship.* New York: Richards Rosen, Inc., 1959.

Rothman, Sheila. *Woman's Proper Place.* New York: Basic Books, 1978.

Rupp, Leila, and Verta Taylor. *Survival in the Doldrums.* New York: Oxford University Press, 1987.

Schur, Sylvia, ed. *New Ways to Gracious Living.* New York: Crown, 1957.

Sermolino, Maria. *Papa's Table d'Hôte.* Philadelphia and New York: Lippincott, 1952.

Shapiro, Laura. *Perfection Salad: Women and Cooking at the Turn of the Century.* New York: Random House, 2001.

Shosteck, Robert. *Five Thousand Women College Graduates Report Findings of a National Survey of the Social and Economic Status of Women Graduates of Liberal Arts Colleges of 1946–1949.* Washington, D.C.: B'nai B'rith Vocational Service Bureau, 1953.

Silverman, Irene. *Nine to Five and After.* New York: Doubleday, 1964.

Simon, Linda. *The Biography of Alice. B. Toklas.* New York: Doubleday, 1977.

Smallzried, Kathleen Ann. *The Everlasting Pleasure*. New York: Appleton-Century-Crofts, 1956.

Smith, Elinor Goulding. *The Complete Book of Absolutely Perfect Housekeeping*. New York: Harcourt, Brace, 1956.

———. *Confessions of Mrs. Smith*. New York: Harcourt, Brace, 1958.

Smuts, Robert W. *Women and Work in America*. New York: Columbia University Press, 1959.

Spigel, Lynn. *Make Room for TV*. Chicago: University of Chicago Press, 1992.

Steward, Samuel M., ed. *Dear Sammy: Letters from Gertrude Stein and Alice B. Toklas*. Boston: Houghton Mifflin, 1977.

Street, Julian. *Table Topics*. New York: Knopf, 1959.

Sunset Cook Book. Menlo Park, Calif.: Lane Book Co., 1962.

Sutton, Horace. *Confessions of a Grand Hotel: The Waldorf-Astoria*. New York: Henry Holt, 1951.

Thoughts for Buffets. Boston: Houghton Mifflin, 1958.

Thoughts for Food. Boston: Houghton Mifflin, 1946.

Toklas, Alice B. *The Alice B. Toklas Cook Book*. New York: Harper & Bros., 1954.

———. *Aromas and Flavors of Past and Present*. With an introduction and comments by Poppy Cannon. New York: Harper & Bros., 1958.

———. *What Is Remembered*. New York: Holt, Rinehart and Winston, 1963.

Tracy, Marian, ed. *Coast to Coast Cookery*. Bloomington: Indiana University Press, 1952.

Turgeon, Charlotte. *Time to Entertain*. Boston: Little, Brown, 1954.

Vanek, Joann. "Time Spent in Housework." *Scientific American,* November 1974.

———. "Household Technology and Social Status." *Technology and Culture* 19, no. 3 (July 1978).

Waldo, Myra. *The Bride's Cookbook*. New York: D. Van Nostrand, 1958.

Waldron, Edward E. *Walter White and the Harlem Renaissance*. Port Washington, N.Y.: Kennikat Press, 1978.

Walker, Nancy, ed. *Women's Magazines 1940–1960*. Boston: Bedford/St. Martin's, 1998.

Weems, Robert E., Jr. *Desegregating the Dollar*. New York: New York University Press, 1998.

Weiner, Lynn Y. *From Working Girl to Working Mother*. Chapel Hill: University of North Carolina Press, 1985.

Weingarten, Violet. *The Mother Who Works Outside the Home*. New York: Child Study Association of America, 1961.

Wellesley-in-Westchester, comp. *Favorite Recipes of Wellesley Alumnae*. Compiled for the Seventy-fifth Anniversary Fund of Wellesley College, 1875–1950.

Welty, Eudora. *Delta Wedding*. New York: Harcourt, Brace, 1945.

White, Walter. *A Man Called White*. New York: Viking, 1948.

Whyte, William H., Jr., and the editors of *Fortune. Is Anybody Listening?* New York: Simon and Schuster, 1952.

Wiegand, Elizabeth. *Comparative Use of Time of Farm and City Full-Time Homemakers and Homemakers in the Labor Force in Relation to Home Management*. Ph.D. diss., Cornell University, 1953.

Williams, E. W. *Frozen Foods: Biography of an Industry*. Boston: Cahners, 1970.

Wine and Food Society of New York. *Newsletter*. New York: Wine and Food Society, 1938–1959.

Wolff, Janet. *What Makes Women Buy*. New York: McGraw-Hill, 1958.

Women's Bureau, U.S. Department of Labor. *The Effective Use of Womanpower*. Report of the Conference, March 10–11, 1955. Women's Bureau Bulletin no. 237. Washington, D.C., 1955.

———. *College Women Go to Work: Report on Women Graduates Class of 1956*. Women's Bureau Bulletin no. 264. Washington, D.C., 1958.

———. *Today's Woman in Tomorrow's World*. A Conference Commemorating the 40th Anniversary of the Women's Bureau. Women's Bureau Bulletin, no. 276. Washington, D.C., 1960.

Wright, Carlton E. *Food Buying: Marketing Information for Consumers*. New York: Macmillan, 1962.

Yagoda, Ben. *About Town*. New York: Scribner, 2000.

Zuckerman, Mary Ellen. *A History of Popular Women's Magazines in the United States, 1792–1995*. Westport, Conn.: Greenwood Press, 1998.

Permissions and Credits

Grateful acknowledgment is made to the following for permission to publish excerpts from letters and other documents:

Rare Book and Manuscript Library, Columbia University
Schlesinger Library, Radcliffe Institute, Harvard University
Sophia Smith Collection, Smith College
WGBH-TV, Boston
Yale Collection of American Literature, Beinecke Rare Book and Manuscript Library

Extracts from the published and unpublished letters of Alice B. Toklas are used by permission of Edward Burns.

Extracts from her papers are used by permission of Ernestine Gilbreth Carey.

Extracts from her letters and other papers are used by permission of Julia Child.

Extracts from published letters of Gertrude Stein are used by permission of Stanford Gann, Jr., literary executor of the Gertrude Stein estate.

Extracts from the published and unpublished writing of Poppy Cannon are used by permission of Cynthia White and Claudia Philippe.

The author would also like to thank Ethan Becker, Mark DeVoto, Marion Gorman, Judith Jones, and Robert Lescher for kindly responding to questions pertaining to copyright.

Portions of this book have appeared, in different form, in *Gastronomica*, *Gourmet*, and *Granta*.

Index

Page numbers in *italics* refer to illustrations.

FOR THE BEST IN PAPERBACKS, LOOK FOR THE Ⓟ

In every corner of the world, on every subject under the sun, Penguin represents quality and variety—the very best in publishing today.

For complete information about books available from Penguin—including Penguin Classics, Penguin Compass, and Puffins—and how to order them, write to us at the appropriate address below. Please note that for copyright reasons the selection of books varies from country to country.

In the United States: Please write to *Penguin Group (USA), P.O. Box 12289 Dept. B, Newark, New Jersey 07101-5289* or call 1-800-788-6262.

In the United Kingdom: Please write to *Dept. EP, Penguin Books Ltd, Bath Road, Harmondsworth, West Drayton, Middlesex UB7 0DA.*

In Canada: Please write to *Penguin Books Canada Ltd, 10 Alcorn Avenue, Suite 300, Toronto, Ontario M4V 3B2.*

In Australia: Please write to *Penguin Books Australia Ltd, P.O. Box 257, Ringwood, Victoria 3134.*

In New Zealand: Please write to *Penguin Books (NZ) Ltd, Private Bag 102902, North Shore Mail Centre, Auckland 10.*

In India: Please write to *Penguin Books India Pvt Ltd, 11 Panchsheel Shopping Centre, Panchsheel Park, New Delhi 110 017.*

In the Netherlands: Please write to *Penguin Books Netherlands bv, Postbus 3507, NL-1001 AH Amsterdam.*

In Germany: Please write to *Penguin Books Deutschland GmbH, Metzlerstrasse 26, 60594 Frankfurt am Main.*

In Spain: Please write to *Penguin Books S. A., Bravo Murillo 19, 1° B, 28015 Madrid.*

In Italy: Please write to *Penguin Italia s.r.l., Via Benedetto Croce 2, 20094 Corsico, Milano.*

In France: Please write to *Penguin France, Le Carré Wilson, 62 rue Benjamin Baillaud, 31500 Toulouse.*

In Japan: Please write to *Penguin Books Japan Ltd, Kaneko Building, 2-3-25 Koraku, Bunkyo-Ku, Tokyo 112.*

In South Africa: Please write to *Penguin Books South Africa (Pty) Ltd, Private Bag X14, Parkview, 2122 Johannesburg.*